The Pitch That Killed

Mike Sowell

MACMILLAN
PUBLISHING
COMPANY
NEW YORK

Copyright © 1989 by Mike Sowell

All rights reserved. No part of this book may be reproduced or
transmitted in any form or by any means, electronic or
mechanical, including photocopying, recording, or by any
information storage and retrieval system, without permission in
writing from the Publisher.

Macmillan Publishing Company
866 Third Avenue, New York, NY 10022
Collier Macmillan Canada, Inc.

Library of Congress Cataloging-in-Publication Data
Sowell, Mike.
    The pitch that killed.
    Bibliography: p.
    Includes index.
    1. Baseball—United States—History. 2. Mays,
Carl, 1891–   . 3. Chapman, Ray, d. 1920.
4. Cleveland Indians (Baseball team) I. Title.
GV863.A1S73   1989   796.357′0973   89-8147

ISBN 0-02-074761-6

Macmillan books are available at special discounts for bulk
purchases for sales promotions, premiums, fund-raising, or
educational use. For details, contact:

              Special Sales Director
              Macmillan Publishing Company
              866 Third Avenue
              New York, NY 10022

10   9   8   7   6   5   4   3   2

Printed in the United States of America

In memory of my father,
Dr. Leon B. Sowell

Contents

You simply can't get out of the way of the bean ball, though you see it coming and you know it's going to crash into your skull. I can still remember vividly how I was fascinated by seeing that ball coming toward my head. I was paralyzed. I couldn't make a move to get out of the way, though the ball looked big as a house. I imagine that a person fascinated by a snake feels much the same way, paralyzed and unable to dodge the deadly serpent about to strike.

The ball crashed into me. It sounded like a hammer striking a big bell. Then all went dark.

Terry Turner
former Cleveland infielder
Cleveland Press
August 17, 1920

Prologue

As the Reverend Dr. William A. Scullen stood to deliver his eulogy, he paused to survey the scene in front of him. There were people occupying every available foot of space in the large cathedral, including the aisles, the sanctuary, and the communion rail. On the altar steps, a small crippled boy sat looking up at the reverend.

It was estimated that two thousand people were inside St. John's Roman Catholic Cathedral in Cleveland that day. Another three thousand had been turned away for lack of space, and they now congregated on the steps or the nearby sidewalks. Some even used automobile tops or stepladders to get to the windows, where they could look in at the proceedings.

The people had begun arriving at the cathedral long before the service was scheduled to begin at 10:40 A.M. They had continued to arrive throughout the morning even as there was no more space for them, and now the onlookers, many with tears in their eyes, lined both sides of Superior Avenue and East Ninth Street for as far as one could see from the church doors. Patrolmen and mounted police guarded the streets in an effort to keep them open to traffic.

In the crowd were representatives of all classes of people in Cleveland. Businessmen, laborers, lawyers, housewives, and newsboys stood side by side.

It was August 20, 1920, a Friday, and the city of Cleveland had come to pay its last respects to one of its most loved citizens. Not since the funeral of the Reverend James M. Hanley, chaplain of the

165th Infantry of the Rainbow Division in the Great War, had there been such a public outpouring of sympathy in the city.

But the man being mourned on this warm summer morning was neither a soldier nor a politician nor even a native son of the city. He was Ray Chapman, a baseball player for the Cleveland Indians. Four days earlier, he had been struck in the head by a pitched ball in a game in New York. Within fifteen hours, Chapman had died of his injuries, making him the first and only ballplayer ever killed on a big-league diamond. His death had touched off a flood of grief and anger both in Cleveland and throughout major-league baseball.

Chapman's funeral originally had been scheduled for St. Philomene's Church in East Cleveland, where he had been married to the former Kathleen Daly less than a year earlier. But that church could seat only one thousand people, and by the public expression of sympathy it quickly became obvious that far more people than that planned to attend the service. On the evening before the funeral, Martin B. Daly, a prominent Cleveland businessman and Chapman's father-in-law, announced the switch to St. John's Cathedral, which was not only much larger but also more centrally located.

That morning, the Cleveland ballplayers arrived in the city after an all-night train ride from New York, where they had beaten the Yankees 3–2 on Thursday. It had been a listless game, with neither team showing much enthusiasm for the task at hand. The Indians had been scheduled to play in Boston on Friday, but Red Sox owner Harry Frazee announced that out of respect to Chapman he was postponing the game to allow the players to attend their teammate's funeral.

Another last-minute arrival that morning was Johnny Kilbane, the featherweight boxing champion from Cleveland and a close friend of Chapman's. Kilbane had been on vacation in the woods of Michigan when his family got word to him of Chapman's death. He made his way to the nearest town and attempted to find a boat to take him to Cleveland. Failing to do so, Kilbane rented a tug to carry him across the lake. He did not arrive in the city until 4:00 A.M., but he was at the church later that morning when the funeral party arrived.

Among those in the party were the ballplayers, who arrived in automobiles and marched into the cathedral in pairs, many of them accompanied by their wives. All the team members except player-manager Tris Speaker and outfielder Jack Graney—Chapman's two closest friends on the club—were present.

Speaker, who had served as best man at Chapman's wedding, remained at the Daly house. The manager had returned to Cleveland with Chapman's body three days earlier and it now was reported that the Cleveland manager, overcome by grief and exhaustion, had collapsed and been ordered to bed by a physician.

Graney, who had been Chapman's roommate on road trips since Ray joined the Indians eight years earlier, was unable to attend for similar reasons. His friends said that upon his arrival that morning at the Daly residence where Chapman's body lay, Graney had become hysterical and had to be physically restrained. Nap Lajoie, the former Cleveland second baseman, had taken Graney—his eyes red and swollen—by force and placed him in an automobile. Lajoie then drove the distraught ballplayer to the country to calm him.

Both Speaker and Graney had been scheduled to serve as pall-bearers. In their absence, the sad task of carrying Chapman's casket into the cathedral was left to catcher Steve O'Neill and outfielder Joe Wood of the Indians; Tom Raftery, a former Indian who had been an usher at Chapman's wedding; Martin B. Daly, Jr., and Daniel Daly, Chapman's brothers-in-law; Howard Monks, an artist and close friend; and William H. Smith, the president of the Pioneer Alloys Company where Chapman was secretary and treasurer.

There had been audible sobbing in the church when Chapman's widow, Kathleen, followed the casket into the cathedral. Behind her came Chapman's parents; his brother, Roy, and his fourteen-year-old sister, Margaret. Chapman's father, Everette, stared straight ahead as he walked down the aisle. The day he had come to bury his son was his sixtieth birthday.

American League president Ban Johnson, sitting in a private pew with Indians' owner James Dunn, silently watched the procession. Nearby sat outfielder Duffy Lewis, first baseman Wally Pipp, and pitcher Ernie Shore of the Yankees.

Cleveland mayor W. S. FitzGerald was absent from the city and unable to attend, but representing him were Law Director Woods and several members of the mayor's cabinet as well as several city councilmen.

There had been more than three hundred floral offerings sent to the cathedral, and they were banked high against the sanctuary rail. Among them was an immense floral blanket from 20,023 persons who had contributed ten cents each toward the "Flower from a Fan" fund. The blanket contained 2,063 flowers, and the remainder of the fund money was to go toward a bronze memorial tablet in Chapman's honor at League Park, the Indians' home field.

Another floral piece, sent by the sandlot ballplayers of Cleveland, was an imitation of a baseball diamond with players at all the positions except shortstop, where Chapman had played. The inscription read: "Gone but not forgotten."

*   *   *

Dr. Scullen, aware of the deep emotions that Chapman's death had stirred both in Cleveland and elsewhere, had chosen his words carefully. He opened his sermon by quoting from the Bible: "I am the resurrection and the life; he that believeth in Me shall not taste death forever."

The huge crowd listened intently as Dr. Scullen went on to speak of the mysteries of life, of Chapman's indomitable spirit and of his strength of character. Chapman was a winner in the game of life, said Dr. Scullen, who then related a dramatic story of the player's deathbed conversion to Catholicism.

"Through all these years," said Dr. Scullen, "that sweet spiritual longing for the Truth was ever there, nay more, he had made definite plans to be received into the Church at the close of the 1920 season, and lo in an instant he was struck unconscious—but the mercy of God intervened, as it always intervenes, and consciousness returned after the operation."

Dr. Scullen paused briefly, then continued.

"When that moment came, when he was asked by his priest-friend if he would die in the faith of his fathers, and his father's fathers, his lips could not speak but the strong clasp of the hand gave assent and a smile broke over his countenance as the last solemn rites of the Church were administered, a smile, we trust, that was but the reflection of the Beatific vision—the smile that was on his lips as he looked into the face of his God."

Dr. Scullen then turned his thoughts to Carl Mays, the man who had thrown the fatal pitch to Chapman. Speaking softly, he said, "May there be no hostility in any heart to the man who was the unfortunate occasion of his accident. He feels it more deeply than you, and no one regrets it as much as he. This great game we play, that is our national pastime, could not produce anybody who would willingly do a thing like that. Remember those would be the words of him who lies here. Do not hold any animosity."

By the time Dr. Scullen concluded his sermon, the size of the crowd outside had increased. Streetcars were halted and traffic was blocked for several blocks.

*　　　*　　　*

In Manhattan, a crowd had gathered in the corridor outside Magistrate Mancuso's courtroom. Its mood was very different from that of the crowd in Cleveland. These people had come not out of respect but out of curiosity. Mays was scheduled to appear in traffic court on a charge of speeding, and the people stood waiting in hope of getting a glimpse of the man whose name suddenly had been thrust into the headlines. Mays had been ticketed more than three weeks earlier, and through a cruel twist of fate, his scheduled court appearance had coincided with the funeral of the man he had fatally beaned.

Shortly before Mays's case was to be heard, there was a bustle of activity in the hallway and someone shouted, "Here he comes!" But the man walking briskly toward the courtroom was not Mays. It was Yankees secretary Charles McManus, who had come to represent the pitcher.

Standing before the judge, McManus explained that Mays had been completely unnerved by the accident and was unable to appear on his behalf in the traffic court. McManus said Mays wished to enter a plea of guilty, which the magistrate accepted. The fine was set at twenty-five dollars. McManus paid the fee and left without further comment. Mays remained at home, out of public sight.

* * *

In the course of an average nine-inning baseball game, there are approximately 200 to 250 balls thrown by the pitchers. There have been roughly twelve hundred games played each season for the more than one hundred years since big-league baseball began in 1871. That adds up to about one-quarter of a million balls hurled toward the plate annually. All told, there have been more than 25 million pitches thrown to batters. Only one of them killed a man.

Many baseball observers viewed this as a tragic but unavoidable accident. As the *New York Tribune* stated the day after Chapman's death: "The extreme rarity of fatal or even of serious accidents in baseball is surprising, when one remembers the vast multitudes who play the game. Consider the number who are drowned while bathing or boating, who meet injury or death while hunting. In the light of such comparisons baseball is singularly free from untoward happenings. Ray Chapman's fate, sad as it is, may be rated as sheer accident. It represents a coincidence not likely to occur again."

Others took a far harsher view of the incident. Their sentiments were expressed in an editorial in the *St. Louis Sporting News* that hit the streets one week after Chapman was laid to rest. It concluded:

> Mays knows what all the world is saying. He can not dodge the finger of accusation by keeping himself from public view. Nor is it "hysteria," as his defenders would charge, when critics everywhere remind us of frequent previous complaints against his style of pitching and recount the disputes it has caused on the ball field.
>
> No one accuses Mays of a direct intent to injure any batter, living or dead, but there are few who do not feel that Mays took the chance and made the batter take the chance, and there are many who wag the head and say such a thing as has happened was bound to happen some day.

Acknowledgments

First of all, I am indebted to Tom Heitz, the librarian at the National Baseball Hall of Fame Library, and his staff for their cooperation and assistance whenever it was needed, and to Lloyd Johnson, formerly the historian at the Hall of Fame Library and now the executive director of the Society for American Baseball Research.

When I began my research in 1985, I was fortunate to make the acquaintance of Ray Chapman's sister, Mrs. Margaret Joy of Huntington, West Virginia. Her memories of her brother, the materials she provided, and her friendship proved to be invaluable over the long months ahead.

A number of other people deserve recognition for helping make this work possible. Jay Cronley gave me advice and encouragement when it was needed. Tom Lindley provided assistance with editing, and Gerald Locklin was the first to read the completed manuscript. Bob Gregory shared his insight and helped keep up my confidence. Steve Love and Kathy Bliss sent photocopied materials whenever requested. I also want to thank my agent, Mel Berger, and my editor, Rick Wolff. And I am grateful to Justin and Russell for their endurance, to Pat for his unfailing support, to my mother for all she has done over the years, and to Ellen, who was at my side from the day the research began to the day the writing was completed.

1

Carl Mays

Where he has gone, Carl Mays has loomed against the Big League background a strange, cynical figure. He has aroused more ill will, more positive resentment than any other ball player on record. And yet his personal habits are quite above reproach. He does not dissipate and he possesses far more than average intelligence. What has made him a solitary genius, lonely and virtually friendless among the ranks of his fellow players? What is the enigma of his contradictory career?

F. C. Lane
Baseball Magazine

1

On the morning of September 28, 1914, two young ballplayers arrived by train at Boston's Back Bay Station. Tired and hungry, they stood holding their suitcases on the platform while deciding where to go next. The train had been running an hour late, and there had been no food left in the dining car when they boarded in Providence, Rhode Island, forty-four miles away.

Checking his pocket, one of the men pulled out two dollars.

"Let's find somewhere around here to eat," he said. "Then we can take a streetcar over to the ballpark."

His companion, a large and boisterous fellow, laughed at the suggestion.

"Come on, kid, follow me," he said in a booming voice. "I know my way around here."

A few minutes later, the two men were in a taxicab headed across town. When they pulled up outside the Brunswick Hotel, just across from Fenway Park, the fare totaled ninety cents. The first man was appalled at the expense, and he made sure to express his displeasure as he forked over his share of the fare. Why, for forty-five cents, he noted, a fellow could buy a decent breakfast.

"Listen, kid," said the big man, "you're in the big time now. You've got to do things big time."

With that bit of advice, he waved for a bellhop and marched noisily into the hotel, attracting the attention of everyone within earshot. His colleague was left standing outside, virtually unnoticed. That was not surprising. Anyone who traveled with Babe Ruth was going to be overshadowed. It happened to be Carl Mays's misfortune

3

that his arrival in Boston coincided with Ruth's. Ruth, a brash and outspoken young left-handed pitcher, burst onto the big-league scene. Mays came in quietly, with little fanfare.

Before they left, both men would leave their marks on the national pastime. Ruth would become the most popular player in the game's history, revolutionizing the sport with his mighty home runs. Mays would leave behind far more tragic memories.

At the time, they were just two bushers called up by the Red Sox, who were playing out the string of the 1914 campaign. The pennant already had been won by Connie Mack's Philadelphia Athletics, with Boston a distant second. Mays and Ruth had teamed up to pitch Providence to the International League championship, and now the Red Sox wanted to give them a brief taste of the big leagues. The ballclub could not have found two more divergent personalities.

The twenty-year-old Ruth was loud, brash, and good-natured, and he both looked and acted like a huge child. He was six foot two and 190 pounds, with broad shoulders, dark black hair that fell over his forehead, a moon-shaped face that featured playful eyes and a wide grin. His full name was George Herman Ruth but his teammates called him "Jidge," a derivative of the New England pronunciation of George. Behind his back, they also called him "The Big Baboon" because of his flat nose and prominent lips, as well as his roughhouse ways.

His father was a saloon-keeper near the wharf area in Baltimore, and Babe had been chewing tobacco and drinking whisky by the time he was eight years old. A year later, his parents had him committed to St. Mary's Industrial School for Boys, which served not only as a reform school but also as an orphanage. Ruth was at St. Mary's off and on for the better part of the next twelve years. During that time, he came under the influence of Brother Matthias, a six foot six, 250-pound man who was referred to by the boys in the school as "The Boss." Brother Matthias not only helped tame Ruth, he also got him started in baseball. Eventually, Ruth's reputation as a ballplayer spread, and in 1914 he began his professional career with the Baltimore Orioles of the International League. He soon was sold to Boston and then shipped to Providence to gain some more seasoning.

By contrast, Mays, a sullen and moody loner, came from a rigid Midwestern background. He was five feet eleven and 185 pounds and had a solid build, with broad shoulders, close-cropped blond hair, close-set blue eyes, a beakish nose, and a dour expression that was accentuated by his tightly drawn mouth. He was, as one teammate described him, a man who always looked as if he had a toothache.

When he arrived in Boston, Mays was twenty-two years old, born November 12, 1891, in Liberty, Kentucky. When he was young, the family moved to Mansfield, Missouri, where Carl's father, William Henry Mays, made his rounds as a traveling Methodist minister. One day, the elder Mays was returning from a sermon in a nearby community when he was caught in a rain shower. He became ill and died soon after. Carl was twelve years old at the time. His mother, Louisa Callie Mays, was left to raise five boys and three girls by herself on the family farm. As an adult, Mays would tell how the family had no gun for hunting so he killed squirrels and jackrabbits by throwing rocks at them.

After a couple of years, Carl's mother moved the family to a farm outside Kingfisher, Oklahoma, to be near her sister-in-law. It was here that Carl was introduced to baseball by his cousin, John Long, who had a baseball and a catcher's mitt. Carl was sixteen when he and John made the semipro team in Kingfisher, where they split five dollars if they won and nothing if they lost. After Carl beat Hennessey one game, he was offered twenty-five dollars a month plus room and board to switch teams. He jumped at the offer, and Hennessey went on to win the state championship as Carl pitched and won five complete games in five days in the state tournament at Enid. Mays's performance earned him a job in Mulvane, Kansas, where he played the following summer. Before getting his mother's permission to leave home to earn money as a ballplayer, Carl had to make a promise. He never would play ball on a Sunday. It was a vow he kept until he made it to the big leagues.

After that summer in Kansas, Mays and his catcher, Jess Myers, hopped a freight train headed west, hoping to make it to California to play winter ball. Instead, they were caught aboard the train and arrested for trespassing in Price, Utah, a small town just outside Salt Lake City. When the sheriff discovered the two train-hoppers were ballplayers, he gave them a choice: They could join the local team for its next game or they could go to jail. They chose to play ball. Mays, playing under the name of Davis, repaid the sheriff by pitching and batting Price to a victory over its rival from nearby Kennelsworth.

After a winter in Price, Mays and Myers slipped out of town by catching another freight north to Boise, Idaho, which had a team in the Class D Western Tri-State League. Although Myers failed to make the team, Mays was signed for ninety dollars a month, beginning his career in organized baseball. Following a successful season, he was sold to Portland, Oregon, of the Northwest League, where he would earn two hundred dollars a month.

Mays won ten games for Portland, but a more important development in his life occurred off the field. One afternoon that summer, an older gentleman came out to the ballpark and introduced himself to Carl. His name was Franklin Pierce Mays, and he was a former state senator and member of the Oregon Supreme Court. Since he and Carl had the same last name, he was wondering if they might be related. After talking for a while, the two men determined there was a distant connection. F. P. Mays invited the younger man out to his house that evening to visit. They discovered they enjoyed each other's company and in the days to follow a strong friendship between the two developed. F. P. Mays's only son, who had been Carl's age, recently had died from pneumonia after being graduated from the University of Oregon. Carl soon became like a second son to the elder Mays and his wife, and before long they invited him to move in with them. To Carl, they became "Uncle" Pierce and "Aunt" Genevieve. They were his adopted parents, and in the years to come, they would provide him with some much-needed guidance and support.

The next year, 1914, Portland sold Mays and outfielder Harry Heilmann, a future Hall of Famer, to Detroit. Mays never got the opportunity to suit up for the Tigers, as they immediately shipped him to Providence of the International League, where he became the ace of the staff.

He was one of the top prospects in the league, but Tigers owner Frank Navin, who also headed the ownership group of the Providence franchise, found himself caught in a financial bind. Several of his players were receiving offers to jump to the rival Federal League, a third major league that was touching off a bidding war in baseball by raiding the American and National leagues for talent. Red Sox owner Joe Lannin quickly seized the opportunity to buy the Providence team. Besides helping out a fellow owner in distress, Lannin also was acting on the advice of his front-office people, who were eager to acquire the rights to Mays. There was only one catch to the transaction. The Tigers demanded the right to retain one player of their choosing from Providence. Fortunately for Boston, the man they selected was veteran left-handed pitcher Red Oldham.

In August, the Grays had pulled within one-half game of first-place Rochester in the International League race when Detroit called up Oldham, who had been threatening to jump to the Federal League. To replace him, Ruth was shipped to Providence from Boston, where he had been given a brief trial with the Red Sox.

*   *   *

Even before Ruth's arrival, the Providence club was a rowdy lot. The locker-room banter was coarse and the humor often was cruel. Ruth would quickly fit into this environment. Mays never did.

Once, early in the summer, Mays, always a good hitter, was sent up to pinch-hit with the tying run on base and two outs. He took with him what the ballplayers liked to refer to as a "pet bat," one he had picked up in Boise two years earlier and had carried with him ever since. Mays waited for a pitch he liked, then swung and hit the ball on the nose. When he did, the bat shattered in his hands. The top half flew toward third base, the ball rolled harmlessly back to the pitcher, and Mays stood at the plate with the bat handle in his hands and a startled expression on his face.

It didn't take long to figure out what had happened. The bat had been sawed through at the label and glued back together, a favorite trick employed by ballplayers who wanted to teach a brash rookie or an overbearing teammate a lesson. In the locker room, Mays confronted the two players he suspected of pulling the stunt. There was an argument, then another player stepped forward to challenge Mays. It took manager Wild Bill Donovan to pull the two men apart.

That evening, Mays, lonely and discouraged, sat down and began writing a letter to Uncle Pierce. In it, he spilled out his troubles and announced he was ready to give up baseball and return to Portland.

"I had about concluded that if baseball was a game where you had to swim continually against the current, I had perhaps better get out and see what I could do in some other profession where the waters weren't quite so deep," he recalled in a later interview with *Baseball Magazine*. "I (got) genuinely discouraged at Providence and, of course, feeling as I did was unable to do good work. In fact, I lost all interest in my work."

Mays had expected sympathy from Uncle Pierce but instead received a terse reply.

"That's fine. If you want to come back, come on. It's a wonderful city, a city of roses. We have wonderful water and the city is clean and not crowded. But if you do come back, don't come to my house because I can't remember anybody by the name of Mays who was yellow. And you won't be welcome."

The harsh words were just what the young ballplayer needed. He decided to stick it out in Providence, no matter what the hardships. It was the turning point of his career. A few days later, he pitched an exhibition game against Washington and held the American League team to three hits. From that point on, Mays was almost unbeatable. But even his success on the ballfield could not gain him acceptance.

"The unpopularity which had come to be as natural as my own shadow still continued to follow me," he told *Baseball Magazine*. "I know when I had won 12 straight games, and lost my 13th after an extra-inning struggle, one of the local newspapermen, who knew me well and hated me cordially, came out with a story in which he panned me for what he called my poor work."

By that time, Mays no longer cared. He would succeed despite what others thought of him.

* * *

Ruth arrived in Providence on August 18. The addition of a first-rate left-hander to go with the right-handed Mays gave Donovan a lethal one-two combination to throw at the opposition. Two days after Ruth joined the club, Mays beat Rochester to move Providence into first place. Ruth won his first game the next day. Then Mays, pitching on only one day's rest, came back to beat Rochester again the following day.

Fueled by the two pitchers, the Grays stormed down the stretch to win the championship. Mays had the satisfaction of clinching the title with a 2–0 shutout. It was his twenty-fifth victory of the season. Ruth won nine games with the Grays, in addition to the fourteen he had won earlier in the year for the Orioles.

Both players were rewarded with promotions to the Red Sox.

2

Ruth got to see a substantial amount of action on the ballfield. He beat the Yankees 11–5 and in the process got his first major-league hit, a double off Leonard "King" Cole.

Mays saw no action on the ballfield in those two weeks. Instead, he spent his time getting acquainted with his new ballclub and his new surroundings.

In 1914, Boston was a smug city that, in addition to its impressive monuments and stately buildings, boasted the highest per capita income of any metropolitan area in the country. It also laid claim to two first-rate major-league baseball teams. The Braves were in the process of pulling off a miracle finish in the National League, coming back from last place in July to win the pennant and, ultimately, the World Series. But not even their shocking four-game sweep of the mighty Philadelphia Athletics for the championship enabled the Braves to win the city's affections away from the beloved Red Sox. Boston's loyalty to its American League team knew no bounds.

The city's passion for the Red Sox had begun to develop just past the turn of the century when the great Cy Young came over to pitch for Boston's entry in the fledgling American League, which claimed major-league status in 1901. Young won sixty-five games in his first two seasons with the club, and on days after he pitched he often stood outside the grandstand selling tickets and talking baseball with the fans.

The team was known as the Pilgrims, or Puritans, and it played its games at the Huntington Avenue Grounds in a park built on an old carnival site. The Pilgrims drew much of their support from the city's Irish population, and the rowdy fans brought signs to the ballpark, shouted at the players through megaphones, and generally created a state of pandemonium. The most ardent of these supporters were the customers of a local tavern run by the colorful "Nuf Sed" McGreevey, a mustachioed Irishman who put an end to every argument by snapping, " 'Nuf said!" McGreevey's followers dubbed themselves the "Royal Rooters" and adopted as their theme song a popular tune called "Tessie," which they sang at every opportunity.

In 1903, the Pilgrims won the American League pennant and issued a challenge to the National League champion Pittsburgh Pirates to meet in a best-of-nine postseason playoff. Boston won the showdown five games to three to claim the first World Series championship.

In 1912, the team had a new name, the Red Sox, and a new home—a twenty-seven-thousand-seat steel-and-concrete structure known as Fenway Park. The facility got its name because it was built in "The Fens," a marshy area of the city. There was some concern that it was located too close to a nearby Unitarian Church, but the club headed off any problems by awarding the minister a lifetime pass to the grandstand.

Playing in their new ballpark, the Red Sox returned to the top of the league standings and followed with a victory over the New York Giants in the World Series.

The nucleus of that club still was intact when Mays and Ruth arrived two years later. In center field was Tris Speaker, the Texas cowboy who rivaled Detroit's Ty Cobb as the greatest all-around player in the game. Speaker's trademark was playing so shallow that he often became involved in rundowns in the infield. From his station just beyond second base, Speaker still was able to sprint back at the crack of the bat and track down fly balls that would elude other outfielders.

On one side of the legendary Speaker was Duffy Lewis, whose ability to race up the enbankment in left field and snag fly balls barehanded prompted Boston fans to dub the area "Duffy's Cliff." On the other side was smooth-fielding Harry Hooper, a legendary flycatcher whose skill and cunning forced a change in the game's rules. Since runners could not tag up and advance on fly balls until they were caught, Hooper would bat the ball forward while running toward the infield before finally securing it in his glove. He became so adept at this maneuver the rules-makers were forced to allow runners to tag up as soon as the ball was touched by a fielder rather than have to wait until it actually was in the player's possession.

At third base was Larry Gardner, the best clutch hitter in the league. The pitching staff headed by Dutch Leonard, Rube Foster, Ernie Shore, and Smoky Joe Wood was as strong as any around.

The team was managed by Bill Carrigan, a stocky catcher whose brand of baseball had earned him the nickname "Old Rough." Carrigan, who had a square jaw and piercing blue eyes, was only thirty years old, but he was a natural leader who commanded his players' unquestioned loyalty and respect.

A former football and baseball star at Holy Cross, he joined the Red Sox in 1906 and quickly established himself as an outstanding handler of pitchers and a dangerous hitter. But Carrigan's specialty was blocking runners off the plate, which he did by planting himself three feet down the third-base line to guard his territory. Once, Detroit's George Moriarty—who had three inches and thirty pounds on Carrigan—reached first base and yelled down to the Boston catcher, "Hey, you Irish SOB, I'm going to come around the bases and knock you on your arse." Sure enough, a few moments later, Moriarty rounded third base and went barreling into home plate. When he did, he was the one who ended up flat on his back. Standing over the fallen player, Carrigan shot a stream of tobacco juice into Moriarty's face and asked, "How do you like that, you Irish SOB?"

But Carrigan was as smart as he was tough. He used his money to buy a bank and a string of theaters in his hometown of Lewiston, Maine, where he resided on a country estate. He also liked to surround himself with college men, as was evident from the Boston roster. Lewis, dapper and well dressed, and Hooper, quiet and studious, both were graduates of St. Mary's College in Oakland. The well-read Gardner and pitcher Ray Collins had been classmates at the University of Vermont. Shore had a degree from Guilford College in North Carolina. Speaker had spent two years at Polytechnic College in Fort Worth before tiring of school and starting his baseball career.

On the field, Carrigan's teams excelled in defensive skills, heads-up play, and above all else, pitching. His tactics were reminiscent of the old school of baseball. When he ordered his pitcher to knock down a batter, he expected to see the man end up in the dirt. The Boston pitchers ruled by intimidation. In 1914, Leonard won nineteen games and lost only five while compiling a 1.01 earned run average, the lowest in the history of the game. Collins had a total of thirty-nine victories in 1913–14. Foster was 14–8 with a 1.65 ERA in 1914, his first season as a starter. Wood, who had a blazing fastball, had compiled an amazing 34–5 record in 1912 and now was attempting to make a comeback from an arm injury.

Already, it was the finest pitching staff in the league. The addition of two prize prospects only made the outlook more promising. Ruth was a hard-throwing left-hander with a good

12

fastball and sharp control. Mays was a right-hander who could make the ball take unnatural dips and curves as it crossed the plate. He had one other quality Carrigan admired. He wasn't afraid to throw the ball inside and knock down the batter.

3

In the spring of 1915, the Red Sox trained at Hot Springs, Arkansas, a popular resort spa and gambling center tucked away in the Ozark Mountains. For all its charms, Hot Springs was not an enjoyable place for the Red Sox that year. An unusually cold and damp spring severely restricted the team's training schedule, and the players spent much of their time on long hikes up and down the mountainsides. Only occasionally were they able to play intrasquad games.

Under such adverse conditions, Carrigan concentrated most of his efforts on getting his pitchers ready. Not surprisingly, Ruth commanded a lot of attention, not only for his ballplaying skills but also for his boisterous behavior. His dining habits alternately shocked and entertained his teammates, as he rarely used such utensils as forks and knives, and his frequent belches and farts at the table amused himself if no one else. When he found an untended bicycle, he would ride it crazily down the street shouting, "Look at me!" He borrowed cars to drive around town, then would forget where he got them. Babe was like an overgrown kid turned loose on the world, but he also was an impressive sight on the field. As a pitcher, he had a lively fastball and a sharp curve. And at the plate, he was a powerful though erratic hitter.

But of the two rookie hurlers in camp, it was Mays who was the most highly regarded. As an indication of his stature, he was singled out by Tim Murnane, a former Boston player and now the city's most respected sports writer, as a pitcher to watch. Carrigan also leaned toward Mays. Not only was he the more polished of the two newcomers, but he had the added advantage of being a right-hander. Ruth was a left-hander on a staff that already featured two outstanding southpaws in Leonard and Collins.

The events in the first week of the campaign seemed to solidify Mays's status. He relieved Collins in the second game of the season and pitched three scoreless innings to beat the defending champion Athletics. The next day, Ruth was knocked out of the box in the fourth inning, and Mays later came on to blank Philadelphia in the ninth.

Carrigan was impressed enough to give Mays a starting assignment in Washington three days later. His pitching opponent would be Walter Johnson, the great fastballer, who was at the height of his brilliant career. Once again, Mays pitched well. He blanked the Senators over the first few innings and even got a base hit off Johnson. But that hit proved to be costly. Mays eventually came around to score, and when he slid home safely to give the Red Sox a 2–0 lead, he bruised his instep. He tried to keep pitching but finally had to leave after six innings with the score tied 2–2.

The injury kept Mays out of action for three weeks, and his absence provided Ruth the reprieve he needed. The Babe was given another starting opportunity, and this time he won. A few days later, he started again, and although he was beaten by the Yankees, he pitched thirteen strong innings. Mays never got another chance to move back into the starting rotation. While Ruth went on to compile an impressive 18–8 won-lost record that year, Mays had to settle for the less glamorous role of "pinch pitcher." He filled in whenever needed, whether as an emergency starter or as a reliever. His record was an unspectacular 6–5.

But Mays endeared himself to Carrigan in a crucial late-season series against the Tigers. Boston and Detroit had been battling all summer for the league lead, and adding to the tension of the pennant race was a simmering feud between Ty Cobb and the Boston pitchers. The Red Sox were angry with Cobb over his rough play during a series in August. For his part, Cobb was convinced the

Boston pitchers had been deliberately throwing at him for the past two years. His conviction had been strengthened the year before when Foster had cracked one of his ribs with an inside pitch, knocking him out of action for two months.

Against this backdrop, a crowd of twenty-two thousand turned out for the series opener September 16 at Fenway Park. The Royal Rooters, equipped with cowbells and horns, marched onto the grounds singing "Tessie" and shouting curses at Cobb and the other Tigers. As a precautionary measure against trouble, a special police detail was assigned to guard the Detroit star.

Midway through the game, the Tigers knocked Foster out of the box, and Mays was brought in to pitch for the Red Sox. In the eighth inning, he faced Cobb for the first time. Mays's first pitch sailed inside, and Cobb scrambled out of the way. The next pitch was right at Cobb's head, sending him sprawling to the ground. He came up cursing and slung his bat at Mays. Walking out to retrieve it, Cobb snarled, "You're a yellow dog!" Mays said something back, and the two men charged at each other. Only the intervention of several other players prevented a fight. When order finally was restored, Cobb returned to the batter's box and took his stance. Mays wasted no time sending another pitch spinning directly at him. This one caught Cobb on the wrist. He threw down his bat and trotted slowly to first base, dodging pop bottles hurled at him from the stands. As he did, he turned toward the mound and shouted at Mays, vowing retaliation. Mays was unperturbed. He glared back at the Detroit star, letting him know he would be waiting.

Eventually, Cobb would have his revenge. But Mays was the winner of this confrontation, which proved to be the pivotal point in the series. When Cobb caught a fly ball for the final out in the Tigers' 6–1 victory, he had to be escorted off the field by two policemen and several teammates wielding bats in the face of an angry mob. That was the highwater mark for Detroit. The Red Sox stormed back to win the next three games of the series, providing the margin of victory as they edged the Tigers by one game for the American League pennant.

Boston followed up by beating the Philadelphia Phillies in the

World Series. Although he didn't see any action in the postseason, Mays took home a winner's check for $3,780.25, which was more than his regular-season pay. He used the money to build his mother a new house in Mansfield, Missouri, where she had returned to live.

4

Over the next three seasons, Mays developed into the best right-hander in the league. He moved into Boston's rotation in 1916 and won eighteen games, tying him with Leonard for second most on the staff behind Ruth's twenty-three victories. The Red Sox repeated as world's champions, beating the Brooklyn Robins in the Series. Mays suffered Boston's only loss to the National Leaguers, losing the third game to Jack Coombs, a former star with the Athletics. Afterward, Ruth, who had pitched fourteen innings to win the day before, made a crude attempt to lighten the mood in the clubhouse.

"Well, if we had to lose one," said Babe, "I'm glad it was to an old American Leaguer."

Mays answered him with a string of epithets.

The next year, Carrigan resigned and the Red Sox slipped back to second place under player-manager Jack Barry, but Mays pitched brilliantly. He won twenty-two games, lost only nine, and compiled an earned run average of 1.74.

He was an odd sight on the mound, bending his body far over to the side and often scraping his knuckles on the ground when he unleashed the ball. The best description of this strange new pitching star was provided by *Baseball Magazine*:

> A pretty wise noodle, a crazy style of delivery, and not much else, have made Carl Mays one of the game's leading pitchers.

> Mays has less "stuff" than a whole raft of other boxmen, whom he outclasses in winning results, but his submarine delivery is mighty effective in torpedoing the batters.
>
> Carl slings the pill from his toes, has a weird looking wind-up and in action looks like a cross between an octopus and a bowler. He shoots the ball in at the batter at such unexpected angles that his delivery is hard to find, generally, until along about 5 o'clock, when the hitters get accustomed to it—and when the game is about over.

Muddy Ruel, who would have a unique perspective on Mays's offerings while serving as his catcher in New York, later gave an even more telling description of the underhand deliveries. In a 1920 interview, Ruel said: "His underhanded motion is not natural and at times some of the balls he throws take remarkable shoots, jumps, ducks and twists. I have caught many balls thrown by Mays which I did not know I had. I have never known how I managed to catch some of them. I have never been able to understand how any batter ever gets a hit off him."

*   *   *

Although Mays was one of the few practitioners to master the unorthodox delivery, the art of underhand pitching was deeply rooted in baseball's past. The early rules of the game barred overhand pitching, and all hurlers threw the ball underhand. It was not until 1883 that pitchers even were allowed to incorporate a sidearm style in their repertoire. After this breakthrough, pitchers began to use the overhand delivery, and finally, in 1885, this more popular method was legalized. But even after it became customary to deliver the ball with an overhand motion, there remained a few hurlers who achieved success with the old style of pitching.

Foremost among these submariners was Charles "Old Hoss" Radbourn. Short and solidly built, with a droopy moustache, Radbourn began his professional career in 1880, when pitchers still were required to throw underhand. Even after the rules were changed, he stayed with the old method. Pitching in the National League and the Players League, Radbourn won 308 games and lost only 191 in twelve years, and by some accounts he never threw a wild pitch in his career. In 1884 alone, he won sixty games for the Providence Grays of the National League, pitching the final twenty-seven games of the season and winning twenty-six of them. The price he paid for this feat was excruciating pain, and most of the time he could not use his right arm at all. He could pitch only after hours of careful limbering up or a massage.

After such a brilliant career, Radbourn's life ended in tragedy. An attack of paresis forced him to give up the game, and he retired and bought a pool hall. One day, the accidental discharge of a firearm caused Radbourn to lose an eye. In his bitterness and grief, baseball's "Old Hoss" spent his last days sitting morosely in a dark corner of the pool hall while the paresis ate into his brain. He died practically friendless and in obscurity at the age of forty-two in 1897.

The next great underhand pitcher was Billy Rhines, who won 114 games from 1890 to 1899 and, more significantly, proved that the ball could be made to curve upward.

Then came the immortal Iron Man Joe McGinnity, who had spent four mediocre years as a conventional pitcher in the minor leagues before retiring to Springfield, Illinois, in 1894 to run a saloon. On weekends, McGinnity pitched for a semipro team and while doing so began to experiment with underhand pitching. This led to the birth of "Old Sal," the name he gave to his underhand offering, which could be a raise ball or a drop ball as the occasion demanded.

"Old Sal" prompted McGinnity to give pro baseball one more try, and in 1899 he caught on with John McGraw's old Baltimore Orioles. After a brief stop in Brooklyn, and a return to Baltimore, McGinnity took "Old Sal" to New York and from 1902 to 1908 he and Christy Mathewson teamed up to pitch the Giants to two championships and four second-place finishes.

Because the underhand motion lessened the strain on his arm, McGinnity was able to achieve such feats as winning five games in six days in 1900, pitching and winning both ends of a doubleheader three times in August 1903, and chalking up a spectacular 35–8 record in 1904. Those legendary accomplishments, plus his previous employment as an ironworker in his father-in-law's foundry in McAlester, Oklahoma, earned McGinnity his "Iron Man" nickname.

After McGraw gave him his release in 1909, McGinnity went on to pitch in the minor leagues until 1923 when, at the age of fifty-two, he won fifteen games and hurled 206 innings for Dubuque, Iowa, of the Three-I League.

It was while he was serving as manager and pitcher for Tacoma of the Northwest League in 1913 that McGinnity caught the eye of a struggling young Carl Mays. Mays had begun his career as a conventional fastball pitcher, but after joining Portland he came down with a sore arm and was unable to raise his arm to throw a baseball or even comb his hair. Only his batting kept him on the team.

Fearing his career was about to come to a premature end, Mays was sitting on the bench one day as Portland played Tacoma. McGinnity was the Tacoma pitcher, and Mays watched with amazement as the forty-two-year-old pitcher baffled the Portland batters with his underhand delivery.

The young pitcher decided to see if the unorthodox style would work for him. With some help from Portland manager Billy Sullivan, who had been the catcher on the Chicago White Sox's "Hitless Wonders" of the early 1900s, Mays went to work on mastering the underhand motion. Slowly, he developed the control and rhythm necessary to resume his pitching career. After a slow start while still learning the new style, Mays rallied to finish the season with a 10–15 won-lost record. More important, he pitched 250 innings and walked only fifty-four batters.

Two years later, in 1915, Mays was throwing his underhand pitch in the big leagues. The only other submariner toiling in the majors at the time was Jack Warhop of the Yankees. A hard-luck pitcher most of his career, Warhop retired after that season with an eight-year record of 69–93. He later would be remembered primarily for serving up the first of Babe Ruth's 714 home runs.

*   *   *

To Mays, the biggest mystery about the underhand motion was why more pitchers didn't employ it. Not that he was complaining.

"If everyone used an underhand delivery, no doubt the batter would become accustomed to it," he said. "But as this is not the case, my particular delivery is hard for the batter to solve."

The conventional thinking in baseball circles was that underhand pitchers lacked the control necessary to be effective, but Mays was disproving this theory. He averaged fewer than three walks per nine innings, putting him among the league leaders in this category. It was the one statistic Mays most prided himself on.

"That's what wins, and control without stuff is far better than stuff without control," he told William B. Hanna of the *New York Sun* and *New York Herald*. "Whenever you hear it said that such and such a pitcher didn't have a thing, you can bet he had control if he didn't have anything else. You can bank on that kind. They'll be winning when they didn't have a thing much oftener than those who have a lot but no control with it."

Yet, for a pitcher with such uncommonly good control, Mays had the curious habit of hitting more than his share of batters. He had five hit batsmen in his rookie season and nine more in his second year. In 1917, he led the league with fourteen hit batsmen. Worse yet, his pitches often came inside directly at the batters' heads. He was branded a "beaner"—a pitcher who throws the bean ball.

The rap against Mays was summed up by a question an unnamed American League player asked F. C. Lane of *Baseball Magazine:* "Mays is a low-ball pitcher," stated the pitcher. "How does it happen that when he puts a ball on the inside, it generally comes near the batter's head?"

Other players, some on his own team, claimed to have heard Mays boast that he was going to "dust off" certain batters. They said Mays was unscrupulous in his pitching methods, a beaner with little regard for the consequences of his actions. When asked to offer proof to validate such charges, often their response was, "He wouldn't have such a reputation if it wasn't true."

Mays was aware of what the ballplayers were saying about him. In an inteview with *Baseball Magazine,* he acknowledged his reputation and offered a defense against such charges.

A twirler has a perfect right to put the ball on either side of the plate. But naturally no one has absolute control, and sometimes the pitcher who is trying to nick the corner of the plate will miss it altogether. Consequently, if the batter is hugging the plate, and many of them do this, he is likely to get hit. If the left hander is guilty, all well and good. But if the right hander is the offender, he is lucky if someone doesn't start the fairy story of bean ball pitcher.

Some newspaper writer set that story in circulation about me sometime ago, no doubt because I had been unlucky enough to hit several men. But he found other writers who were willing to join in the hue and cry, so the consequence was that in several cities of the circuit I have had to labor under the handicap of an evil reputation.

The players claim not to be influenced particularly by what they read, but quite a few players have been willing to believe the bean ball story, and in consequence I have been saddled with a reputation that I do not think I deserve.

It is very easy to give a player such a reputation. And it is very difficult for him to combat the stigma for he hasn't the ear of the public. Everyone who has ever had experience along that line knows how next to impossible it is for a private individual successfully to refute scurrilous reports that are set in circulation about him.

That has been my experience and I merely wish to say that I am not a murderer nor do I aim to take any unfair advantage of anyone. I depend largely on a peculiar delivery that I have perfected which acts in a manner almost directly contrary to that of the average right-handed pitcher. And due either to the freak breaks of this delivery or my desire to take the corners of the plate to which I am entitled, I have been unfortuante enough to hit a number of batters, though very seldom on the head.

*   *   *

There also was Mays's continuing feud with Cobb. After his first confrontation with the submarine pitcher at the end of the 1915 season, Cobb had sworn revenge. Ultimately, he made good on his vow.

It happened one year during another Boston–Detroit showdown, when several of Mays's pitches sailed in at Cobb's head. Finally, the Tiger star walked out toward the mound and warned Mays another such pitch would result in retribution. The next pitch was aimed directly at Cobb's head. He fell to the ground to dodge the pitch, then stood up and fired his bat at Mays.

When play resumed, Cobb pushed a bunt between the pitcher's box and first base. His intent was to make the first baseman field the ball, forcing Mays to cover the bag. The ploy worked, and when Mays arrived at the base, Cobb leaped at him feet first, his spikes tearing into the pitcher's leg. Mays ended up sprawled on the ground, his pants leg soaked with blood. With a savage grin on his face, Cobb looked down at the fallen pitcher and hissed, "The next time you cover the bag, I'll take the skin off the other leg."

*   *   *

While Mays was vilified by his opponents, he was despised by many of the players on his own ballclub. On the field, he was belligerent and argumentative, raging at anyone who stood in the way of his winning. He shouted at fielders who made errors behind him and belittled others for their shortcomings. Off the field, he was contemptuous of the lifestyles of the players who liked to drink, smoke, or chase women, all vices that he shunned. He was intelligent and articulate, but he pulled no punches when pointing out the faults of others.

"He was sulky," said one teammate. "He was not congenial. You would ask him a question and he would brush you off. I was never on a club that a fellow was disliked as much as Mays."

Even those who professed to like him had trouble understanding him. After Mays joined the Yankees later in his career, Colonel Huston of the New York club was prompted to observe: "Mays is one of those unlucky fellows who seem to have a special knack for getting in wrong. I was associated once with just such a man. He was an admirable character. He hadn't a conspicuous fault that you could really put your finger on. But he antagonized everybody who came within the sound of his voice. I knew him for just what he was and yet in spite of it all he used to make me hot under the collar. One of the last times I was in his office, I felt so insulted that I got up and left. But when he later told me that I ought to know him better than to act that way, I knew that he was right."

Mays himself was hardpressed to understand the cause for his growing alienation from his peers. All he knew was that such problems had dogged him throughout his baseball career.

In a 1920 interview with *Baseball Magazine,* he recalled: "When I first broke into baseball, I discovered that there seemed to be a feeling against me, even from the players on my own team. When I was with Boise, Idaho, I didn't have a pal on the club until the season was half over. Then the fellows seemed to warm up a bit and we were on very good terms for the balance of the season."

Two years later, when Mays joined Providence, he once again found himself an outcast. "I got a still bigger dose of the same unpleasant medicine and that began to get on my nerves," he remembered. "My fellow players on the Providence team didn't seem to like me and I wondered why. I always have wondered why I have encountered this antipathy from so many people wherever I have been. And I have never been able to explain it, even to myself."

It was the same way in Boston. Speaker, the head of one clique on the team, disliked Mays because of his surliness and his hot temper. Hooper, who also had a big following in the clubhouse, regarded Mays as "an odd bird."

Another of Mays's teammates who often found himself in conflict with the pitcher was his old colleague, Ruth. Several times, the two stars came close to fighting, and it was a matter of dispute as to which one actually backed down from such a confrontation.

The consensus in the clubhouse was that Mays avoided pushing Ruth too far because he knew that if the team had to make the choice of which one of its stars to keep, it would be the Babe. Others claimed Mays was afraid of Ruth, who was an imposing physical specimen. But Mays, although three inches shorter, also had a solid build and a rugged physique.

"Moreover, he was known to have a cold, calculating mind," wrote Lane of *Baseball Magazine*. "Even the most hot-headed of his critics would think twice before engaging in a physical combat with Carl Mays. Babe Ruth, big, burly, and blunt of speech, was at outs with Mays for long periods, but the two never came together. Some of the younger players in the clubhouse used to hope they might. Although Babe would appear to have a considerable advantage in weight and strength, it would have been no one-sided encounter."

In Boston, Mays came to accept his status as an outcast on the team. He professed not to know what it was about himself that turned people away from him, but then again he claimed he was not particularly concerned about finding out. "I have been told I lack tact, which is probably true," he once said. "But that is no crime."

Rather than worry about his lack of popularity, Mays accepted it as a badge of honor. If others did not accept him on his terms, then so be it. His philosophy was summed up in the interview with *Baseball Magazine:* "It was long ago made very apparent to me that I was not one of those individuals who were fated to be popular. It used to bother me some . . . but I was naturally independent and if I found that a fellow held aloof from me I was not likely to run after him."

5

Whatever else they said about him, no one questioned Mays's ability on the mound. He had another superb season in 1918, turning in a record of 21–13 and leading the league with thirty complete games and eight shutouts. True to form, he was among the leaders in another category, also. He hit eleven batters, the second-highest total in the league.

Mays capped his season by pitching a three-hitter to beat the

Chicago Cubs 2–1 in the final game of the World Series. It was his second victory of the Series and gave the Red Sox their third championship in the past four seasons. The team's celebration, however, was somewhat subdued. Reduced gate receipts due to the war limited the winning players' payoff to only $1,102.51 per man—the smallest winner's share in World Series history.

*   *   *

For Mays, the extra money was sorely needed. Eight days after the final game of the Series, he was married to Marjorie Fredricka "Freddie" Madden, a student at the New England Conservatory of Music. Following a small ceremony in the New Old South Church, Copley Square, Boston, the newlyweds left for a honeymoon in Mansfield, Missouri.

Carl and Freddie had little time to spend together before he received the inevitable induction notice from the army. Sworn into the service on November 6, he was slated for early shipment overseas, but he never made it out of St. Louis. Shortly after the recruits arrived there, the city was hit by the influenza epidemic that had started on the East Coast. Even though he never got within one thousand miles of the fighting, Mays's military stint was a grim experience. Ten of the eighteen men inducted with him died from the flu, and his entire unit was placed in quarantine. It was while he was isolated in St. Louis that he heard the Armistice had been agreed to on November 11.

A few weeks later, Mays received his discharge and returned home to his bride. That winter was perhaps the happiest period of his life. He had proven himself as one of the top pitchers in baseball, and now he had a new wife to share his successes. He was a young man with the world at his fingertips.

Two years later, he would look back at those days and recall: "I had no just complaint to offer against my experience as a professional ball player. It is true I had never been popular, but this had ceased to bother me. And if I was not popular, I was at least rated as a successful pitcher. In other words, I had made good in my chosen profession.

"I remember a conversation I had with my wife about this time in which I told her my baseball career had been singularly free from trouble. I said to her in a joking way that perhaps it would be necessary for me to do something out of the ordinary to get my name in the papers.

"But I needn't have been impatient. For could I have looked into the future, I would have seen trouble enough headed in my direction to satisfy the most ambitious trouble seeker who ever lived."

6

There were storm clouds gathering even before Mays reported to spring camp in 1919. Over the winter, Red Sox owner Frazee, in an effort to reduce the team's payroll, traded pitchers Ernie Shore and Dutch Leonard, both proven winners, and hard-hitting outfielder Duffy Lewis to the New York Yankees. In return, the Red Sox received Ray "Slim" Caldwell, a once-promising pitcher whose effectiveness was being destroyed by his frequent bouts with the whisky bottle, three second-line players, and fifteen thousand dollars in cash.

The loss of two front-line pitchers in exchange for the undepend-able Caldwell came at a bad time for Ed Barrow, the Boston manager. For the past few months, he had been tinkering with the notion of shifting Ruth from pitcher to either first base or the outfield to take advantage of his sensational slugging.

Filling in at first base or in the outfield when he wasn't pitching in 1918, Ruth had led the league in home runs with eleven—just four less than the current major-league record. Ruth, who had tired of double duty as a pitcher and outfielder and preferred to remain in the lineup every day in left field, was eager to make the move, but it went against conventional baseball logic. Left-handed pitchers were a scarce commodity, and Ruth was one of the best in the league, as evidenced by his record streak of 29⅔ consecutive scoreless innings in World Series play. No matter how promising the Babe was as a hitter, Barrow would be giving up a lot by taking him off the mound. The problem was only compounded by the loss of Leonard, the team's other left-handed starter, and Shore.

To make matters worse, Ruth had gotten himself an agent and demanded a raise from seven thousand dollars to fifteen thousand. It was a figure that would have put him behind only Detroit's Cobb, the premier player in the game. Frazee was adamant in his refusal to pay Ruth such an exalted sum, so Babe became a holdout for the first time in his career. While the Red Sox were preparing to depart for spring training, the Babe returned to the eighty-acre farm he had bought in Sudbury, twenty miles west of Boston, and made a great pretense of becoming a farmer. He tramped about his land in a huge overcoat and posed for photographers chopping wood left-handed. Seeing one such picture in the newspaper, Frazee scoffed, "Can you imagine him not playing baseball?"

But the Boston owner also was in a bind. He had made a deal with his friend John McGraw of the Giants to move his team's training camp from Hot Springs, Arkansas, to Tampa, Florida. From there, the Red Sox and Giants would launch a barnstorming tour north to raise money. Without Ruth, the trip could become a financial disaster.

In addition, Mays also had refused to sign his contract. Rather than hold out as Ruth was doing, he at least agreed to report to training camp from his home in Missouri in hopes of reaching a settlement.

Meanwhile, the remainder of the team set sail from New York harbor aboard the steamer S.S. *Arapahoe* on March 17 for a cruise down the Atlantic coast to Florida. It was an ill-fated journey. For three days, the boat was tossed about in stormy waters, and the players spent most of their time below deck battling the effects of seasickness.

One of those who never got his sea legs was pitcher Sam Jones. He was standing aboveboard clutching the railing one day when Burt

Whitman of the *Boston Herald* stopped by to talk about the upcoming season.

"How do you think you'll do this year, Sam?" asked the writer.

"Well, Burt," replied Jones, "if I can put as much on the ball this season as I've put on the briny all the way down here, I ought to go undefeated."

Once they landed in Jacksonville, the ballplayers climbed aboard a train for the 250-mile ride across Florida's orange-grove country to Tampa. Upon their arrival, they were paraded in automobiles from the train station down a brick road to the "The Tampa Bay," a spacious inn set among the palm trees a mile from downtown.

At the hotel, Barrow finally received some good news. He was handed a telegram informing him that Ruth was on his way south. Shortly after the team sailed from New York, Frazee had summoned the Babe to New York, and the two had agreed upon a three-year deal calling for ten thousand dollars a season. Ruth caught the next train to Tampa, and Frazee wired the good news ahead to the team.

Now, all that remained was to bring Mays back into the fold.

* * *

In dealing with Barrow, who was in charge of all player contracts outside of the special exception in Ruth's case, Mays was faced with a considerable adversary.

During a baseball career that spanned three decades, the fifty-year-old Barrow had been involved in every phase of the game, from team manager to league president. He managed his first team at age nineteen, when he took over the local semipro team in Des Moines, Iowa. Before his thirtieth birthday, he helped launch a short-lived baseball league in Ohio, and among the players he brought in was a young infielder named Honus Wagner, who went on to become the greatest shortstop in the history of the game.

Barrow's itinerary as a manager included stops in Detroit of the American League, Indianapolis of the American Association, and Toronto of the Eastern League. Eventually, he became president of the Eastern League, and when his seven-year reign ended in 1917 the organization had been upgraded one level to the highest classification in minor-league ball and renamed the International League. Barrow stepped down only when his friend Ban Johnson persuaded him to take the managerial reins of the Red Sox.

Barrow's style as a field manager was similar to his style as a league administrator. A gruff-looking man whose face was dominated by massive black eyebrows, he demanded obedience and he was known to chew out subordinates for the slightest mistake. If necessary, he was willing to enforce his rule with threats of physical retaliation. Barrow had proven his toughness at an early age. As a teenager in Des Moines, he had been made circulation manager of the newspaper because he could beat up all the other paperboys.

Barrow also was a notoriously hard-nosed negotiator who knew how to bully players into signing on the ballclub's terms. Frazee was so amazed at his manager's hard-line methods that he affectionately dubbed him "Simon" because of his similarity to the notorious stage character Simon Legree. And since he received a percentage of the team's profits, Barrow had good reason to keep the payroll as low as possible.

*　　　*　　　*

Mays vowed to return home if he didn't get a fair offer, but he did agree to train with the team while he and Barrow continued to negotiate. Although fifteen pounds overweight, Mays was confident he could prove to the manager he was the indispensable leader of the pitching staff.

On March 26, four days after practice began, Mays was preparing to leave for the baseball field when he was paged to the front desk of the hotel. The desk clerk handed him a telegram, and Mays quickly read through it. The words on the page left him stunned. The house that he had built in Mansfield had been burned to the ground. The only thing that had been saved was a box of possessions waiting to be shipped to Boston.

Mays was devastated by the setback. A year later, he told *Baseball Magazine*:

I had a very nice home, of which I was extremely fond and not a little proud. We fitted it up in a manner which was pleasing to us both, and I put into that home most of my earnings as a base ball player.

Furthermore, I stored in that home all the little momentos and souvenirs that I wished to preserve, and my wife did, also.

But about the time we had everything settled to suit us, the house caught fire and burned to the ground. Everything in it was totally destroyed, and as it was insured for but a fraction of its true value, I found myself practically wiped out.

He also was convinced the fire was no accident. Not long before, he confided to a few of his teammates, some of his mules had been shot and several hens stolen. Unfortunately, he had no way to prove his suspicions. All he could do now was start to rebuild his life. A few days later, he signed on Barrow's terms. It was a three-year deal that reportedly called for only three thousand dollars per season.

After signing the contract, Mays returned to Missouri to settle the insurance on the burned house. He would rejoin the team on its way north to Boston to open the season.

7

The season started off well enough. On Opening Day, Mays threw a four-hitter to beat the Yankees 10–0 in the Polo Grounds. After the rest of the series was rained out, the Red Sox moved down the coast to Washington and won twice more. Mays won the second of those games, allowing just one earned run in a 6–5 victory over Walter Johnson.

Then Barrow faced his first crisis of the year. Ruth was becoming increasingly hard to handle, and Barrow had assigned coach Dan Howley to be the big fellow's roommate and "keeper."

"Don't worry, Manager, I'll take care of that guy if I have to put a ring through his nose," vowed Howley.

But Howley proved to be no match for Ruth, who continued to flout the manager's rules. That night, the Babe missed bed check again and still hadn't returned to the hotel by 4:00 A.M. when Barrow finally retired to his room.

The next day, Ruth went hitless as the Red Sox suffered their first loss. That evening, Barrow gave the porter in the Washington hotel two dollars to let him know when Ruth got in.

"I don't care what time it is," he said. "Come to my room and tell me."

The porter nodded.

At 6:00 A.M., there was a knock on Barrow's door.

"That fellow just came in," reported the porter.

Barrow put on his dressing gown and slippers and went down the hall to Ruth's room, where there was a light shining under the door and voices inside. When Barrow knocked, the light went out and the talking stopped. The door was unlocked, so the manager pushed it open, walked in, and turned on the lights. What he saw was like a scene out of a vaudeville routine. Howley had ducked into the bathroom, leaving his rumpled bed empty, while Ruth was lying in his bed with the sheets pulled up to his chin, calmly smoking a pipe.

"Do you always smoke a pipe at this time of the morning?" asked Barrow.

Babe puffed calmly on the pipe. "Oh, sure. It's very relaxing. It helps me get back to sleep."

Barrow paused for a moment, then walked over to the bed, grabbed the sheets and yanked them back. Ruth still was fully clothed, all the way down to his shoes.

"You're a fine citizen, Babe!" roared Barrow. "I must say, you're a fine citizen!"

Wheeling about, he stormed out of the room, shouting, "I'll see you at the ballpark!"

The next day, Barrow walked into the locker room and slammed the door behind him. He then proceeded to lecture the entire team on the importance of obeying his rules, but it was clear his remarks were aimed at Ruth. Stung by Barrow's words and still embarrassed by being caught red-handed a few hours earlier, Babe finally stood up and threatened to flatten the manager on the spot.

An uncomfortable silence fell over the room as Barrow walked over to where Ruth was standing.

"If you think you can punch me in the nose, Babe, I'd like to see you try it," the manager growled.

The two glared at each other for a few seconds. Finally, Barrow, who was more than twice as old as the Babe, slowly began to remove his coat.

"The rest of you fellows get out of here—all except Ruth. I have some business I want to settle with the Babe."

After the players filed out the door, Barrow was left standing by himself. Ruth, knowing when to back down, had departed with the others.

Just before game time, Barrow was sitting on the bench writing out the lineup card when he looked up to see Ruth on the dugout steps staring down at him. Barrow ignored him and turned his attention back to the lineup card.

"Am I playing today, Manager?" asked Ruth.

Barrow continued writing.

"Go in and take your uniform off," he said without looking up. "You're suspended."

The Babe disappeared for the rest of the afternoon as the Red Sox beat the Senators 6–1 for their fourth victory in five games. He reappeared at the train station that evening when the team boarded the Federal Express to return to Boston for its home opener the following day. The train had not yet arrived in Baltimore when Ruth sought out Barrow in his drawing room.

"Will you speak to me, Manager?"

Barrow waved Ruth in and the two talked. It was a heart-to-heart discussion, with Ruth reminiscing about his boyhood and the hard times he suffered while growing up on the streets in Baltimore. In turn, Barrow, whom Babe often called "Mr. Barrows," gave Ruth a stern but fatherly lecture. Among other things, the young ballplayer was told that it was suicide for him to stay out late and to be even the least bit careless about what he ate.

Occasionally, Ruth made a forceful denial or contradiction, but for the most part he was attentive. In the eyes of Melville E. Webb, Jr., of the *Boston Globe,* Ruth showed "as much restraint as the Colossus could con."

Others may have been skeptical, but Barrow was convinced of Babe's sincerity. Finally, Ruth looked his manager in the eye and asked, "Manager, if I leave a note in your box every night when I come in, and tell you what time I got home, will you let me play?"

Barrow thought about it a few minutes and finally agreed to Ruth's proposal. By the time the lengthy conversation ended, the train had passed through not only Baltimore but also Philadelphia. In Boston the next morning, Barrow announced that "everything had been fixed up" and that the suspension had been lifted.

For the rest of the year, whenever Ruth returned to the hotel at night, he left notes addressed "Dear Eddie" or "Dear Manager" with his time of arrival. Barrow never checked to see if the Babe was telling the truth.

8

Mays had the honor of pitching the Red Sox's home opener in Fenway Park. It was not a pleasant experience. The Yankees scored four runs in the ninth inning and won 7–3 although only three of their runs were earned. Despite pitching a complete game, Mays was tagged with his first loss of the season. It was a sign of things to come.

Never in his career had Mays experienced the frustration he did that spring. Among all the Boston pitchers, he was the only one who continued to pitch well, and yet time after time his performances were wasted. The Red Sox simply could not score any runs for him.

His defeat in the home opener was the beginning of a stretch during which he lost four of five starts and left one game without a decision. In those five starts, Boston scored a total of nine runs. In addition, Mays lost one game in a relief appearance.

Even Ruth stopped hitting. One month into the season, he was batting .180 with only one home run, and the writers were starting to get on him. After Ruth went hitless one game, it was reported, "He didn't hit a thing, not even an umpire." By mid-May the slumping Red Sox had fallen into the second division. In an effort to reverse his team's fortunes, Barrow felt compelled to back out on his agreement with Ruth and press him into part-time service as a pitcher. The Babe pitched well, but still Boston continued to flounder.

As the team struggled and his own personal fortunes took a nosedive, Mays grew surlier than ever. And the worse his mood, the more vocal he became in his criticism of his teammates, whom he blamed for his troubles. At one point, he marched into Barrow's office and accused several players of "laying down" when he was on the mound. Barrow dismissed the charges as ridiculous, but Mays continued to brood.

As poorly as the Red Sox were playing, there were plenty of targets for Mays's anger. For whatever reasons, he directed most of his animosity at Jack Barry, the veteran second baseman. Although on the downside of his career, the light-hitting Barry was a flashy fielder and one of the most popular figures in the game. In 1911, he had been the shortstop of the world-champion Philadelphia Athletics' legendary "$100,000 Infield," which also included Eddie Collins at second base, Home Run Baker at third, and Stuffy McInnis at first. Boston had acquired Barry in 1915 and moved him to second base to strengthen its infield in its drive for the pennant. A respected leader on the field and a player-manager for that one season in 1917, Barry had a lot of supporters on the ballclub.

Mays cared little about Barry's past achievements or his status in the clubhouse. He was contemptuous of the Boston second baseman, and at one point he went to Barrow and threatened not to pitch with Barry playing behind him. Inevitably, the writers picked up on the trouble and reported there was a "plot" against Barry, with Mays the ringleader.

Soon, the discontent on the team was the subject of rumors among the press and fans, and there was talk of several trades to shake up the team. Considering Mays's value to the team, it wasn't surprising that most of the trade talk centered on Barry, who reportedly would be shipped to Philadelphia for Bobby Roth, a hard-hitting outfielder. Both Frazee and Barrow remained silent on the matter.

*   *   *

Ty Cobb had a matter he wanted set straight that spring. His opportunity to do so came in late May, when the Red Sox arrived in Detroit on the first part of a western swing. The Boston players were on the field warming up before the game when Cobb marched up to Mays on the sidelines.

"Say, will you answer a question for me?" he demanded.

"That depends on the question," answered Mays. "If it's a fair question."

"I said a fair question. Will you answer it?"

"Yes. If it's a fair question and I can answer it. Go ahead."

Cobb looked the pitcher square in the eye. "Do you try to hit me?"

"What do you think, Ty?"

"Never mind that. You aren't answering my question. Yes or no. Do you try to hit me?"

Mays paused. "Once more, Ty. What do you think?"

"That isn't the point. I think you do."

"Well," said Mays, "if you think I do, Ty, that makes me a better pitcher. As long as you're feeling that way about it, I'm the more effective."

Cobb bristled at the suggestion. "Are you? Some day I'll drive one back at you, and with a silver plate in your knee you won't be so effective."

Shrugging his shoulders, Mays answered, "Well, if that's the case, I won't make a fuss over it and turn to the stands for sympathy like you do."

"You haven't answered my question," Cobb insisted. "Let's settle that. Do you try to hit me?"

"No, I don't try to hit you, and I don't try to hit anybody, but if I do hit you, I don't care. I've had them try to hit me, and I've never squealed."

"All right," said Cobb. "We'll bury the hatchet. It's a case of each man looking out for himself. If you hit me or I cut you, we'll let it go at that."

"Right-o," said Mays.

*   *   *

Mays's troubles with his teammates began to come to a head on that road trip. The Red Sox wrapped up the series in Detroit by losing to the Tigers 5–3 when Mays, pitching in relief, gave up three runs in two innings for his fourth consecutive loss. Afterward, he was packing his belongings for the trip to Cleveland when he discovered his glove was missing. He went around the locker room demanding to know who had taken it. When no one spoke up, Mays angrily reported to Barrow that the glove had been stolen.

The next morning in Cleveland, Mays went out to buy a new mitt. Since he was scheduled to be the starting pitcher that afternoon, he hurriedly oiled the glove in an effort to break it in properly. In his haste, he overdid the job. When he went out to pitch, the glove was so oily it made the ball slick and difficult to control.

At one point, the ball became so slippery Mays called time and asked umpire Ollie Chill to replace it. Chill refused, claiming there was nothing wrong with the ball. When Mays explained his problem, the umpire suggested he borrow a glove from one of the other Boston pitchers. Mays walked over to the dugout and asked if anyone would lend him a mitt. His request was met with stony silence. Mays turned to the umpire and shrugged his shoulders. Finally, Chill tossed him a fresh baseball.

Mays got beat 3–2 for his fifth consecutive defeat, with the winning run scoring after an error by Barry. It was the normally smooth-fielding second baseman's second error of the day. Barry, as well as McInnis, also got thrown out at home due to some poor base running.

It probably was no coincidence that in Mays's next start four days later in Philadelphia, forty-one-year-old journeyman infielder Dave Shean played second base and Barry was on the bench. Mays beat the Athletics 7–1 to end his losing streak, but the Red Sox still were in sixth place with a 10–14 record, nine games behind front-running Chicago. The chances of overtaking five teams, including the powerful White Sox and Indians, already seemed remote.

*   *   *

Bryan Hayes, a member of the Philadelphia customs office and a boxing instructor at the Racquet Club, took advantage of the Memorial Day holiday to go to the ballgame with a group of friends. Like many of the fans in Philadelphia's Shibe Park that day, Hayes was more interested in seeing Boston slugger Babe Ruth than the hometown Athletics, who had been the doormat of the league for the past few years. The day before, Ruth had hit a line shot that cleared the right-field fence and struck the roof of one of the houses on adjacent Twentieth Street and bounded on until it was lost from view. Philadelphia writer James Isaminger called Ruth's homer "the longest hit made on these grounds in history."

Sitting a few rows behind the Red Sox dugout and dressed stylishly in a new straw hat, Hayes was rooting for Ruth to hit the ball out of the park again.

Boston led 2–0 in the bottom of the second when the Athletics began to hit the ball hard off the Red Sox's six-foot-four pitcher, Big Bill James. After three runs had crossed the plate, giving Philadelphia the lead, several rooters excitedly began pounding on the tin roof that covered the visitors' dugout. Inside the dugout, the Boston players cursed the terrible din.

Hayes was about to say something to the man next to him when he noticed someone leap from the dugout holding a baseball in his right hand. The ballplayer was Carl Mays. Without warning, he cocked his arm and fired the ball into the stands with a sidearm motion.

Many of the people sitting in the area never even saw the ball thrown into their midst. It would not have made much difference. There was not time to react as the ball grazed a woman's head before striking Hayes, breaking his straw hat and leaving him temporarily dazed. In the resulting confusion, an unidentified Boston player reached out and punched another man sitting behind the dugout.

Fortunately for Hayes, his hat absorbed most of the blow, leaving him with no more than a bump on the head, a broken hat, and an angry disposition. He stayed to watch the remainder of the game, which Boston won 6–4, then went to the ballclub's offices to lodge a complaint. He was met there by Athletics manager Connie Mack, who pleaded with him not to take legal action in the matter. Hayes was too angry to listen. He left the ballpark and went down to the police station, where a warrant was issued for Mays's arrest. Before the warrant could be served, Mays and the other members of the Red Sox, having completed the series, already had packed their bags and left town.

*   *   *

The victory in Philadelphia was only a brief respite for Mays. In the seven games he started in June, the Red Sox scored a total of eight runs. In three of his four losses, Boston was shut out. In the two games he did win that month, he had to be nearly perfect, prevailing 2–0 and 2–1. By the end of June, Mays's record was 5–9.

The Red Sox remained mired in the second division, and finally, on June 27, an attempt was made to shake up the team by trading Barry and outfielder Amos Strunk to the Athletics for Braggo Roth and second baseman Red Shannon. Barry refused to report to Philadelphia and announced his retirement.

The team's only bright spot was Ruth, who had recovered from his early batting slump to raise his average well over .300. He was hitting the ball so well Barrow finally pulled him off the mound and let him concentrate on playing the outfield and batting.

*　　　*　　　*

When the Red Sox returned to Philadelphia to open a three-game series July 1, Mays gave little thought to the Memorial Day incident or the outstanding warrant for his arrest. He was standing in the hotel lobby waiting to check in when one of his teammates hurried over and grabbed him by the arm.

"You better get out of here," the player said. "There's a constable over there who says he has a warrant for your arrest."

Mays looked over to see Barrow talking to a stranger. It appeared the Boston manager was trying to delay the man. Mays didn't need any more prompting. He grabbed his suitcase and quietly slipped out the exit. He returned to the station and made good his escape by catching the next train back to Boston.

*　　　*　　　*

The following week, the Red Sox were scheduled to depart on a two-week western swing that would take them to St. Louis, Chicago, Cleveland, and Detroit. Mays threatened not to accompany the team, claiming Barrow had reneged on an agreement to pay the fine the pitcher had incurred in Philadelphia. Barrow responded that it was not the club's responsibility to settle Mays's legal debts. The *Boston Globe* reported that Barrow was unmoved by Mays's threats to walk out and had said that the pitcher "could go fishing or anywhere else he elects."

The day before the trip was to begin, the club backed down and paid the fine. The matter was settled in the morning. That afternoon, Mays reported to the ballpark in Boston for the second game of a doubleheader. He pitched the final two innings in relief to save a 5–4 victory over the Athletics.

On July 8, Mays was with his teammates as they boarded the train and headed for Chicago. Although his differences with Barrow appeared to have been patched up, Mays's days with Boston were rapidly coming an end.

*　　　*　　　*

The Red Sox's game against the first-place White Sox on Sunday, July 13, started out as a typical display of the ineptness that had plagued them all season. The Red Sox already trailed 4–0 in the second inning when catcher Wally Schang attempted to throw out a baserunner at second base. Instead, the peg hit Mays in the back of the head.

After the side had been retired, with the score still 4–0, Mays was seething. He stormed off the mound in a rage, ignoring the jeers and catcalls from the rooters in Comiskey Park. By the time he neared the dugout, he had built up a full head of steam. Instead of joining his teammates in the dugout, he threw down his glove and headed for the clubhouse.

"I'll never pitch for this ballclub again!" he shouted as he stormed past the bench.

Barrow wasn't even aware Mays was gone until someone came over and told him. The manager's first thought was that his pitcher had suffered a cut on his scalp when he was hit by Schang's errant throw. Barrow told pitcher Sam Jones to go check on Mays, then he turned his attention back to the ballgame.

When Jones walked into the clubhouse, he saw Mays sitting by his locker, undressing.

"Barrow wants you back on the field," said Jones.

Mays ignored his teammate and continued to peel off his uniform. Jones started to say something else, but Mays cut him short.

"Tell Barrow I've gone fishing."

When Jones returned to the dugout and relayed the message, Barrow rushed a relief pitcher out to warm up. He also dispatched another messenger to the clubhouse.

Mays heard the man enter the room, but he refused to look up from his locker. Instead, he sat there weeping. In a few minutes, the other player silently slipped out the door.

Outside, the White Sox were in the process of roughing up Boston reliever George Dumont for seven more runs over the next four innings to pile up an 11–3 lead. Meanwhile, Mays left the clubhouse and caught a taxi back to the hotel where the Red Sox were quartered. There, he picked up his bags and checked out, leaving behind a handwritten note.

Although the contents of the note never were made public, James O'Leary of the *Boston Globe* later claimed to have seen it. In the note, reported O'Leary, Mays indicated he was despondent over some personal problems.

Despite a late rally, the Red Sox lost the game 14–9. Mays was charged with the defeat, but that was of little concern to him by now. He already was at the train station, where he paid his own fare for a ticket back to Boston. That night, he was on his way home. Mays had taken Barrow at his word. He was going fishing.

9

On the overnight train ride to Boston, Mays had time to plan his next step. He would settle his accounts in Boston, then he and Freddie would drive to her parents' home in Hopewell, Pennsylvania, to ride out the storm. He knew that if he was patient, he could force the Red Sox to send him to another team.

But first, Mays must get his side of the story before the public. He didn't have to wait long to do so. When the train arrived in Boston on Monday morning, Mays was greeted by Burt Whitman.

The official announcement by the Red Sox regarding Mays's departure was that the pitcher had headed to Chicago to rest for the upcoming series there. But the *Boston Herald* writer knew better, and he had correctly guessed that Mays would be arriving at Trinity Station.

Normally, Mays was guarded in his comments to the press, but he welcomed the opportunity to talk to Whitman. Mays knew exactly what he wanted to say.

"I'll never pitch another ball for the Red Sox," he told Whitman. "I intend to fix up my affairs here and then go fishing in Pennsylvania.

"And I want to say it right here, and I can't put it too strongly, manager Ed Barrow is a gentleman and a fine fellow, but I'm convinced that it will be impossible for me to preserve my confidence in myself as a ballplayer and stay with the Red Sox as the team is now being handled.

"So far this year, I have won only five games and have lost eleven. I have pitched better ball than ever before, but I have never known where I was at. The entire team is up in the air, and things have gone from bad to worse. The team cannot win with me pitching so I am getting out. And that's all there is to it.

"I do not say that I will not play any more ball. Maybe there will be a trade or a sale of my services. I do not care where I go. I have enough confidence in my ability as a pitcher to believe that I can finish better than .500 even if I went to the Philadelphia Athletics."

Mays paused before going on. He had a favor to ask of Whitman.

"Please do not make it appear as if I were throwing down the team," he said. "That would be putting it wrong. I believe it ought to be up there fighting for the lead right now, but there is not a chance the way things are being handled."

When Whitman noted that some people might interpret such action as akin to deserting his team, Mays shook his head and laughed.

"You can desert the army or a wife and children," he said, "but you just can't possibly desert some twenty able-bodied baseball players."

*   *   *

Mays's arguments didn't win him any supporters in the sporting press. The writers were only too eager to condemn him for his actions.

Ernest Lanigan noted in *The Sporting News* that Barrow had dug into his own pocket to pay the fine Ban Johnson slapped on Mays for throwing the ball into the stands in Philadelphia. Lanigan said Mays's action "shows how he appreciates good treatment."

James Isaminger of the *Philadelphia North American* claimed the one-hundred-dollar fine levied for the Memorial Day incident had not been paid by the Red Sox, and the refusal of the team to do so was one of the reasons Mays walked out. "But the real reason was that he was jealous of the salary paid to Babe Ruth," wrote Isaminger.

In Boston, the *Globe*'s O'Leary, pointing out that the pitcher had just signed a three-year contract at his own insistence in the spring, noted that Mays was more than happy to pitch for the Red Sox as long as he felt he had a chance to gain a share of World Series money. "Now that the team is in the doldrums, and its prospects at low ebb, he hops out," said O'Leary.

The Boston players also closed ranks to rebuke Mays. They issued a statement claiming the team's poor showing was due to the condition of the pitching staff early in the season and to "the general ill luck they have been up against shortly after the opening." Every one of Mays's teammates signed the statement.

*   *   *

Despite the press's indignation, it soon became apparent that Mays had correctly gauged management's response to the walkout. The Boston owner was Harry Frazee, and he was not as concerned with the principles involved in the matter as he was with the financial considerations. Regardless of all else, Mays was a valuable commodity, and Frazee was sorely pressed for money.

The thirty-nine-year-old Frazee was not a traditional baseball man. He had made his mark at the theater, not the ballpark. He was a short, plump man with a soft face and swarthy complexion. His flashy clothes and diamond rings set him apart from his peers in baseball, but Frazee was a charming and shrewd operator who knew how to get along in any crowd.

He was from Peoria, Illinois, and he had worked as a bellhop before getting into the theater business in Chicago. Eventually, he bought his first theater there and later he would add the Longacre

Theater in New York to his holdings. Occasionally, Frazee ventured out of show business and into other productions. In 1915, he helped promote the Jack Johnson–Jess Willard heavyweight championship fight in Havana, Cuba.

In 1916, a year after the fight, one of Frazee's Broadway productions, a comedy titled *Nothing but the Truth,* had a hit run at the Longacre. Frazee was riding high, and when the opportunity came to venture into baseball, he jumped at it. Red Sox owner Joe Lannin, whose team had won two championships in the three years since he had purchased the club, had grown weary of the responsibility of running his baseball operation. He was in failing health and the ballclub was becoming a financial drain. On November 1, 1916, Lannin announced he had sold the club for $675,000 to a three-man group headed by Frazee. The three men put up less than half of the total cost in cash. The rest was covered in the form of notes from Frazee to Lannin, putting the new owners on shaky ground financially from the start.

Although Frazee knew little about baseball and had only a limited amount of money at his disposal, he jumped into the sport with the same boom-or-bust philosophy it took to survive on Broadway. In his first month as owner, he heard the Washington Senators were considering an offer of fifty thousand dollars for pitcher Walter Johnson. Frazee immediately made a public bid of sixty thousand.

That attempted purchase failed, but Frazee kept trying. In 1918, when all sixteen major-league teams were losing front-line players to the military service, Frazee beefed up the Red Sox by picking up pitcher Joe Bush, catcher Wally Schang, and outfielder Amos Strunk—all valuable members of Connie Mack's Athletics—for sixty thousand dollars and three second-line players. Frazee was accused of trying to buy a pennant, a charge that would seem ironic in light of his later actions with the Red Sox.

By the summer of 1919, Frazee's fortunes had taken a turn for the worse. He didn't have a hit play, and he was hard-pressed for cash. His baseball team had plunged into the second division and his biggest drawing card—the irrepressible Ruth—had become a constant source of irritation over salary matters.

Then came word of Mays's defection. Frazee was in New York when he received the news. Most baseball people assumed the pitcher would be suspended for his actions, but Frazee had more pressing concerns than enforcing discipline on his baseball team.

Reaching Barrow by telephone, Frazee instructed his manager: "Don't suspend this fellow. The Yankees want him and I can get a lot of money for him."

*   *   *

Frazee always had gotten along well with the Yankees' co-owners, Colonels Jacob Ruppert and Tillingham Huston. In 1918, when Ruppert had challenged Ban Johnson's decison to call a premature halt to the season because of wartime demands, Frazee had sided with the New York owners. Together, they had been able to force a compromise settlement with Johnson.

Now, in another time of trouble, Frazee turned to Ruppert and Huston.

The Yankees' owners were an unlikely pair, with little in common outside of the appellation "Colonel."

Brash and outgoing, Huston was a fat man with little concern for his appearance. Often he wore the same suit for a week at a time. He was known as "the man in the iron hat" because of his ever-present dusty derby.

Ruppert, on the other hand, was a reserved man, meticulous in his dress. Every article of clothing he wore was custom made, and he often wore as many as four outfits in a day.

The two had bought the Yankees in 1915 from Frank Farrell and Big Bill Devery, a Tammany politician. The ballclub wasn't much back then, and each man had to put up only two hundred thousand dollars.

Ruppert, who had become president of his father's brewery at age twenty-nine and increased the family fortune sevenfold, belonged to New York's famous Seventh Regiment and gained his military title when appointed an aide to Governor Hill. He was a New York Giants fan and had only seen the Yankees play one time before he was talked into making the purchase.

Huston had been a civil engineer in Ohio at the outbreak of the Spanish-American War in 1898. He organized a company of engineers and led them to Cuba, and after the war he stayed on to accumulate a fortune at the head of his own engineering firm, dredging harbors and building sea walls, roads, railroads, public buildings, and private residences. It was during this time that Huston, known as "Cap" for his army rank of captain, met Giants manager John McGraw, who had taken his team to Cuba for spring training. The two became friends, and when Huston went in with Ruppert to buy the Yankees, McGraw helped them secure the services of his friend Harry Sparrow as business manager.

The day after the United States entered the Great War in Europe in April 1917, Captain Huston again enlisted in the army. In January 1919, he returned from the war, a full colonel, but he still preferred to be called Cap.

Despite their differences in personality, Ruppert and Huston shared one trait. Both had an intense desire to win. Under their leadership—and with their money—the Yankees had become a vastly improved ballclub by 1919. It was making a run at its first championship, and the addition of a pitcher such as Mays could prove to be all it needed to beat out the White Sox and Indians.

The Yankee colonels would be only too happy to work out a deal with their old friend Frazee.

*   *   *

The Yankees weren't the only team interested in bidding on Mays's services. For all of the problems he could cause, Mays still was a highly prized commodity who would have been a welcome addition to any of the contenders. Frazee was prudent enough to recognize he could parlay the controversy into a sizeable financial profit.

In Chicago, owner Charles Comiskey had put together a powerful team that had jumped into the lead early in the season and showed no signs of surrendering its hold on first place. The White Sox lineup featured some of the greatest stars in the game. At second base was the smooth-fielding Eddie "Cocky" Collins, the premier infielder of his day. At third was the cat-quick Buck Weaver, a .300 hitter who still played with the boundless enthusiasm of a rookie. In the outfield was the great Shoeless Joe Jackson, considered the best natural hitter ever to play the game. On the mound, Chicago had knuckleballer Eddie Cicotte, who had won forty games over the previous two seasons, plus hard-throwing Lefty Williams and spitballer Urban "Red" Faber.

Chicago had broken Boston's stranglehold on the championship by winning the American League title in 1917 and now appeared on the verge of establishing a dynasty of its own.

If Comiskey could get a proven winner such as Mays, the pennant would be as good as won.

The White Sox owner immediately offered Frazee twenty-five thousand dollars for the pitcher.

Washington, Detroit, and Cleveland also made inquiries, with Indians owner Jim Dunn showing the most interest. The Indians had the best batting attack in the league but were thin in pitching. Even before the walkout by Mays, Dunn had tried to work a deal for the pitcher. Initially, the Red Sox wanted outfielder Jack Graney and second baseman Bill Wambsganss, both starters, plus reserve first baseman Doc Johnston. Now, the offer being discussed was pitchers Guy Morton, Fritz Coumbe, and Hi Jasper plus cash for Mays.

*   *   *

Within a matter of days, it appeared that any speculation over Mays was academic. Johnson, disturbed that no disciplinary action was being taken against the recalcitrant pitcher, decided to get involved in the affair. The AL president believed that if Mays was allowed to force his team to trade him to one of the contenders simply by walking off the job, other players would follow suit. The result, in his view, would be anarchy.

So Johnson sent word to the eight owners that he wanted no transaction made for Mays until the pitcher returned to the Red Sox in good standing. His intent was clear: Frazee must take some form of disciplinary action to put Mays back in line.

In reply to this directive, Colonel Huston of the Yankees stated his club would cease negotiations for Mays if the other club owners would do likewise.

That was all the assurance Johnson needed. Believing his wishes would be respected, he sat back and waited for Mays to admit defeat. Johnson had no idea who the real loser would be in this battle.

10

Throughout the turmoil he had created, Mays remained secluded in Pennsylvania. When he wasn't hunting or fishing, he passed the time at the local barber shop in Hopewell, visiting with the local residents. That was where he was when he received a telephone call on the night of July 29—seventeen days after his walkout. The man on the other end of the line identified himself as Colonel Huston of the Yankees.

"I called to find out if you would be interested in pitching for the Yankees. If you are, there's a good chance of my swinging a deal for you tonight."

"How about the money?" asked Mays.

"We'll have no problem there. Just pack your bag, and by the time you get here we'll be ready to talk contract."

With a verbal assurance from Mays that he would sign with New York, Huston got back in touch with Boston's Frazee. The deal was set. In exchange for Mays, Frazee would receive forty thousand dollars and two pitchers—Allan Russell, a thirty-one-year-old right-hander with a 5–5 record and a career mark of 26–36, and Bob McGraw, a twenty-four-year-old right-hander with one victory in three seasons of infrequent use.

*   *   *

American League president Ban Johnson was spending the weekend in St. Louis with his friend J. G. Taylor Spink, publisher of *The Sporting News,* when the news broke.

Johnson was a huge man with an ego to match his girth. He was an autocratic leader who ruled with an iron hand, and more than any other man he was responsible for the success of the young league. While some disagreed with his methods, no one disputed his right to the title "Father of the American League."

Johnson was born in 1864 in Norwalk, Ohio, where his father was an educator at a Midwestern college. Ban was graduated from law school in Cincinnati and worked briefly for a law firm there before becoming a reporter for a Cincinnati newspaper. Soon, he developed into a well-known baseball writer and through his work he became friends with Charles Comiskey, who at the time was managing the Cincinnati baseball club.

Comiskey convinced him to leave the newspaper business for baseball, and in 1894 Johnson became president of the Western League. Being an old newspaperman, the young baseball executive recognized the importance of the media to the game. Whereas baseball writers used to be thrown out of the park if they didn't write to suit the owners, Johnson courted the writers and saw to it they always had plenty of good copy.

Six years later, Johnson's organization was ready to challenge for status as a major league. Comiskey moved his St. Paul, Minnesota, franchise to Chicago, and the war with the National League was on.

The league reorganized as the American League and began playing a schedule in 1901. Johnson was an untiring fighter in the struggle, and within two years his league gained recognition with the signing of a peace settlement known as the Cincinnati Agreement.

The American League continued to prosper, and in 1919 the fifty-five-year-old Johnson was the most powerful man in baseball.

He had just sat down at the breakfast table with Spink when he opened the newspaper to the sports pages. Across the top of the page was the headline: "CARL MAYS TRADED TO NEW YORK."

The old czar was furious. Not only did he feel betrayed, he saw the move as a challenge to his dictatorial rule of the league. Johnson immediately suspended Mays and issued instructions to his umpires not to allow him to participate in a game in a New York uniform.

"Baseball cannot tolerate such a breach of discipline," he announced. "It was up to the owners of the Boston club to suspend Carl Mays for breaking his contract and when they failed to do so, it is my duty as head of the American League to act. Mays will not play with any club until the suspension is raised. He should have reported to the Boston club before they made any trade or sale."

*　　　*　　　*

In Cleveland, Dunn and Speaker sensed a double cross.

"Mr. Johnson must have notified all the clubs the same as he did us," said Speaker. "We would have offered Boston just as much money as did New York and given them a better deal in the way of players, but called everything off when Johnson said there would be no deal for Mays this season."

Dunn claimed his trade talks with the Red Sox had occurred before Mays's walkout. Although still interested in a deal, the Indians owner said that after Mays walked out on his team Barrow told him "all bets" were off because a principle now was involved. According to Dunn, Barrow reported that Frazee had stated Mays would pitch for the Red Sox or no one.

*　　　*　　　*

Having swung the deal for Mays, the Yankees were in no mood to back down. Colonel Ruppert, in a wire asking Johnson to lift the suspension, questioned the league president's authority to interfere in a matter between the Red Sox and one of their players. Ruppert also claimed that if Johnson was going to take action against Mays, he should have done so while the player was refusing to report to Boston rather than wait until he was a member of the New York team.

Johnson wasn't swayed by such arguments. He said the suspension would remain in effect, but he did propose a special league meeting in New York to iron out the problem.

The Yankee colonels rejected this idea and said they would refuse to attend such a meeting, claiming the outcome was predetermined. Instead, they met with Johnson in a stormy session during which they brought out all of their past and present objections to Johnson's handling of his office.

Among other things, the colonels charged Johnson with conflict of interest in the matter. They were aware of Johnson's stockholding interest in the Cleveland club and that, they claimed, had motivated him to keep Mays from playing for New York since both the Yankees and the Indians were in contention for the pennant.

Johnson defended his stock holdings as a matter of necessity in helping Dunn purchase the Indians and keep the franchise financially viable. As he pointed out, it was not the first time he had resorted to such tactics to prop up shaky franchises in the young league. More to the point, Johnson adamantly maintained that Mays was a contract-breaker and that to allow him to be traded under such circumstances would be to encourage insubordination by other dissatisfied players.

The meeting accomplished little more than to accentuate the depth of feelings on the matter. The battle lines were formed, and the other owners had no choice but to take sides on the matter.

The majority lined up behind Johnson. These were the Loyalists, consisting of Cleveland's Dunn, Detroit's Frank Navin, Washington's Clark Griffith, St. Louis's Phil Ball, and Philadelphia's Connie Mack and B. F. Shibe.

On the other side were the "Insurrectionists," led by Ruppert and Huston of the Yankees and supported by Chicago's Comiskey and Boston's Frazee. Although outnumbered five to three, the Insurrectionists held control of the league's five-man board of directors. Dunn and Griffith were the only Loyalist members of this policy-making body.

*   *   *

Despite the storm he had unleashed, Mays received a warm greeting from most of his new teammates. When he first arrived in the Yankees' clubhouse, the players came over one by one to welcome him and shake his hand. Only one man hung back. Truck Hannah, a broad-shouldered catcher, sat in front of his locker with his back to the newcomer.

Mays, who recognized the catcher from his days in the Northwest League, walked over to offer a greeting. When he did, Hannah suddenly spun around and swung at him, hitting him in the chest. The unexpected blow staggered Mays, knocking him backward across the room and into some lockers. The other players were too startled to react as Hannah jumped across a table and charged at Mays as if to finish him off. But just as unexpectedly as he had attacked, the big catcher abruptly stopped and extended his hand.

Smiling, he said, "Now we're all even."

Mays nodded as if he understood.

"What was that all about?" someone asked Mays later.

Mays explained that he always had been particular about presenting a neat appearance on the field, even going so far as to keep several pairs of freshly polished shoes in his locker.

"But every time I'd go up to bat when I was pitching against the Yankees, Hannah would squat down there underneath the bat with that big quid of his, and he'd splatter tobacco juice all over my shoes. So every time he'd come to bat, I'd deck him."

I I

On August 7, before a doubleheader between the Yankees and Browns at the Polo Grounds in New York, an injunction was served on the umpires. It was a court order obtained by the Yankee colonels and it restrained league president Johnson, his umpires, and agents from interfering with the contract between the Yankees and Mays or with the established schedule between the New York team and the other members of the American League.

When the second game of the doubleheader began, Mays strode out to the mound to make his first start as a Yankee. The crowd of sixteen thousand stood and cheered, and they cheered even louder when the submarine pitcher struck out the first three batters he faced.

Mays pitched a six-hitter to beat the Browns 8–2 and when he retired the final batter, he was mobbed by his new teammates. The press immediately dubbed him "The Injunction Kid."

*   *   *

Off the field, the legal maneuvering continued. The Yankees offered to settle the matter peacefully at a special owners meeting in New York, but only Comiskey and Frazee, the other two Insurrectionists, attended. The attitude of the Loyalists was expressed by St. Louis's Phil Ball, who wired: ". . . Your business sagacity and acumen in Mays matter does not appeal to us. Your sportsmanship smells to heaven. We decline your invitation."

Ruppert shot back this reply: "Refusal not unacceptable in view of your gratuitous insult in reply to polite invitation."

Huston further fanned the flames with a bitter verbal attack on Johnson, referring to him as "a carbuncle on the league organization."

Ruppert's next move was to summon the five-man board of directors, which was controlled by the Insurrectionists. With only the three Insurrectionist votes present, the board reinstated Mays in good standing with the Yankees.

*   *   *

From his vantage point, Mays followed the proceedings with a certain amount of amazement. In an interview the following year, he would recall: "I came to New York in a display of brilliant fireworks. There were court proceedings and more court proceedings. There was talk of a disruption of the entire league. The whole thing looked to me like a tempest in a teapot.

"Perhaps if I had been inclined to be swell-headed, I would have got all puffed up about the desperate struggle that was taking place over my own unimportant self. But I have never been criticized for undue egotism. That is one fault, at least, which has not been laid to my charge."

Nor could anyone accuse Mays of being overwhelmed by the legal battle raging around him. Going about his business on the field, he beat Cleveland in his second start with New York. He had a chance to win his third consecutive game when he faced the Tigers in Detroit on August 14.

The umpire behind the plate that day was Clarence "Brick" Owens, a rough character who had begun his umpiring career quite by accident. As a sixteen-year-old ballplayer in 1901, Owens had bought a revolver with the intention of using it in the pregame Fourth of July ceremonies at a game in Chicago. Instead, he carelessly shot himself in the hand. Although his hand was heavily bandaged, he decided to go to the ballpark anyway, and while there he was pressed into service as an umpire. The pay was fifty cents. That was the beginning of a long journey that eventually led Owens to the American League as a member of Ban Johnson's umpiring crew in 1916. Along the way, he picked up his nickname when a hoodlum nailed him with a brick while he was calling a game in Pittsburg, Kansas.

On this particular day, the Yankees and Tigers were tied 3–3 when New York got a runner to second base with two outs in the top of the tenth inning. Mays, always a good hitter, was allowed to bat for himself. A hit would have driven in the go-ahead run, but instead he took a pitch for a called third strike to retire the side.

To show his displeasure with the call, Mays hurled his bat high in the air toward the bleachers down the right-field line. Before the bat even had time to hit the ground, Owens majestically signaled that Mays was ejected from the game. The Yankees eventually won 5–4, but afterward all anyone wanted to talk about was Mays's spectacular bat toss.

The Sporting News, which was firmly behind Johnson in the legal dispute over Mays, took note of the incident and wondered: "Is Brick Owens in contempt of court? Or will the three members of the board of directors who reinstated Mays sit on his case and discipline him for what amounts to flouting of their authority?"

*　　*　　*

Although the Yankees could not maintain the pace set by the White Sox and Indians, Mays continued to pitch well down the stretch. His record in New York was 9–3, giving him an overall mark of 14–14. More important, his nine victories allowed the Yankees to edge the Tigers by one-half game for third place, a crucial difference since only the top three teams shared in the receipts from the World Series.

Detroit's Navin immediately moved to block the disbursement of the prize money by filing a formal objection to the final standings, arguing that games won by New York with Mays pitching were illegal because the pitcher was under suspension. At stake in the dispute was roughly thirteen thousand dollars, a hefty sum that only added to what already was being contested: Johnson's control over the league.

Ruppert's reply to the action was predictable: "This protest from Mr. Navin verifies my opinion of the gentleman's sporting caliber, and it is my belief, based upon his well-known timorousness, that without the suggestion of support from the self-constituted powers in baseball he would not have the temerity to champion his untenable position so boldly."

At the time, Pirates president Garry Herrmann still was the chairman of baseball's three-man National Commission. But Herrmann's hold on his position was tenuous. The other National League owners, many of whom felt they had been treated unfairly by Herrmann in the past, were pushing for a neutral party as head of the commission. Only Johnson, exercising the control he then had over the AL owners, had saved Herrmann the previous year. To repay this personal debt Herrmann now sided with Johnson and agreed to hold up the payment of the third-place money.

Next, it was the Yankees' turn to strike a blow, which they did with an attempt to have the temporary injunctions on Mays's behalf made permanent. During a preliminary hearing on the matter,

Johnson was forced to admit he had not suspended Mays until two days after the Yankees purchased his contract and that he had sent telegrams to all AL owners except Frazee to tell them not to negotiate for Mays. Johnson said he had omitted Frazee because he was waiting for the Red Sox owner to discipline Mays.

That evidence persuaded New York Supreme Court Justice Robert F. Wagner, later a U.S. senator, to make the injunctions permanent on October 26. According to Wagner, it was the right of clubs to regulate their own affairs without interference from the league president.

The Yankee colonels were jubilant.

"Our fight has not been for Mays alone," they announced, "but to safeguard the vested and property rights of the individual club owner against the continual encroachments on club rights by the president, who has never been clothed with the powers that he has taken unto himself."

It was only a temporary victory. The fighting continued through-out the offseason, and feelings still were running high when the two sides got together at a league meeting in New York in December. On the eve of the meeting, Comiskey learned from Navin that the five Loyalists planned to vote the Insurrectionists off the board of directors and install a new board.

"Nothing but the vanity of one man [Johnson] stands in the way of peace in baseball," said Huston upon hearing the news.

The meeting was held behind closed doors, but the shouts of the owners could be heard out in the hallway. At one point, Ruppert screamed, "You can't drive us out of baseball!"

With five votes, the Loyalists held the balance of power, and they put it to good use. Comiskey was voted out as vice-president and replaced by Navin. Ruppert, Comiskey, and Frazee were replaced on the board of directors. Their seats plus the one vacated earlier by Dunn were taken by Ball of St. Louis, Shibe of Philadelphia, Navin of Detroit, and Benjamin Minor of Washington.

Johnson claimed he had signed a contract in 1910 making him president for twenty years at an annual salary of thirty thousand dollars, so no election for president was held.

When it was all over, Huston told reporters, "They rode over us with a steamroller and we are going to send the steamroller right back at them."

To do so, the Yankees again turned to the courts, where they sought to remove Johnson from office and force him to produce the contract he claimed to have signed in 1910.

In early February 1920—with spring training rapidly approaching and the Mays affair still not settled—the Yankees filed a five-hundred-thousand-dollar suit against Johnson and the Loyalists on the ground that the AL president "conceived the idea of driving the New York club out of baseball and to this end did various acts injurious to the New York club, including the suspension of Mays, [and] making public the plans which the New York club had for a new baseball site, preventing the acquisition on favorable terms."

By now, the Insurrectionists were talking with the anti-Herrmann faction in the National League about joining forces to form a new twelve-team circuit.

Realizing that something had to be done before the American League was irreparably torn apart, Tigers president and league vice-president Frank Navin stepped forward as a peacemaker. He persuaded the owners to convene in Chicago on February 10.

Once more, it was a raucous gathering. One writer said, "There were many times when all were talking at once." At one point, Ball and Ruppert almost came to blows.

After three exhausting sessions throughout the day and late into the night, the owners finally emerged at two o'clock the following morning with a settlement. It was almost a total defeat for Johnson. Mays was reinstated without penalty as a member of the Yankees, New York's third-place finish was recognized, and the prize money would be paid to the team immediately. As a further blow to Johnson's formerly autocratic power, a two-man committee of Ruppert and Griffith was appointed to review all penalties of more than one hundred dollars and suspensions in excess of ten days. In case of a tie vote by the committee, a federal judge in Chicago would decide the issue. In return, the Yankees agreed to call off their lawsuits.

Johnson, the father of the American League, was drawn and pale as he left the meeting room and walked past the reporters without saying a word. His power had been shattered, reducing him almost to a figurehead leader. In his bitterness, he would not forget those who had brought about his defeat.

*   *   *

Mays spent the winter in Missouri, where he supervised the erection of a hunting and fishing lodge on his property. Shortly before it was time to report for spring training, he sat down to write a letter to the Yankees expressing his gratitude for the ballclub's efforts in his behalf.

"I sure am going to fight hard to help the Yankees win," he wrote. "The club deserves success after all this trouble, and I am going to do more than my share to help you win."

A few days later, Mays began to pack his bags for Florida, believing he had weathered the storm. He never imagined the worst of his troubles still were ahead of him.

II

Ray Chapman

From the half dozen pictures of Chapman in our files, we sought one suited to the conventional border of black. But every one of them showed the great Cleveland shortstop with a smile. So we said, "Why not?" In Chapman, the smile was characteristic of the man. So let his friends remember him as he looked in life.

Baseball Magazine
October 1920

12

One month after the 1919 baseball season ended, the Hotel Winton in downtown Cleveland was the site of one of that city's most publicized social events. Among those in attendance were local politicians, community leaders, and nationally prominent athletes.

Even if the guest of honor had not been such a well-known figure, it would not have been difficult to guess his occupation. The decor of the private dining room made that obvious. The centerpiece of the oval banquet table was a decorative baseball diamond made of green cloth and measuring four feet across and eight feet in length. Home plate was located at the head of the table, and around the "playing field" were miniature ballplayers. In keeping with this ballpark theme, the dinner rolls were baked in the shape of baseball bats. Also placed around the table were baseballs cut in half and filled with nuts.

Seated at the head of the table, looking out on the field from behind home plate, was Ray Chapman. It once had been written of the Cleveland shortstop, "He was as much at home in the ballroom as on the ball diamond." When sports editor Ed Bang of the *Cleveland News* penned that line, he never imagined that the ballpark and the ballroom would be brought together in such an unconventional manner. Having seen it happen, Bang, like the other eighteen guests present, was quick to express his approval. He made a note to himself to compliment Carl M. Snyder, the manager of the hotel and the man responsible for the decor, in an upcoming newspaper column.

There was good cause for such an elaborate display. In two days, on October 29, Chapman would marry Kathleen Daly, the daughter of a wealthy Cleveland businessman. The wedding of the popular ballplayer and the beautiful young socialite was being billed as "the social event of the fall" in the city. To prepare for the occasion, some of Chapman's closest friends had gathered for his bachelor dinner.

"We're here to get Ray properly married," proclaimed Tris Speaker, who had just arrived from a hunting and fishing expedition in Canada.

The silver-haired Speaker, the manager and star center fielder for the Indians, seemed to be almost as excited as Chapman. The two men had been teammates for the past four seasons, and in that time a strong bond had developed between them. They had become best friends, as close as any two brothers. During the baseball season, they shared a seven-room apartment in the Hotel Winton. In the offseason, they often hunted together, either near Speaker's home in Texas or in the woods around Chapman's home state of Kentucky. Their friendship even extended into their social lives. Speaker went with Jane McMahon, who was the first cousin and best friend of Chapman's fiancée. At the wedding, Miss McMahon would serve as Kathleen's bridesmaid, Speaker as Ray's best man.

There were two other members of the Cleveland ballclub present. Outfielder Jack Graney, talkative and good-natured, swaggered around the room talking about the good times he and Chapman had enjoyed in seven years of playing ball together. The two men roomed with each other on the road, and one year they went so far as to take Graney's pet dog, Larry, with them on the team's travels. Larry kept everyone entertained by performing tricks at the ballpark before the games, and his death during the 1917 season had been cause for great mourning throughout the league.

Catcher Steve O'Neill also was there. Easygoing and personable, he was the perfect straight man for Chapman's pranks. O'Neill recalled the time at spring camp when Chapman organized a contest to see which player could hit a golf ball the farthest. Chapman got

O'Neill so worked up over the competition the catcher was willing to bet he could drive the ball over the fence at New Orleans's Pelican Park. This set off a spirited round of wagering, with Chapman pretending to be O'Neill's most enthusiastic backer. After all the bets had been placed, Chapman pulled out a new golf ball and got down on his hands and knees to carefully place it on a mound of dirt, which he patted into the shape of a tee.

"I'll tee it up for you, Steve," Chapman said helpfully. "Now, Stevie-boy, I'm betting all I got on you. Take a healthy swing."

Using a 2-wood, O'Neill stepped up and took a mighty cut at the ball. He hit it squarely, as well as he ever hit a ball in his life. When he did, the ball literally exploded off the tee, with pieces flying in every direction. O'Neill stood there in astonishment, his mouth hanging open as the other players struggled to contain their laughter. He didn't realize he had been set up until he heard Chapman call out in mock seriousness, "Say, Steve, did you see it go, though?"

The other men gathered around the table represented an interesting mix.

Seated to Chapman's right was his future father-in-law, Martin B. Daly, a self-made millionaire and one of Cleveland's most prominent citizens. Daly had only a grammar-school education when, as a young man in the 1880s, he left his home in Sandusky, Ohio, to go to work in the oilfields of western Pennsylvania. The oil-and-gas industry still was in its infancy, and through his hard work and inventiveness Daly earned a reputation as one of the country's leading authorities on artificial and natural gas. He was appointed to head Standard Oil's gas company in Toledo, Ohio, and shortly after the turn of the century he moved to Cleveland to become president of the newly founded East Ohio Gas Company. With his experience and his clout in the community, Daly had the ability to pave the way for his son-in-law when he left baseball to begin his career as a businessman, and that was exactly what the elder gentleman planned to do.

Also seated at the table was Cleveland Mayor Harry L. Davis, a genial man who was serving his second term as leader of the city.

Davis was a devoted Republican whose two passions in life were politics and baseball. He rarely missed a Cleveland home game, and he considered it one of his greatest honors when some of the more prominent followers of the team formed a club to support the Indians and named it the "Harry L. Davis Rooters."

Another noteworthy guest was Johnny Kilbane, the featherweight boxing champion of the world and one of the top sporting personalities of his day. Kilbane, one of Chapman's most loyal friends, was an especially interesting figure. When he was eighteen, he quit his job as a railway clerk in Cleveland to become a professional boxer. In 1912, the same year Chapman joined the Cleveland ballclub, Kilbane won the world title by beating long-time champion Abe Attell. Kilbane had held the crown ever since, while Attell had drifted into other pursuits. Unknown to anyone in this room, one month earlier Attell had played a prominent role in a gambling plot that resulted in the fixing of the World Series.

One by one, these men stood up and expressed their affection for Chapman and wished him well in his marriage. As they did, the ballplayer's face lit up and he thanked his friends profusely. He always had been outgoing and cheerful, but his happiness and excitement never had been more evident than on this night. Several times, amid the laughter and conversation, he could be heard whistling one of his favorite tunes. The significance of the song was not lost on those present. Its title was "Good-Bye, Boys, I'm Through."

13

Chapman had come a long way in his ten years as a professional ballplayer. Born on January 15, 1891, on a small farm outside Beaver Dam, Kentucky, his background was common to many of the players of the era. When Ray was fourteen years old, his father, Everette Chapman, moved west in search of a better life. He settled in Herrin, a booming little mining town in the heart of the southern Illinois mining country. Through his work in the mines and, later, his position as constable of the town, he was able to provide a modest income for his family.

There were three children. The oldest, Roy, contracted spinal meningitis as a baby and was left handicapped, unable to walk normally or speak plainly. Ray was the second oldest. Another child died as an infant. There was one sister, Margaret, who was born just before the family left Kentucky.

To help supplement his father's income, Ray worked a series of odd jobs, from delivering groceries to—when he was older—going down into the mines. For the rest of his life, he carried his membership card in Local 986 of the United Mine Workers, a reminder of his humble beginnings.

Chapman also was the star player for the local semipro baseball team in Herrin, and one day he caught the eye of Dick Kinsella. A well-known baseball scout who liked to scour the mining towns in southern Illinois for talent, Kinsella had put together enough capital to purchase the Springfield, Illinois, ballclub in the Three-I League. It was a rough circuit, as evidenced by a remark Ty Cobb once made when asked his assessment of an umpire: "He licked somebody in the Three-I League. He ought to do."

Chapman, only nineteen years old, signed with the Springfield club in the spring of 1910. He was five foot ten and 160 pounds with dark hair, a square jaw, and an ever-present smile on his face. He also was faster than anyone else on the squad, and he had a unique method of breaking out of the batter's box, like a sprinter exploding out of the starting blocks, literally plunging himself toward first base.

One player offered the following description of Chapman: "He was a very flashy player. And he could run. He was a beautiful runner, the way he would pick up his knees. He was very fast, had a good arm, and was a good fielder, although he was at times a little erratic. And he was very jolly, a jolly guy. Always laughing, talking, singing. That's what made him popular with a lot of people. A friendly fellow—very friendly with everybody."

The natural abbreviation of his name was "Chappie," and the nickname fit his temperament. He had a happy personality and a lighthearted manner that spilled over to all those around him. Even Springfield's hard-line manager, Dick Smith, was affected by the youngster's unfailing cheerfulness.

"You know, kid," he told Chapman one day, "even if you never played a game, you'd earn your pay just by sitting on the bench and being such a cheerleader."

But Springfield had a veteran ballclub, and Chapman played sparingly, filling in at every position except pitcher and catcher. In July, Kinsella, short of funds, sold the young ballplayer to league rival Davenport, Iowa.

That was the break Chapman needed. He returned to Davenport in 1911 and, playing full time, batted .293 with fifty stolen bases and seventy-five runs scored. Late in the season, Bill Armour, president of the Toledo Mud Hens of the American Association, was on a scouting trip through the area when he saw Chapman in action. He immediately wired Cleveland owner Charles Somers, who also had controlling interest of the Toledo club, for permission to sign this player who was "setting the circuit on fire with his speed and fielding ability." Chapman played the final month of the season in Toledo, where the local newspaper called him "the swellest fielder we have seen on the job in a long while."

He returned to Toledo in 1912 and started the campaign in spectacular fashion. On Opening Day, he had three hits and scored the winning run with a daring steal of home. A few days later, Chapman had five hits in five at-bats, including a drive that rolled under the center-field fence to allow him to circle the bases for a home run. The Toledo fans dubbed him "Cyclone" for the way he was tearing up the league. Late in August, he was batting .310 with 49 stolen bases and 101 runs in 140 games when he received instructions to report to the big-league club in Cleveland.

14

Cleveland was one of the western outposts of the American League, an energetic city that prided itself on its growth and progressivism.

In the first official U.S. census in 1850, it ranked thirty-seventh among American cities in population. By 1910, it had leaped all the way to sixth with a population of 560,000. That marked the largest gain of any of the leaders and led Clevelanders to brag that their city "holds the long-jump population record."

Roughly one-third of this population was foreign-born, adding to the city's cosmopolitan atmosphere. Located on Lake Erie, at the mouth of the Cuyahoga River, Cleveland had become an industrial, financial, and manufacturing center. Among those who had come to the city to make their fortunes were multimillionaire John Rockefeller, who had founded Standard Oil in Cleveland, and Charles F. Brush, the inventor of the arc light, which Cleveland used to become the first city to illuminate its streets with electricity.

Nine makes of automobile of national reputation were being turned out in Cleveland, and the city was establishing itself as the leading producer of automobile parts. The streets were filled with noisy Winton and Stearns gasoline cars as well as the quiet and refined Baker and Rauch & Lang electric autos, which could go as many as one hundred miles without recharging.

In the face of its industrial growth, Cleveland was taking steps to maintain the scenic beauty that had earned it the nickname "The Forest City." A boulevard system stretched in a thirty-six-mile arc around the city, connecting a chain of parks comprising more than twenty-two hundred acres.

The ballpark was on the eastern edge of the city, at the busy intersection of East Sixty-sixth Street and Lexington Avenue, allowing fans arriving at League Park to take a trolley car to within twenty feet of the entrance to the playing grounds.

When Frank Robison had the park built in 1891, he chose this site because it was serviced by two of his trolley companies' lines. But to gain such a strategic location, he had to make certain concessions. The owners of two residences and one saloon on the block had refused to sell their property to Robison, so he constructed his ballpark around them. As a result, when the park first opened the scoreboard was on a fence at Kellacky's saloon and the dimensions of the playing field were among the oddest in baseball.

The left-field foul pole was a distant 375 feet from home plate. From there, the outfield fence stretched straight across to dead center field, where it took a ninety-degree turn toward the right-field line. The distance to the corner in center field was 420 feet. Yet, the right-field foul line measured only 290 feet from home plate.

In 1909, club president Ernest S. "Barney" Barnard had the old wooden park dismantled and replaced by a steel-and-concrete structure. Among the improvements was a forty-foot screen erected above the right-field fence to cut down on the number of fly balls sailing onto adjacent Lexington Avenue.

When Detroit slugger Wahoo Sam Crawford first saw the screen the following year, he defiantly proclaimed: "So that's Barney's dream. I'll show him." True to his word, Crawford went out and sent a drive over the fence in one of his first at-bats in the remodeled park.

The screen did more than cut down on cheap home runs. It also was a constant source of concern for right fielders, forcing them to make split-second decisions on fly balls. If the outfielder went back to catch the ball, he risked its hitting the fence and bouncing back to where the second baseman had to come out and retrieve it. Or the outfielder might prepare to play the rebound only to watch the ball land short of the fence. Balls that hit the screen might rebound or simply fall straight down. Some even got stuck in the screen.

The stands were double-decked, but ten years earlier there had been only a single deck behind home plate, a covered pavilion on the first-base line, and a small bleacher section. On the roof behind home plate had been a small press box and a box for the team officials.

Jack Kilfoyl, the president of the club in those early years, was sitting in this perch one day early in the 1902 campaign when a throw from center fielder Jack "Bullet" Thoney sailed into the private box. After diving for cover, Kilfoyl sent word that he wanted to speak with his manager, Napoleon "Larry" Lajoie, immediately after the game.

"Larry, you'll have to get rid of Thoney," said a still-shaken Kilfoyl. "I don't propose to take my life in my hands when I come to see my club play."

"Well, I'll see if we can't trade him," said Lajoie.

"Don't wait," answered Kilfoyl. "He might kill me tomorrow."

The home-team clubhouse was located beneath the stands on the first-base side. When he first walked in the door, Chapman looked around and saw some of the most famous ballplayers in the game.

On one side of the room was the legendary Lajoie, whose popularity in Cleveland was so great the team was called the Naps in his honor. Lajoie had started his career in 1896 after signing his first contract on the back of an envelope. He became a sensation with Philadelphia of the National League because of his hitting and fielding, but in 1901 he jumped to the city's entry in the newly formed American League. When the Phillies obtained an injunction to prevent him from playing, the Athletics shipped him to Cleveland. Three times the big Frenchman led the AL in batting, and his .422 average in 1901 gave him the distinction of becoming the first player in the league to break the .400 mark. Even now, at thirty-six years of age, Lajoie was on his way to a .365 batting average.

Nearby was twenty-five-year-old outfielder Shoeless Joe Jackson, already regarded as one of the greatest hitters in baseball. Jackson had batted .408 the previous year, only to finish twelve points behind Ty Cobb in the race for the batting championship. In his second full season, Shoeless Joe was making another run at the .400 figure and would fall short by only five percentage points.

Across the way was center fielder Joe Birmingham, an outstanding all-around ballplayer with one of the best throwing arms in the game's history. Once, Birmingham hauled in a fly ball to deep center field at Sportsman's Park in St. Louis and rifled the ball home in time to nail the speedy Bobby Wallace, who was trying to score from third base. The play so amazed the spectators that a tape measure was brought out, and it was determined the throw had traveled 370 feet in the air.

The manager of the ballclub was thirty-eight-year-old Harry Davis, who had been manager Connie Mack's right-hand man in Philadelphia. Known as "Home Run Harry" for his slugging feats in the early days of the AL, Davis had played on four of Connie Mack's pennant winners and had been the first baseman in the original "$100,000 Infield" in 1910.

Despite his success as a ballplayer, Davis had been a failure as a manager. His heavy-handed manner had alienated the team, and more than once there had been violent shouting matches between the manager and his players in the locker room. The Naps, who had finished third the previous season, had fallen all the way to sixth place by the end of August, and Davis had accused the players of quitting on him.

Stepping into such a volatile atmosphere, Chapman made an immediate impression. He was touted as "the boy wonder" and "a kid phenom" by the Cleveland newspapers, and he lived up to his billing. In his debut against the Chicago White Sox, he had a bases-loaded walk and a bunt single in four at-bats, scored twice, forced two White Sox errors with his aggressive baserunning, and fielded flawlessly. The Naps, losers of 15 of their previous 17 games, beat the White Sox 7–2.

Three days later, Davis resigned as manager and was replaced by the easygoing Birmingham. The Naps responded by winning 21 of their final 28 games. Chapman fueled the surge by finishing the season with an 11-game hitting streak and 20 hits in his final 42 at-bats. For his 31 games with Cleveland, he batted .312 with 29 runs and 10 stolen bases.

15

Chapman's days in the mines were over. He returned to Herrin a hero, an authentic major-league ballplayer. The city fathers rewarded him with an appointment as sidewalk inspector.

"This preliminary taste of politics just whetted my appetite for more," he joked. "Guess I'll be mayor of Herrin when I grow up and retire from baseball."

That day seemed far away. Chapman enjoyed another solid season in 1913, batting a steady .258 and leading the league in sacrifice hits with forty-eight. He also teamed up with his boyhood idol, Lajoie, to form one of the strongest middle infields in baseball. Watching the two execute a double play, one writer marveled at "the quickness and dispatch with which the ball streaks from one to another of these men."

The ballclub rewarded Chapman with a boost in salary from twenty-four hundred dollars a season to thirty-five hundred dollars. To the young ballplayer, it was a small fortune. He always had liked fine clothes; now he could buy silk shirts whenever he wanted and have his suits tailormade in big cities such as Boston and New York. He shared his newfound wealth with his family, sending them clothing and watches from these faraway places.

Then came the first setback of Chapman's career. At the team's spring camp in 1914, he broke his leg in two places while sliding into third base at the end of practice.

"I don't see why I'm so unlucky," Chapman moaned as the leg was set in a cast. "My heart is in my work, and I was working as hard as any man could. I wanted to be the best shortstop in America."

The Cleveland manager was almost as distraught as the ballplayer.

"More than half my team is out of the game," Birmingham glumly told newsmen.

It was not too great an exaggeration. With Chapman missing almost one-third of the season, Cleveland, which had finished in third place the year before, fell all the way to last, losing a club record 102 games.

Henry Edwards of the *Cleveland Plain Dealer* later wrote of that campaign:

"The first six weeks of that season with Chapman in the hospital in Cleveland was like traveling with the mourners. Never a song, never a funny story, never a thing to bring a smile. It was the most discouraged aggregation of ball players I ever saw, and it remained such until Chapman rejoined the team."

Chapman barely had recovered from that misfortune when he suffered another setback in 1916. Tagging out a runner at second base, his spikes caught in the bag and he plunged forward to the ground with a severely twisted knee. He spent two weeks in the hospital and was out of action for more than a month. Hobbled by the injury even after he returned to action, Chappie turned in a batting average of .231, the worst of his career.

It was not until 1917 that Chapman finally achieved the stardom that had been predicted for him after his sensational debut. He did so in convincing fashion. Playing every game that season, he batted .302, stole fifty-two bases, and scored ninety-eight runs. He also established a major-league record with sixty-seven sacrifice hits, beating the old mark by fifteen. To top it off, he fielded his position brilliantly, leading both leagues in assists and putouts by a shortstop. He had become, according to writer F. C. Lane in *Baseball Magazine,* the greatest shortstop baseball had seen since the incomparable Honus Wagner of Pittsburgh.

"For sheer versatility for excellence of performance in every department of the game [Chapman] has proved for one season at least a not unworthy rival to the Dutchman at his best," wrote Lane.

Chapman's sudden burst into stardom coincided with Cleveland's emergence as a contender in the American League. Bolstered by the addition of Speaker from the Red Sox the previous season, the long downtrodden Indians were showing signs of life.

In 1917, Cleveland rose to third place, and in 1918 it made a strong run at the championship before finishing second to Boston. A late surge by the Indians in 1918 moved them within four games of the White Sox in the last week of August, when Speaker was suspended for pushing an umpire. Even at that, there might have been time to overtake the leaders, but the schedule was called to a premature halt on Labor Day because of America's involvement in the Great War in Europe. On August 31, Cleveland was officially eliminated from contention despite a 2–1 victory over Chicago. After the game, owner Jim Dunn climbed up to the press box and bitterly announced his team would not go to St. Louis for its final game. "The players have arranged to enter essential employment, and they want to report early Tuesday morning," he said. "I am with them heart and soul in their desire to do so." The next day, a Sunday, the St. Louis Browns put nine players on the field and had their pitcher throw ten pitches—five for each game of the scheduled doubleheader. St. Louis then claimed both games by forfeit. It made little difference to Cleveland ballplayers, who, assured of a second-place finish, already had scattered about the country to fulfill their wartime obligations.

*   *   *

For Chapman, military experience was simply another adventure. He enrolled in the naval auxiliary reserve force as a second-class seaman, hoping to earn his commission and go to sea as a "gold striper." As part of his training, he sailed the Great Lakes on the steamer *H. H. Rogers*. "It is one of the greatest experiences of my life, cruising around on the lakes," he wrote to his friends.

When Chapman was not shipbound, there was plenty of time for sports. He competed for the naval reserve in a track competition against the soldiers from Camp Custer, winning the hundred-yard dash with a time of 10.8 seconds. At a meet against a team from Camp Grant, he so easily outdistanced the field that the *Cleveland Plain Dealer* reported the other fourteen runners "looked like an audience gathered to watch him."

Chapman also served as captain of the football and baseball teams. In football, the naval reserve was the only team to defeat Pittsburgh University that fall. Chapman's enthusiasm for the sport was evident during a game at League Field. While many of his teammates still were stretched out on the ground after a touchdown, Chappie could be seen doing handsprings across the field in celebration of the score.

Shortly after he completed his training, the armistice was signed and Chapman was mustered out of the service. His commanding officer, Lieutenant J. H. Clark, later said of him: "We could easily see why Chapman was said never to have had an enemy in baseball, the way he handled himself while attending the school. Chappie always acted a gentleman and endeared himself to every gob and officer on the ship."

16

Chapman's popularity as a ballplayer had opened doors for him off the playing field, also. He made friends in powerful places, and he mingled comfortably in their circles. In the words of Ed Bang: "He was his 100 percent self all the time, no frills or furbelows, and it was this trait that won him fast friends among the heads of manufacturing, industrial and mercantile concerns as well as among the newsies on the street corner." In 1916, Chapman's celebrity led to a meeting with an attractive young woman prominent in the Cleveland society scene. Her name was Kathleen Daly.

The daughter of oilman Martin B. Daly, she had been raised in affluence. The Daly home was on the city's prestigious Euclid Avenue, along the stretch known as "Millionaires' Row." The scenic drive was known for its beauty and had managed to remain free of all forms of commercialism that might spoil its splendor. In fact, it was not until 1917 that streetcars were allowed through it.

Kathleen had been educated in the finest private schools in Cleveland, and she spent her summers vacationing in Florida. She was cultured and privileged, and once had had the honor of christening a ship at the shipyards in Toledo. She also was very athletic, as evidenced by her skill and grace as an ice skater. And, with her light brown hair and blue eyes, Kathleen was as beautiful as she was sophisticated.

One of her interests was baseball, which she had come to enjoy while attending games with her father, himself an avid fan. In an era when few women went to the ballparks, Kathleen followed the game closely enough to know the scoring symbols and to be able to keep her own scorecard. She was twenty-two years old when she was introduced to Chapman, with the meeting arranged by a member of the Indians staff after Mr. Daly mentioned his daughter's interest in the Cleveland shortstop.

From the beginning, their romance was played out against the backdrop of baseball. During their courtship, Kathleen would arrive at the Indians' home games in a chauffeur-driven automobile and sit in the Daly family's box seats along the first-base line. Before play began, Ray would lean against the wooden stands and visit briefly with her. Afterward, she would wait outside the ballpark until he emerged from the locker room, and they would ride together to the Daly house for supper. In the evenings, Ray would entertain the family with his singing while Kathleen's younger sister, Margaret, played the piano. In time, his visits became more frequent and lasted longer.

The Daly family never had encountered anyone quite like the young ballplayer. He brought to their household the playfulness of the locker room, only without its coarseness. Once, a dressmaker's dummy was left on the stairway landing, frightening a house guest who mistook it for an intruder. The next day, Ray hung a sign on the dummy: "Hi, my name is Mr. Smith and I'm going to be staying here for a while." For several days, he set a place at the supper table for Mr. Smith and carried on imaginary conversations with him. "Oh, is that right?" Ray would respond to something he imagined the dummy saying. "Well, we'll just have to see about that." Soon, everyone was talking to Mr. Smith and treating him as an honored guest.

Chappie also was a talented singer who often was asked if he ever considered performing on stage. It was a proposal that must have appealed to him. He loved music and he loved the theater. He also knew how to play to a crowd. A story told by his friend John Reid Alexander of Owensboro illustrated that point.

One winter, Chapman was a guest at the home of Alexander, who owned an up-to-date brand of phonograph and an extensive collection of records by John McCormack, the famed Irish singer. One evening, Alexander was playing one of McCormack's records for some friends when Chappie walked into the room.

"As I live, it is my old friend John McCormack himself!" shouted Alexander as he rushed over and grasped Chapman's hand. "Friends, I have a treat in store for you. You have been listening to songs on the machine by McCormack. Well, here is McCormack in person!"

Chapman picked up on the prank and walked to the phonograph.

"I see you have nothing but my old songs. You ought to get some of my latest hits."

Chapman then attempted to leave the room, but Alexander blocked his path and announced that "McCormack" would honor the group by singing some of his favorite songs. The only song Chapman could remember was "In the Shade of the Old Apple Tree," which was repeated over and over in response to vigorous applause. When he was asked to sing some of McCormack's later songs, Chapman finally was able to beg off.

Still, word of "McCormack's" visit spread around town, and the following day he was booked for three engagements in schoolhouses and before patriotic societies. This forced Chappie to wire to Louisville for the words to some of the songs sung by the real McCormack, and he honored every engagement. The satisfied audiences never knew they hadn't heard the real thing.

*　　　*　　　*

In 1918, Ray gave Kathleen a diamond ring and formally asked for her hand in marriage. When he told his mother, he jokingly added, "Well, Mama, if anything happens to me and I don't get married, you'll have a nice diamond ring."

Mrs. Chapman worried that her son was making a mistake by marrying out of his social class. "Ray, she's used to so much and they're such a wealthy family," she warned him. "You should marry a girl more your equal, your money. A nice girl from around here." Always, Ray would smile and assure his mother he was doing the right thing.

Upon his release from the military service in December 1918, he and Kathleen set the date for their wedding. They would be married shortly after the end of the 1919 baseball season.

*　　　*　　　*

Mr. Daly had bold plans for Chapman. Often, he joked with his friends that he was not just gaining a son-in-law, he was adding a business partner. He used his influence to get William H. Smith, the president of the Pioneer Alloys Company, to take in Chapman as secretary-treasurer of the company. The idea was for the ballplayer to learn the ropes of the business world in order to take over his own company someday.

In return, Mr. Daly asked only one thing. He wanted Chapman to consider retiring from playing baseball after his marriage and devote full time to being a businessman and a husband. Traveling around the country playing ball is no occupation for a family man, pointed out the patriarch of the Daly family.

Chapman promised to take the matter under consideration.

17

On the eve of the 1919 season, Chapman still had one unfulfilled goal in his career. He had not played on a championship ballclub. It was a dream shared by all Cleveland baseball fans.

Since the city fielded its first major-league ballclub in 1879, it never had managed a first-place finish. There had been four different franchises with six different names and eight different owners in four different leagues but no pennants. In the past nineteen years alone, Cleveland had been led by nine different managers.

The campaign began on an optimistic note. In early June, the Indians were in first place as they embarked on a swing through the East. But in Boston, Chapman suffered an attack of lumbago, a painful rheumatic condition affecting the muscles in the lower-back region. It was a month before he was able to return to the lineup, and in his absence, the Indians lost 16 of 25 games to fall from first to third, 5½ games behind the White Sox and 3½ behind the Yankees. "Hurry up and kick that lumbago out of your system, Chappie!" urged a headline in the *Cleveland Press*. Finally, on July 13, the same day Mays walked off the mound in Chicago, Chapman returned to the starting lineup, his midsection wrapped tightly. He had a single in three at-bats as Cleveland beat Washington 5–4.

The Indians were hopeful of launching a winning streak, but less than a week later they were jarred by another setback. The Red Sox, demoralized by the controversy surrounding Mays's walkout, had arrived in town and dropped the first two games of a series. Cleveland now had won all nine games between the two teams thus far in the season, prompting Indians manager Lee Fohl to start a left-hander named Hi Jasper in the Friday game. The choice of pitchers was approved by Tris Speaker, who, unknown to all but a few insiders on the club, had become a sort of assistant manager without portfolio. Speaker advised Fohl on personnel moves and lineups, and the two men even had gone so far as to devise a set of signs to enable the center fielder to signal to the dugout when he wanted a pitching change made.

Jasper, a thirty-two-year-old journeyman who had toiled for the White Sox and Cardinals from 1914 to 1916 without much success and now was trying to catch on with Cleveland, pitched well through the early innings against the Red Sox. Despite surrendering a home run to Babe Ruth, he made it into the eighth with the score tied 3–3. In the bottom of the inning, he was pulled for a pinch-hitter when the Indians loaded the bases. The move paid off when Joe Harris blasted a three-run triple to cap a four-run outburst, giving the Indians a 7–3 lead.

Considering Boston's offensive problems, the game appeared well in hand as relief pitcher Elmer Myers took the mound to start the ninth. But Myers didn't have his good stuff, and there was a growing sense of uneasiness among the crowd at League Park when the Red Sox scored one run to chop the lead to 7–4 and then loaded the bases. There were two outs, and the next batter was Ruth.

The fans were shouting at Fohl to do something when the Cleveland manager finally emerged from the dugout and looked out toward the right-field corner, where three relief pitchers were warming up. Two of the hurlers were right-handers. The third was Fritz Coumbe, a left-handed curveball specialist.

Fohl glanced out to center field to pick up the signal from Speaker. The sign came back for a right-hander, but when Fohl waved to the bullpen he called for the left-handed Coumbe, who had a tendency to get pitches up high where Ruth liked them.

In the outfield, Speaker was shouting: "No! No! Not Coumbe!"

It was too late. Fohl had returned to the bench, and Speaker turned his back to the plate in disgust.

Ruth swung at and missed Coumbe's first offering. The next

pitch was a high curveball, and Ruth pounced on it. From the time the ball jumped off the bat with a loud crack, the Indians knew disaster had struck. Right fielder Elmer Smith could only stand and watch helplessly as the ball sailed high above the right-field screen and onto the top of a laundry building on the far side of adjoining Lexington Avenue. The grand slam gave the Red Sox an 8–7 lead. Demoralized, the Indians went out meekly in the bottom of the ninth.

After the game, the Cleveland players sat stunned in front of their lockers with their heads bowed. Speaker was particularly disconsolate. Fohl hurriedly dressed and left the room.

Speaker still was sitting at his locker when the clubhouse boy walked up. "Mr. Dunn wants to see you in his office," he said. Speaker nodded numbly. A few minutes later, he ascended the metal stairs to Dunn's private quarters on the second level above the ticket windows. Dunn and Barnard were waiting for him when he entered. Speaker was surprised to see sports writers Ross Tenney, Bang, and Edwards also were in the room.

Dunn wasted no time getting to the point. "Lee has resigned as manager, Tris, and we want you to take over."

Speaker was silent for a moment, then declined the offer. Dunn, however, was adamant. He wanted the star center fielder to run the ballclub. The two men discussed the proposition for several minutes before Speaker finally gave in.

"I don't want the job," he told Dunn. "I'd rather be a player. I believe I'd be more useful to you that way. But I'll take it on one condition. Lee Fohl has to ask me."

The request by Fohl was only a formality. The next day it was announced that Speaker had taken over the Indians. Coumbe cried when he learned of Fohl's resignation. A few hours later, the pitcher was shipped to the minor leagues.

Under Speaker's leadership, the Indians chased the White Sox all the way to the wire, almost overtaking them with an incredible surge in the final two weeks of the season. Cleveland began its final charge on September 10, when Slim Caldwell, a onetime star who was picked up by Speaker late in the summer after the Red Sox gave up on him, pitched a no-hitter against the Yankees in the Polo Grounds. Sparked by Caldwell's gem, the Indians won ten games in a row and thirteen of their final seventeen. But once again, they had waited too late. Although gaining five games on the White Sox, they still were 3½ games behind when time ran out.

The Indians' frustration at finishing second became more pronounced when the White Sox mysteriously collapsed in the World Series, losing to the underdog National League champions from Cincinnati. Chapman, who had been friends with Chicago star Shoeless Joe Jackson when the slugger played in Cleveland five years earlier, attended the Series and came back with an uneasy feeling. He told his family he did not place any wagers on the games because "something didn't seem right."

Chapman gave no more thought to the matter. He had more pressing concerns on his mind that fall.

18

On October 29, in a ceremony held at the Daly house, Ray and Kathleen were married. The nuptial service was read by the Reverend Joseph Smith, pastor of St. Philomene's Church. The marriage was, according to the newspapers, the culmination of "a romance of the ball diamond."

At the wedding dinner that evening, the guests joined tenor Frank Gafney in singing "Believe Me, If All Those Endearing Young Charms."

The next day, the newlyweds left for an extended vacation in Florida. There would be time later for them to think about baseball and their future.

*   *   *

Chapman was at work at Pioneer Alloys one day that winter when he received an unexpected visitor. One of his cousins was passing through town and wanted to see the business. Chapman took him on a tour of the plant, waiting until the last before leading him to a room on the first floor. Taking a seat behind the desk, Ray propped his feet up and said proudly, "Henry, this is my office."

With the baseball photographs on the wall and business reports on the desk, the room was symbolic of all Chapman had achieved in his life. He had succeeded in one occupation and now was learning another. He was a bona fide businessman—the secretary-treasurer of a profitable company. His future outside baseball seemed secure.

Because of his success, there was concern among Cleveland baseball fans that Chapman was about to announce his retirement from the game. The rumors persisted throughout the fall, and they received added impetus when it was learned that Boston shortstop Everrett Scott had expressed the desire to be reunited with Speaker and the other former Red Sox now playing in Cleveland.

Chapman denied such reports, assuring all who asked him that he would return for at least one more season.

"I'll play next year, for I want to help give Tris Speaker and the Cleveland fans the first pennant Cleveland ever has won," he told the newspapers. "Then I will talk quitting."

Chapman's decision was not made without some regrets. He was only twenty-nine years old, still in the prime of his career. He knew it would not be easy to give up the game.

On one occasion, he wistfully remarked to Ed Bang: "Well, I guess I'll be a real businessman. But, gee, it'll be hard to pull away from Spoke and the rest of the boys."

*   *   *

Chapman told the family of his retirement plans when he visited in late February 1920 on his way to the Indians' training camp in New Orleans. As usual, the visit seemed too short. Chapman's trips home had become more infrequent in the past few years, as he spent more and more time in Cleveland. This year, he went hunting with his uncle in Kentucky, then traveled over to Herrin. He stayed only a few days before departing for nearby Carbondale, where he would meet the rest of the Cleveland ballplayers en route by rail to spring training in New Orleans. Kathleen, who was making her first trip to spring training, also would be on the train.

On the morning of March 3, Chapman boarded the train in Carbondale and prepared to head south. He stopped on the steps of the passenger car long enough to turn and wave good-bye to the rest of the family. It was the last time they ever saw him alive.

III

The Pennant Race

Mays alone, or Ruth alone, yes. Scarce both of them. They'll be as jealous of each other as prima donnas before the season begins.

John B. Sheridan
The Sporting News

19

In late December 1919, Ed Barrow's shower was interrupted by the ringing of the telephone in his New York apartment. With a towel wrapped around his midsection and water still dripping off him, he picked up the receiver. The caller was Frazee.

"I need to see you," said the Red Sox owner. "Meet me at the Hotel Knickerbocker at six o'clock."

There was a sense of urgency in the owner's voice that left Barrow with an uneasy feeling. That afternoon, he left his apartment on Riverside Drive in New York and took a cab to the hotel. Frazee was sitting in the café with a friend of his, actor Frank McIntyre. They motioned Barrow over and got right down to business.

"Simon, I'm going to sell Ruth to the Yankees."

Barrow let the news sink in for a few moments before answering.

"I thought as much. I could feel it in my bones. But you ought to know that you're making a mistake."

"Maybe I am, but I can't help it," said Frazee.

Ruth had hit the incredible total of twenty-nine home runs in 1919, which accounted for all but four of the total accumulated by the Red Sox. It also bettered the previous major-league standard of twenty-seven, set by Chicago's Ed Williamson in 1884. But the twenty-four-year-old slugger was becoming increasingly difficult to please. Although the Babe had signed a three-year deal calling for $10,000 a year the previous spring, after the season ended he once again demanded a new contract. Now, he was threatening not to play unless his salary was doubled.

Frazee, financially strapped because of losses in his show-business ventures, was in no position to meet such demands. He had a $250,000 loan that had to be paid off, and the bank would not renew the notes until he could pay half the amount due. Frazee's only hope of raising that kind of money was to peddle Ruth to his trusted allies in New York, the Yankee colonels. Not only were they willing to provide Frazee with the $125,000 he needed, Ruppert even agreed to loan the Red Sox owner $300,000 in exchange for a mortgage on Boston's Fenway Park. In return, Ruppert wanted to make a deal for Ruth.

"I can't turn that down," Frazee told Barrow. "But don't worry. I'll get you some ballplayers, too."

Barrow shook his head.

"Listen, losing Ruth is bad enough. Don't make it tougher for me by making me show off a lot of ten-cent ballplayers that we get in exchange for him. There is nobody on that ballclub that I want. This has to be a straight cash deal, and you'll have to announce it that way."

The announcement was made January 5, 1920. That same day, it was ruled that the Volstead Act, which prohibited the manufacture, sale, import, or export of liquor in the United States, was constitutional. Prohibition would take effect in less than two weeks, but the baseball fans in Boston and New York were more concerned with the effect of the Ruth sale.

In Boston, the reaction was predictable. Bostoners had come to think of Ruth as one of their own, and there was outrage that such a popular figure would be sold off to bail out an absentee owner. One newspaper carried a cartoon of Faneuil Hall and the Boston Public Library—two other well-known landmarks—with "For Sale" signs on them.

In New York, there was ecstasy. The Yankees' lineup of shortstop Roger Peckinpaugh, first baseman Wally Pipp, third baseman Home Run Baker, second baseman Del Pratt, and left fielder Ping Bodie already had been dubbed "Murderers' Row" in 1919. The addition of Ruth to such an array of sluggers almost was too good to be true. For good measure, New York also added hard-hitting outfielder Duffy Lewis, attempting a comeback after being discarded by the Red Sox, and muscular young Bob Meusel, a power hitter just up from the minor leagues. Even if Baker carried through on his threats to resign, the team was overloaded with power.

There was only one catch. Ruth was reluctant to leave Boston, where he had a cigar business as well as a burgeoning social life. To soothe Babe's wounded pride, the Yankees agreed to give him a $1,000 bonus up front and $20,000 spread out over the next two seasons in periodic payments of $2,500. As a final gesture, they even offered to pay him $500 for each home run he hit over his record total of twenty-nine. They had no idea that agreement would end up costing them an additional $12,500 when Ruth belted the incredible total of fifty-four homers that first year in New York.

Any final traces of regret Ruth had at leaving Boston were removed when Frazee, attempting to justify such an unpopular transaction, blamed the Red Sox's demise in 1919 on Babe's drinking and rowdy behavior.

"It would be impossible to start next season with Ruth and have a smooth-working machine," said the Red Sox owner.

When he heard Frazee's statement, Ruth exploded. Indignant, he announced he was glad to be leaving Boston.

"Frazee is not good enough to own any ballclub," said Babe in his parting shot.

20

A carnival atmosphere surrounded the Yankees when they set out for spring training that March. On the train ride from New York to Florida, Dixieland bands and large crowds turned out at every stop to greet the team. The reception in Miami was just as enthusiastic.

To record the event, a record thirteen reporters accompanied the club south. The horde of writers had little trouble coming up with fresh material to provide their readers back home.

In the exhibition opener in Miami, Ruth, allegedly suffering from a hangover, ran into a palm tree in the outfield and knocked himself out.

Meusel seemed intent upon following in the Babe's footsteps, both on the field and off. The rookie regularly broke curfew, drank till all hours of the night, and often played as if he were hung over. One reporter, noting Meusel's "utter disregard for training rules," warned him to shape up.

By the third week of the spring season, the writers were wondering if manager Miller Huggins would be able to control this strange mix of prima donnas, hotheads, troublemakers, and carousers. Finally, Huggins called a team meeting and read the players the riot act. He not only imposed a curfew, he ordered every player to put in an appearance at the breakfast room before nine o'clock each morning.

A few days later, Bodie, dubbed "The Wonderful Wop" by the writers, became piqued at some perceived slight and stormed out of camp to return to his home in Hoboken, New Jersey.

Compounding the problems, Ruth was off to a slow start at the plate, and as his batting woes mounted so did his irritability with the press. After one of Babe's outbursts against the newspaper hacks, Mays cut him short with the admonition, "Babe, as soon as you do something noteworthy, the writers will start to react more positively." Ruth glowered at the pitcher, then walked away.

The slugger also was tormented by the fans. During a game in Jacksonville, a man in the outfield bleachers taunted Ruth for striking out in his previous at-bat.

"You're a big bunch of cheese!" shouted the heckler.

At the end of the inning, Ruth stalked over to the bleachers and confronted the man. There were some harsh words, then the fan dared Ruth to come into the stands. When Babe accepted the challenge, the man pulled a knife on him. It took pitcher Ernie Shore to go into the crowd and rescue Ruth.

21

Miller Huggins was an unlikely leader for such a volatile collection of ballplayers. A small man with prominent ears, he was known to the fans as "The Rabbit" when he played second base in Cincinnati and St. Louis from 1904 to 1916. Now, he was more commonly referred to as "The Mighty Mite" or simply "Hug."

He was only five foot six and 140 pounds, and with the Yankees, he always seemed to be wearing a uniform that was two sizes too large. His jaw bulged with loose-leaf chewing tobacco and often he had to stretch his neck to lecture his players, most of whom towered above him.

Huggins was born in 1879 in Cincinnati's famous old Fourth Ward, then one of the roughest in the city. Despite his lack of size, Hug quickly learned to fight his own battles in his neighborhood.

As a teenager, he played second base on the Shamrocks, a fast semipro team in Cincinnati, and in 1899, he played on a team organized by Colonel Julius Fleishman, who later became mayor of Cincinnati. Fleishman recognized Huggins's skill and sent him to Mansfield, Ohio, to begin his pro career. In 1900, Fleishman engineered Huggins's sale to the St. Paul club in the American Association. An accomplished fielder and above-average batter, Huggins made it to the major leagues with Cincinnati in 1904.

While a member of the Reds, Huggins still found time to study law for three years. He was graduated from the Cincinnati Law School, but he never had the opportunity to practice the profession.

Huggins was the classic example of the self-made ballplayer. Early on in his career, while he was at St. Paul, he realized he never would make the major leagues as anything but a second baseman and a leadoff hitter because of his small stature. Since his size prevented him from reaching curveballs thrown away from him, he spent one winter swinging at a ball suspended from his basement ceiling by twine. Then he decided to become a switch-hitter, so he set about to teach himself to bat left-handed. Away from the ballpark, he threw the ball, chopped wood, drove spikes, used his knife and fork, ate, drank, walked and talked left-handed. He worked at it winter and summer for three years before finally mastering the art of switch-hitting. At the end of those three years, he went up to the major leagues, and in thirteen seasons there he would log a .265 batting average, 324 steals, and 1,002 walks.

Huggins also was handicapped by a weak throwing arm. To offset this, he took a position deep in the field and much farther toward center field than was customary. This way, he always kept the ball on his left hand. He always was going toward his play and rarely had to go to his right to make the pickup, turn, and throw.

Huggins was traded to the Cardinals in the winter of 1910 and became manager of St. Louis in 1913. He had few friends and was introspective, but his courage, determination, and resourcefulness were never questioned. Although his record as manager in St. Louis was unspectacular—the Cardinals finished in the second division three of the five years Huggins guided the team—he earned respect for the job he was doing with inferior talent.

In St. Louis, Huggins was noted for keeping his players happy and working together. He always took a player's side when he was holding out for more money.

It was Ban Johnson who was responsible for Huggins moving to the Yankees following the 1917 season. Ruppert and Huston had suffered through three losing years as owners and were looking for some new leadership.

With Huston overseas in the service, Ruppert, whose knowledge of baseball and his players often was shaky, met with manager Wild Bill Donovan and told him in his heavy German accent: "You're a good man, Don-vans, but somebody has to go."

Huston's choice to take over the position was Brooklyn's Wilbert

Robinson, his old hunting, drinking, and singing companion. Ruppert interviewed Robinson but didn't want to hire him.

At this point, Johnson stepped into the picture. Angry at the National League for luring Browns executive manager Branch Rickey across town to the rival St. Louis Cardinals, the AL president wanted to retaliate by having the Yankees swipe the Redbirds' manager.

"You'll get a good man," Johnson advised Ruppert, "and we'll be taking a good man away from the enemy."

The aristocratic Ruppert wasn't convinced, having a dislike for Huggins because of his practices of wearing a cloth cap and smoking a pipe in public, traits that the Colonel considered working class. But the Yankee owner did agree to at least meet with Huggins.

Johnson introduced the two, and Ruppert was impressed by the little man's baseball knowledge. Although Huggins was reluctant to join the Yankees, J. G. Taylor Spink of *The Sporting News* convinced him to take the job and the deal was done.

Huston, furious that his recommendation to hire Robinson had been ignored, immediately wired his protest from Europe, but it was too late. As a result, Huston never warmed to Huggins and in future years he could be counted on to listen sympathetically to the players' complaints about the manager.

Taking over a team that had come in sixth in 1917, Huggins guided the Yankees to first-division finishes the next two years. But the New York fans and sports writers, taking their cue from Huston, found Hug drab and colorless.

Ruth's arrival on the team only aggravated the problem. From the start, the big and boisterous Ruth bristled at any attempt by the tiny Huggins to tell him what to do. Before long, the Babe's lack of respect for Huggins's authority was producing friction. Ruth referred to the manager as "Little Boy," and the impressionable Meusel and others had been quick to follow Babe's lead in his disdain for the manager. When Huggins would walk up and down the bench, some of the players would discreetly spit tobacco juice on his socks.

Mays also made known his contempt for the New York manager. The pitcher had brought his auto with him to spring training, and often Huggins asked to borrow it. When he did, Mays complained to others that the manager was too cheap to buy gasoline for the vehicle.

22

From the beginning, the mood in the Indians' spring-training camp in New Orleans was lighthearted. The day the players checked into their quarters at the DeSoto Hotel the first week in March, Kathleen and the other wives in the traveling party each received a box of a dozen roses. The attached cards said simply: "With the compliments of Tris Speaker."

The Cleveland manager was determined to make the five-week stay in the South as pleasant and productive as possible for his ballclub to put it in the right frame of mind for the season ahead. To ensure the proper atmosphere, he had prepared for his first spring training as manager with painstaking thoroughness. It could even be said that he left no stone unturned in his planning. Putting aside his personal desire to train closer to his home in Hubbard, Texas, Speaker had decided the team should return to the facility in New Orleans for the fifth year in a row. The facilities were good, the climate mild, and only once since 1916 had a practice been called because of rain.

There was, however, one drawback to the site. The infield at Pelican Park was in horrible condition and had been the source of numerous complaints by the players. Rather than the traditional soil, it was composed of a crushed substance consisting of bits of seashells, small stones, and pebbles. Even bits of glass could be found in the field. Jules Heinemann, the president of the New Orleans ballclub, had ignored repeated appeals for improvements in the playing field, so Speaker decided to take the matter into his own hands. He dispatched Indians groundskeeper Frank Van Dellen to New Orleans during the winter to remove the troublesome filler and replace it with good soil. By the time camp was to begin, the infield measured up to major-league standards.

Speaker had arrived in New Orleans on February 27, hoping to be the first on hand so he could personally greet each of his players when they reported over the next few days. Much to his chagrin, he discovered he had been beaten to town by Guy Morton, a sore-armed pitcher who had come over early from his home in Vernon, Alabama.

There was one other thing Speaker hadn't counted on upon his arrival. The weather was unseasonably cold throughout that first week. It even snowed one day, forcing Jack MacCallister, who served as Speaker's right-hand man, to invoke an unwritten rule: "Practice is called off whenever it snows in New Orleans in March."

There was little for the players to do but busy themselves in such activities as handball, running, and even leapfrog while waiting for the sun to break through. Not even Speaker could control the weather, they laughed. To the fans in Cleveland who worshiped him, it was one of his few signs of mortality.

*   *   *

With his rugged good looks and his colorful past, Speaker was a larger-than-life figure. He was a trained aviator capable of taking up an airplane alone, a crack shot with a rifle, an expert horseman, and an authentic Texas cowboy who had learned to rope a calf before he swung a baseball bat.

Speaker was born in the small Texas town of Hubbard, south of Fort Worth, but there were conflicting records about the date of his birth. He would maintain he was born on April 4, 1888. Other records listed the year as 1883. Although it was a discrepancy that would play a major role in his career, it was of little concern in 1905 when Speaker dropped out of Polytechnic College in Fort Worth after two years to earn his living as a baseball player. He talked himself into a tryout as a pitcher with the Texas League team from Cleburne, which picked him up only because it was short of players.

The same day he joined the team, Speaker pitched brilliantly in a 1–0 loss to Waco.

The next afternoon, he went to center field to shag fly balls during practice. Manager Ben Shelton was hitting fungoes to the outfielders, and he soon discovered the only way he could hit a ball the newcomer couldn't catch was to knock it over the fence. The manager was so amazed he called Speaker over and told him, "Son, you have the makings of a great pitcher, but you can be an even greater center fielder." Speaker knew little about playing the outfield, but he agreed to make the switch. It wasn't long before he was setting new standards for the position. He played perilously shallow and was so near the infield he often threw out batters at first base or became involved in rundowns on the bases. Yet his speed, quick reflexes, and unerring ability to gauge the flight of balls enabled him to race back at the crack of the bat and catch drives to the deepest parts of center field. Sparked by Speaker's batting and fielding, Cleburne won the Texas League pennant that year.

Two years later, in 1907, Speaker was sold to Boston of the American League for four hundred dollars. He was with the major-league team for only three days during training camp at Little Rock, Arkansas, before being transferred to the local team as "ground rent" for the Red Sox's use of the ballpark. Speaker batted .350 for Little Rock and rejoined Boston in the fall. He became a regular in 1909, and for the next seven seasons in Boston he batted over .300. Red Sox manager Rough Carrigan would taunt the opposition with the cry "Speaker spoke!" after every Speaker hit, earning him the nickname "Spoke." He also was called "The Gray Eagle" because of his prematurely silver hair and his ability to cover so much of the outfield.

Speaker led the Red Sox to the world championship in 1912 when he batted .383, stole fifty-two bases, and hit a league-leading ten home runs. In 1915, he slumped to a .322 batting average and saw his totals in doubles, runs batted in, and stolen bases decline, but still he paced Boston to another title.

Although Speaker continued to rival Detroit's Cobb as the greatest all-around player in the game, there were whispers being heard that the Boston star was on the downside of his career. His batting average had declined for three consecutive seasons, and Red Sox owner Joe Lannin was convinced that Speaker had knocked five years off his age when he had entered professional baseball. According to Boston's records, the star ballplayer was thirty-two years old, not twenty-seven as he claimed.

In Lannin's eyes, Speaker no longer was worth the $17,500 he had been paid under the terms of a two-year contract that now had expired. That was a salary unheard of in baseball and was more than even Cobb was making in Detroit. Plus, the rival Federal League had been forced out of business, and with the demise of the two-year-old third major league, there no longer was any outside competition to drive up the salaries.

That winter, Lannin sent Speaker a contract offer for nine thousand dollars. Speaker sent it back unsigned, and when the Red Sox reported for spring training at Hot Springs, Arkansas, in 1916, he remained at his home in Texas. Carrigan finally persuaded Speaker to report to camp by working out a deal that would allow the player to be paid by the game while waiting to meet with Lannin to work out a contract when the team returned East to open the season.

The Red Sox were in Brooklyn for a final preseason tune-up with the Dodgers when Speaker hit a dramatic ninth-inning home run off Rube Marquard to give Boston a 2–1 victory. After the game, an exuberant Lannin rushed up and threw his arm around Speaker's shoulder.

"That was great, Tris! And I'll tell you this now. Your terms are okay. We'll sign when we get to Boston tomorrow."

Speaker returned to his hotel room believing the salary squabble was behind him. But Lannin long ago had decided that the time had come to get rid of the great center fielder. "I'd rather fire a man than cut his salary," Lannin had confided to a business associate. "For if I cut his salary, he will not do his best work. The owner who has a declining star on his hands had better dispense with his services altogether than to have any such unsatisfactory arrangement."

Acting on this premise, Lannin had been discreetly shopping

Speaker around. In Cleveland, Ed Bang of the *News* was clearing up some matters in the newsroom before the start of the season when a wire story caught his eye. It was a report out of Boston concerning Lannin's unhappiness with Speaker. Playing a hunch, Bang called Indians executive Bob McRoy and urged him to make an offer for the Red Sox star.

"He can be had for the right price," said Bang.

With this prodding, McRoy got in touch with Lannin, and before long, a deal was worked out. Even as Speaker was accepting congratulations for his game-winning homer in Brooklyn, the die had been cast. That evening, McRoy contacted Speaker in his hotel room.

"Tris, how would you like to go to Cleveland?" he asked.

Speaker wasted no time in giving his reply.

"I wouldn't consider it."

Cleveland had finished seventh in 1915 and never had won a pennant. If Speaker were exiled to such a club, he almost certainly would be forfeiting his hopes of the World Series money he could earn in Boston. He had no intention of making such a costly move.

McRoy was silent for a few seconds. Then he hit Speaker with the news.

"Well, we've made the deal for you. We've already bought you."

Speaker was stunned. He had been traded for pitcher Sad Sam Jones, infielder Freddie Thomas, and the record sum of $57,500. Lannin had wanted second baseman Bill Wambsganss, but McRoy had convinced him to accept Thomas and Jones instead. Jones later developed into a top pitcher, but to angry Red Sox fans the deal appeared to be little more than a cash transaction.

Speaker reluctantly reported to his new team but only after he forced Lannin to agree to give him ten thousand dollars of the purchase price. The Cleveland fans were ecstatic, and with good reason. That first season, Spoke batted .383 to end Cobb's nine-year reign as the American League batting champion.

He turned in two more solid seasons but in 1919, burdened by the additional duties of managing, his batting mark fell below .300 for the first time in eleven years.

In the spring of 1920, Speaker drove himself relentlessly in his determination to resurrect his skills. From the time he set foot on the practice field, he was engaged in some activity. He demanded the same hustle from his players. It had been customary for players to stand around while awaiting their turn in batting practice, but Speaker would dash down to first base, grab a mitt, and engage in infield drills. Following their manager's lead, the other Cleveland players busied themselves when not on the field by warming up pitchers or fielding bunts along the sidelines.

Speaker had other theories that he put into effect. He did not believe in using a batting cage, and for batting practice he put a catcher behind the plate and had him signal for curves and fastballs. "We can secure better results with the catchers receiving and the pitchers putting real stuff on a ball rather than using the cage," he insisted.

His skills as a leader and motivator were unquestioned. He played no favorites and he was straightforward with all of his players. As a result, there were no signs of disharmony on the club despite the extensive platooning of players. The best assessment of Speaker as a manager was delivered by Henry Edwards in the *Plain Dealer:* "He combines the gray matter of a thinking veteran with the effervescence of a college boy. He is the carefree rookie one moment, the critical manager the next. He is the happy-go-lucky practical joker one moment, the stern disciplinarian the next."

Added one of his players in later years: "Speaker would laugh and have a good time, but when it was time to play ball, that was serious. That wasn't no fun making."

*　　　*　　　*

As he led his team through practice that spring, Speaker could not help but be optimistic. He had at his command an experienced and powerful ballclub.

The pitching staff was headed up by Stanley Coveleskie, thirty years old and a spitballer with legendary control. It was said that Coveleskie once pitched seven innings without a single ball being called. Every pitch either was hit or was a strike. Covey was the workhorse of the staff. He had won forty-six games in the past two seasons, and on days he wasn't scheduled to pitch he would go down to the bullpen on his own in the late innings if the score was close. He would warm up slowly and start throwing harder if it appeared he might be called upon. When he was loosened up, he would look out to Speaker and nod his head to signal he was ready.

Rivaling Coveleskie as the ace of the staff was Jim "Sarge" Bagby, whom Ty Cobb called the smartest pitcher he ever faced. Bagby had a fadeaway pitch and outstanding control, but most of all he relied on his knowledge of the hitters. He knew their weak points and their strong points, and he always threw to their weaknesses. In the past four seasons, he had not won fewer than sixteen games and in 1917 he was a twenty-three-game winner.

Then came thirty-two-year-old knuckleballer Slim Caldwell, a onetime star for the Yankees and Red Sox whose weakness for alcohol almost ruined his career. When Speaker signed him the previous summer, he added a unique clause in the pitcher's contract. It read: "After each game he pitches, Ray Caldwell must get drunk. He is not to report to the clubhouse the next day. The second day he is to report to Manager Speaker and run around the ballpark as many times as Manager Speaker stipulates. The third day he is to pitch batting practice, and the fourth day he is to pitch in a championship game." Speaker's strategy was to give Caldwell two days to drink and two days to sober up enough to pitch. The pitcher never again showed up at the ballpark drunk.

Caldwell had one other claim to fame. In his first game for the Tribe at League Park, he was struck by a bolt of lightning from a thunderstorm that rolled in off nearby Lake Erie. Caldwell was knocked flat on his back on the pitcher's mound, but after a few moments, he stood up and frisked himself to see if everything still was in place. He then resumed pitching, finishing with a complete game. As best as anyone could figure, the lightning had hit the metal button at the top of his cap, surged through his body, and exited through his metal spikes, leaving him only with a slight burn on his chest. From then on, the players swore Caldwell had lightning in his pitches.

The first baseman was Doc Johnston, who was dubbed "The Human Telescope" for his ability to stretch out his body to pull down errant throws. Johnston also was known for his constant chatter, and it once had been suggested that he install a mirror behind the bag so he would have someone to talk to in the field.

At second base, the slick-fielding Bill Wambsganss was coming off his best season. Quiet and studious, Wamby had come up as a shortstop, joining the team in 1915 when it was playing in Chicago. One look at the newcomer's strange name prompted Ring Lardner of the *Chicago Tribune* to write the following verse:

> The Naps bought a shortstop named Wambsganss
> Who is slated to fill Ray Chapman's pants.
> But when he saw Ray
> And the way he could play,
> He muttered, "I haven't a clam's chance."

But Wamby made the switch to the other side of the bag and found his niche playing alongside Chapman. Although he had a reputation as a good field–no hit ballplayer, Wamby had raised his batting average to a solid .278 with sixty runs batted in and sixty runs scored in 1919. In the field, Wamby and Chapman had come to know every move the other man was going to make. They spent hours working on executing the double play, and they were as smooth a pair of fielders around the second-base bag as there was in the game. On more than one occasion, Chapman told Wamby, "Bill, you're the only second baseman I'll ever play next to."

At shortstop, Chapman appeared primed for another outstanding season. Watching him in action at the team's first practice session, Ed Bang observed: "Chappie still retains his youthful beauty and his speed. He shook a mean pair of dogs getting down to first base during the workout."

Completing the infield was third baseman Larry Gardner, who had played on three of the championship teams in Boston. Even at thirty-four years of age, Gardner still was an outstanding fielder and the best clutch hitter in the league.

The right fielder was Elmer Smith, a powerful left-handed hitter who had come into his own the previous season by hitting a team-leading nine home runs.

In left field was the team's veteran, Jack Graney, who had broken in with Cleveland twelve years earlier. A patient hitter, he was known as "Three-and-Two Jack" for his ability to run the count out full to wear out pitchers. Graney had the distinction of recording a number of "firsts" in baseball. He was the first batter faced by Babe Ruth when the Babe broke into the big leagues in 1914. Graney hit a single off the young left-hander. When Cleveland experimented with identifying the players by attaching numerals to their jerseys in 1916, it was Graney, batting leadoff, who became the first man to appear in a game wearing a number on his uniform.

Battling Graney for the starting job in left was Charlie Jamieson, a speedy outfielder who had come to Cleveland the previous season as a throw-in in a trade with Philadelphia. The Indians were supposed to receive Gardner and pitcher Elmer Myers in exchange for outfielder Bobby "Braggo" Roth. The deal appeared set, but Speaker, serving as Lee Fohl's assistant, insisted on Philadelphia's including Jamieson in the transaction. Connie Mack, who had obtained the spare outfielder and part-time pitcher for the waiver price, had no objection. Jamieson responded to the opportunity to play in Cleveland by batting .353.

The missing ingredient on the ballclub was catcher Steve O'Neill. When his teammates headed south to open training camp, he remained behind in New York, locked in a contract dispute.

O'Neill was a rare commodity: a player who combined intelligence with his outstanding skills behind the plate. Speaker called him the smartest caller of pitches he ever had seen, and O'Neill's powerful throwing arm also was legendary. He was one of the few catchers that Ty Cobb rarely tried to steal on.

Earlier in his career, O'Neill had been branded a one-dimensional ballplayer, an outstanding defensive catcher who couldn't carry his weight as a batter. One year, his batting average was a feeble .184. But through his hard work, O'Neill made himself into a solid hitter, and in 1919, he hit an impressive .289 while catching 123 games.

Now, he wanted to be rewarded for his performance. He returned Dunn's first contract offer that winter unsigned, and scheduled a trip to Cleveland in January to discuss the matter with the Indians' owner. But just as O'Neill was to depart his home in New York, his wife became ill. When Dunn failed to receive word of the catcher's change in plans, he broke off the negotiations, peeved over what he regarded as O'Neill's obstinacy.

A few days later, Ed Bang was in New York before spring training when he happened to run into O'Neill. The ballplayer expressed his regret over the misunderstanding and said he feared his service with the Indians was over.

"But I still want to play ball," he insisted. "If not with the Indians, I'd like to go to the Yankees. I've heard they're interested in me."

Bang immediately contacted Dunn in Chicago to let him know what he had learned. The owner assured him he would clear up the problem. One week into training camp, word arrived in New Orleans that O'Neill and Dunn had just worked out an agreement in Cleveland. The catcher was on his way south. When Speaker heard the news, he boasted, "That's just about the last little link in our pennant chain."

23

In mid-March, the growing unrest among the New York players erupted into a short-lived rebellion. The blowup was triggered by the distribution of the disputed thirteen thousand dollars in prize money from the 1919 World Series.

The payment of the money had been held up until February,

when the Yankees had won the battle over Mays's eligibility and validated their claim to third place. When Ruppert and Huston finally had been able to pay out the money, they sent shares not only to the active players but also to pitchers Bob McGraw and Allan Russell—who had been traded to Boston at midseason in exchange for Mays—as well as team secretaries Mark Roth and Charles McManus, trainer Al Woods, and groundskeeper Phil Schenck.

When word got out that two former teammates plus four office employees had received full shares, the New York players were incensed. They felt they had been shortchanged, and they wanted Ruppert and Huston to reimburse them for the six extra shares paid out. The two colonels dismissed the complaint out of hand.

On March 20, the Yankees were in Jacksonville to play the world champion Cincinnati Red Legs in the first game of a Jubilee Day doubleheader. The Brooklyn Dodgers and Washington Senators were scheduled for the second game, and a capacity crowd of five thousand was on hand even though ticket prices had been boosted to between one and two dollars.

Shortly before it was time for the Yankees to take the field, Ruppert and Huston received a note stating it was urgent they report to the team's locker room immediately. When the two owners did, they were met by Pratt, Peckinpaugh, and pitcher Bob Shawkey. The players informed the colonels they had been chosen by the rest of the team to present a grievance demanding an immediate settlement of the dispute over the division of the thirteen thousand dollars.

Neither Ruppert nor Huston was willing to negotiate under such conditions. The only concession they were willing to make was an offer to take the matter under consideration.

Pratt, Peckinpaugh, and Shawkey returned to the locker room to consult with their teammates. Some of the militant players wanted to go out on strike. Others favored holding up the start of the game to underscore their demands. After a lengthy and sometimes heated discussion, the players finally decided to take the field. At one o'clock, they emerged from the locker room, sullen but in uniform.

In the other clubhouse, a similar confrontation was taking place over an entirely different matter. Edd Roush, Cincinnati's star center fielder, had declared that unless he was given five box seats for his family and friends, he would lead the Red Legs in a walkout. Frank Bancroft, the Reds' seventy-one-year-old business manager, steadfastly refused to provide the tickets. During the discussion, Roush began shouting at the older man.

Fearing for the old man's safety, Charles Ebbetts, the owner of the Dodgers, and Harry Sparrow, the Yankees' business manager, tried to intervene on Bancroft's behalf. When they did, Roush became belligerent. He cursed Ebbetts and Sparrow, then pushed Sparrow against a wall. Bancroft became so frightened by the outburst, he quickly pulled five tickets from his pocket and handed them over to Roush.

It was not the first time the elderly Bancroft had been bullied. When Cincinnati won the World Series the previous fall, the players voted not to give him a share of the receipts although he had been with the team for forty-nine years.

Oblivious to the dramas that had been played out in the opposing clubhouses, the fans applauded loudly when the two teams appeared on the field. The players rewarded them with a thrilling game that went down to the final inning before it was decided. Meusel hit a tremendous home run to deep center field in the second inning, and in the bottom of the ninth Ruth and Lewis hit back-to-back doubles to give New York an 8–7 victory.

But the matter had not been forgotten. For the next few days, the New York players continued to press their grievance over the division of the money. Finally, Ruppert and Huston settled the dispute by agreeing to donate to the players a sum equal to the two original shares already paid out to McGraw and Russell.

That came to $915.70, which would be divided among the twenty-nine team members. For their troubles, the players received $38.15 apiece.

*　　　*　　　*

Back in Miami, Huggins was sitting in the hotel lobby when he was approached by a couple of reporters. The New York manager was told there was talk going around that several opposing players were planning "to get Mays" for what they perceived as his habit of throwing bean balls.

"What do you propose to do about this, Hug?" one of the writers asked.

Huggins shrugged his shoulders.

"The howlers are not worrying us because we figured on hearing a lot about Mays' 'bean ball.' We were prepared for such talk last season after Mays joined us, but it didn't materialize at that time.

"Those who are peeved because Mays landed with the Yanks and remained with the Yanks are responsible for the howl. Had Mays landed with Cleveland, Chicago or any other club, there would have been no talk about the 'bean ball' or unusual delivery. Those who are panning Mays are jealous of his success and the position he holds with regard to the rumpus in the league."

Besides, added Huggins, "Mays wouldn't harm anybody."

24

Chick Fewster was a frail youngster who looked out of place among all of the Yankee sluggers that spring. He was five foot eleven and weighed only 160 pounds, but he was a pesky hitter and his slick fielding was one of the highlights of training camp.

Mays called Fewster "the best young second baseman I ever looked at." Huggins also had a high opinion of the twenty-four-year-old infielder. The Yankees manager already had set aside a spot for Fewster in the lineup and had plans to bat him leadoff, using his speed to get on base ahead of the Murderers' Row.

On March 25, shortly before it was time to break camp and head north, the Yankees and Dodgers met for yet another in their series of exhibition games.

In the bottom of the first inning, Fewster stepped up to lead off for New York. On the mound for Brooklyn was a big right-hander named Jeff Pfeffer, one of two brothers to pitch in the big leagues under the same name. Although his older brother, who had played ten years earlier, had been known as Big Jeff, the younger Jeff was a strapping six foot three and one of the hardest throwers in the National League. It was warm and sunny on this day, and Pfeffer already was cutting loose with the ball even though the game had just begun. He ran the count to 2–2, then threw a curveball inside. As the Brooklyn pitcher watched in horror, the ball curved in on Fewster, who had a habit of crowding over the plate, and struck him at the base of the skull, just above and back of the ear.

When the ball hit, Pfeffer heard a "dull, crushing sound." All the way in the outfield, Zack Wheat could hear what he described as "a terrible wallop."

Fewster dropped straight to the ground, his body quivering in spasmodic bursts. For a moment, no one could move as the stricken player lay writhing in the dirt by home plate.

It took ten minutes to revive Fewster, and when he finally did regain consciousness, he sat up and looked about in a daze. He could not remember what had happened. He thought perhaps he had fainted.

Spotting the ball nearby, he asked, "What's the matter? Did the ball hit me?"

By the time he was taken to the locker room, Fewster was losing his ability to speak. He attempted to write out messages, but seemed unable to put his thoughts together.

In the days to come, Fewster would lose all recollection of being hit or even seeing the ball pitched. His skull had been fractured and a blood clot prevented his vocal nerves from functioning. In the immediate aftermath of his injury, Fewster's vocabulary consisted of only two words and it was feared he might never speak normally again. A month later, he still would require a wheelchair to get around. It would be midseason before he would return to the ballclub.

The man who threw the ball was visibly upset by the incident. He also was puzzled. The pitch had not been wild. In fact, it appeared to have been in the strike zone when it struck Fewster. Why then, wondered Pfeffer, had the batter not tried to dodge the ball?

"Fewster never moved a muscle while that ball came toward him," the pitcher claimed. "I thought perhaps he might have been hypnotized by the ball, as I have heard of such instances. The batter getting his eyes fixed on the ball seems to be fascinated by it, like a bird before a snake, and can't seem to make up his mind to move until it is too late."

Another player who was badly shaken by the beaning was Carl Mays. Fewster, it seems, was one of the few men on the ballclub Mays considered his friend.

25

Opening Day in Cleveland was the coldest in memory. A cold front had plunged temperatures into the forties and a brisk north wind only added to the discomfort. Occasionally, the sun peeked through the clouds to provide some much-needed warmth, but otherwise there was little relief from the frigid weather that enveloped League Park. Even longtime fan H. O. Van Hart, who had attended every opener since 1901 and had made it a custom to observe the occasion by changing to his summer clothes, had been forced to break tradition and wear his winter garments. Others in the crowd of 19,984 pulled up the collars on their overcoats, rubbed their hands together, and stamped their feet in an effort to keep warm.

On the playing field, Indians owner Jim Dunn was oblivious to the weather. For him, the season could not begin soon enough.

A flamboyant fifty-three-year-old Irishman, Dunn reveled in the attention he commanded as owner of the Cleveland ballclub. He was a highly visible figure in his front-row seat at the ballpark, cheering for his team whether things were going well or they were in the midst of a losing streak. And when he rooted, claimed *The Sporting News,* "the rafters tremble." Personable and well liked by his players, Sunny Jim, as his friends called him, also could be a bit pompous. Once he had traveled to New Orleans to visit his team in spring training. Upon disembarking from the train, he was startled to hear two Dixieland bands strike up a tune of welcome.

"This is all very nice," he whispered to one of his companions, "but don't you think they have overdone it a bit?"

Only later did someone spoil the fun by informing Dunn the bands had been there to greet the grand exalted ruler of the Elks, who happened to be on the same train.

Unlike most owners of the era, Dunn's background was in business, not baseball. He had started out in the contracting business in his hometown of Marshalltown, Iowa, and eventually became the senior member of the Dunn-McCarthy Company, builders of railroads. In 1908, while completing a contract on the Cleveland Belt Line railroad, Dunn became convinced of the city's potential as a baseball town. It was then that he made the decision to buy into the game if he ever had the opportunity. In 1916, he got his chance after meeting American League president Ban Johnson, who was casting about for someone to take over the Cleveland club from the financially strapped Charles Somers. Dunn indicated his interest, but admitted he could lay his hands on little more than $15,000 in cash at the moment. Johnson agreed to lend him $100,000 on behalf of the league, and White Sox owner Charles Comiskey, whom Dunn had helped establish in Chicago, came up with another $100,000. Dunn's friends in Chicago and Marshalltown put up the remainder of the $500,000 purchase price.

Dunn's impact on the team was immediate. When he first arrived in Cleveland to take command of the franchise, he was introduced to the local newspapermen. Sizing up the new owner, the *Plain Dealer*'s Edwards wanted to know what role Dunn intended to take with the team.

"I never went into anything yet that I did not run myself," said

Dunn. "If that means I must be president of the club, I'll be president."

"You do know you've taken over a rotten ballclub?" asked Edwards.

"But I will give Cleveland a pennant winner in three years," shot back Dunn. "Cleveland will not support anything but a winner, and I am going to give it one regardless of cost."

Dunn showed he meant business by taking advantage of the opportunity to purchase Speaker that first year. He also put up fifteen thousand dollars—then a substantial amount of money—for first baseman Lou Guisto, who never panned out.

He failed to meet his deadline for delivering a championship ballclub, but after four years in charge he was getting closer. Standing on the pitcher's mound of his ballpark on April 14, 1920, Dunn was convinced he at last was on the verge of achieving his goal.

At precisely three o'clock, umpire Billy Evans shouted "Play ball!" and Dunn handed Mayor Davis a brand-new Reach baseball. Davis, whose pleasant personality and infectious smile had served him well in winning the past three mayoral elections, proudly held up the ball for all to see and stepped onto the pitching rubber, ready to deliver the first pitch of the season. His task on this day would be more than a mere ceremonial toss to the catcher. In the batter's box was Browns third baseman Jimmy Austin, a switch-hitter batting from the left side, and he was fully prepared to take a cut at the mayor's offering. An eleven-year big-league veteran, Austin was forty years old, but he still could send line drives whistling off his bat. Undaunted, the Republican mayor stared in at him with the disdain he normally reserved for a Democrat.

"Pitch to his weakness, Harry," advised Dunn. "That guy never could hit one high and on the inside."

Davis nodded in agreement.

Hampered by his overcoat, the mayor stiffly went through his windup and tossed the ball high and inside. Austin swung and missed, and the fans let loose a loud roar.

Davis and Dunn clapped each other on the back and walked

Ray Chapman was born on January 15, 1891, in Beaver Dam, Kentucky. (*Author's collection*)

romising shortstop for the Cleveland ns, Ray Chapman during his early days he team. (*Courtesy of the National Base- ibrary, Cooperstown, New York*)

Chapman played a total of nine years in the major leagues, all with the Cleveland Indians. His lifetime batting average was .278. (*Author's collection*)

In his bachelor's days with an unidentified date at a Chicago park. (*Author's collection*)

Chapman and his buddy, John Reid Alexander, who fooled guests into believing that Ray was the famous Irish singer John McCormack. (*Author's collection*)

Ray's bride-to-be, Kathleen Daly, at the Ship Building Company where she christ ship on November 11, 1916. (*Author's colle*

Mays always claimed that pitching "high-and-tight" to batters was part of the game. (*Courtesy of National Baseball Library, Cooperstown, New York*)

Mays compiled a lifetime record of 208–126, ding a record of 26–11 in 1920. (*Courtesy of nal Baseball Library, Cooperstown, New York*)

Carl Mays showing his "submarine-style" pitch. (*Courtesy of National Baseball Library, Cooperstown, New York*)

Jack Graney, shown early in his career with Cleveland around 1908–1909. Graney was friends with Chapman throughout his career in Cleveland. (*Courtesy of National Baseball Library, Cooperstown, New York*)

Steve O'Neill, Cleveland catcher and one of Chapman's teammates and best friends from the time Ray joined the club in 1912. (*Courtesy of National Baseball Library, Cooperstown, New York*)

Cleveland's famed double-play combination of second baseman Bill "Wamby" Wambsganss and shortstop Ray Chapman. (*Courtesy of National Baseball Library, Cooperstown, New York*)

Cleveland's manager and center fielder Tris Speaker. A close friend of Chapman's, he fell into a deep depression after Ray's death. (*Courtesy of National Baseball Library, Cooperstown, New York*)

Tris Speaker—"The Gray Eagle"—at bat. (*Courtesy of National Baseball Library, Cooperstown, New York*)

Ray Chapman at the peak of his career. (*Courtesy of National Baseball Library, Cooperstown, New York*)

Joe Sewell, the young shortstop who was called up by Cleveland to replace Chapman in the lineup. (*Courtesy of National Baseball Library, Cooperstown, New York*)

as Connolly, the umpire vas behind the plate the the fatal beaning. (*Cour-National Baseball Library, town, New York*)

CLEVELAND					NEW YORK			
	ab	bh	po	a		ab	bh	po	a
Jameson lf	5	2	1	0	Ward 3b	4	0	1	5
Chapman ss	1	0	0	3	Peck'p'h ss	4	0	3	3
Lunte ss	1	0	0	2	Ruth rf	4	1	1	0
Speaker cf	4	0	0	0	Pratt 2b	3	1	1	4
Smith rf	4	0	2	0	Lewis lf	4	0	0	0
Gardner 3b	3	1	2	1	Pipp 1b	3	0	12	0
O'Neill c	4	3	8	0	Bodie cf	4	2	4	0
Johnston 1b	4	1	10	0	Ruel c	3	2	5	0
Wambs's 2b	4	0	4	2	Mays p	2	0	0	4
Covel'skie p	3	0	0	3	*Vick	1	1	0	0
					Thorm'len p	0	0	0	0
					†O'Doul	1	0	0	0
Totals	33	1	27	12	Totals	33	7	27	17

Innings	1	2	3	4	5	6	7	8	9	
Cleveland	0	1	0	2	1	0	0	0	0	—4
New York	0	0	0	0	0	0	0	0	3	—3

Errors—Ward, Ruel. Two-base hit—Bodie. Home run—O'Neill. Double play—Pipp (unassisted). Base on balls—Off Mays 1, Covaleskie 2. Struck out—By Mays 3, Covaleskie 4. Hit by pitched ball—By Mays (Chapman.) Umpires—Connolly (plate) and Nallin. Time—1 hr. 55min.

*Batted for Mays in 8th.
†Batted for Thormahlen in 9th.

Box score of fatal game.

Chapman's grave in Lake View Cemetery in Cleveland. (*Author's collection*)

triumphantly off the field, surrendering the mound to Coveleskie. The Cleveland pitcher finished what the mayor had started, throwing three more pitches past Austin for the strikeout. The first batter had gone down on four strikes. The season was under way.

*   *   *

Covey was unhittable that day, holding the Browns to just five hits and not allowing a runner past second base. He got all the offensive support he needed from Doc Johnston, the Indians' superstitious first baseman. Doc had been the hitting sensation of the spring for the Indians, earning himself a spot high in the batting order, but his lucky number was seven, and he pleaded with Speaker to bat him in that spot in the lineup. Speaker obliged, even though it meant Johnston would be placed below the light-hitting Wamby.

It was Johnston's single in the second inning that touched off a four-run outburst off St. Louis right-hander Alan Sothoron, a longtime Cleveland nemesis. The previous season, Sothoron had beaten the Indians five times in six games. A strikingly good-looking man who once had been voted the most handsome player in baseball, Sothoron was a top-notch pitcher, but he had some unusual quirks. While he could throw the ball to the plate with the best of them, he was strangely incapable of throwing it to first base to hold on a runner. To overcome this bizarre handicap, he had been forced to resort to tossing the ball underhand to the base in the style of a bowler.

Johnston singled again in the fifth to drive in another run, making the final score 5–0. In addition to pitching a shutout, Coveleskie, using his pet bat "Able," also had a run-scoring single. When Covey retired the final St. Louis batter, his teammates hoisted him onto their shoulders and carried him off the field as the fans who had weathered the cold stood and cheered.

In the clubhouse, no one was more satisfied by the events of the day than Chapman. Less than two weeks earlier, his back had stiffened on him and he had feared a recurrence of the problems that had plagued him the previous season. But after several days of treatment and restricted workouts, the pain had vanished as mysteriously as it had arrived. Even playing the opening game under such adverse weather conditions, he had not experienced any discomfort.

Chapman had other reasons to celebrate. Not only had the team won, but his totals included two base hits, a stolen base, and a sacrifice hit. If this was to be his final season as a ballplayer, he had wanted to start it on a good note. He could not have asked for a better beginning.

26

Opening Day 1920 found Huggins in a foul mood. Under the best of circumstances, the Yankee manager, who suffered from chronic neuritis and dental problems, could be an irritable man. The events of the past few hours had only served to worsen his temperament. The Yankees were in Philadelphia to start the season, and Huggins had been forced to leave his best pitcher behind in New York. There still was an outstanding warrant against Mays as a result of the Bryan Hayes incident one year earlier, so he did not dare to venture into the city. Consequently, Huggins was forced to rearrange his pitching rotation for the first few days of the campaign.

Adding to the manager's displeasure, a railroad strike resulted in the cancellation of the train the team was booked on. Secretary Harry Sparrow scrambled to make other accommodations, and as a result the players griped loudly over having to endure a ride in the day coaches.

Things didn't get much better for the Yankees once they arrived at their destination. It was overcast and chilly, and overcoats and furs were the garb of the day among the twelve thousand fans at

Shibe Park. Had it not been for the debut of Babe Ruth in a Yankee uniform, the crowd would have been considerably smaller.

Most of the fans who came out to see Ruth did so to hurl abuse at the big slugger. When he batted in the first inning following a solo home run by Wally Pipp, he was greeted with cries of: "Pipp's crabbing your act, Babe!" "He's stealing your stuff!" and "You haven't got a hit in your bag!" Ruth responded by slashing a single to right for his first hit as a Yankee. It went for naught when Philadelphia's Scott Perry fanned Duffy Lewis to retire the side.

In the fourth, Babe came up with runners on first and second and no outs. This time, he struck out as the fans cheered wildly.

In the bottom of the eighth, the score was tied 1–1 and the Athletics had runners on first and second with two outs. Joe Dugan lofted an easy fly ball to right field for what should have been the final out of the inning, but at this crucial moment, Ruth stumbled backward, raised his glove unsteadily, and muffed the catch. Both runners scored, and the fans shouted gleefully at the Babe.

Perry retired the Yankees in order in the ninth to complete the 3–1 victory, and the Athletics, who had lost 104 games the previous year, had gotten the Yankees' season started on a sour note.

The next day, play was about to begin when a small boy appeared on the field carrying a large hatbox. He boldly marched straight to home plate to speak to umpire Dick Nallin.

"I have a present for Mr. Ruth," said the boy.

The players gathered around home plate and the fans strained to see what was going on as the Babe carefully untied the package and pulled out a brown derby. It was of the low-cut style that had been popular at the turn of the century and since had come to symbolize the German dialect comedian. The implications of the hat were clear to all in attendance at Shibe Park. In baseball language, "to win the brown derby" meant making a crucial misplay.

Unabashed, Ruth grinned widely and placed the derby atop his head where, according to the *New York Times,* "it reposed like a sofa cushion on Grant's tomb for it was about seven sizes too small."

Babe's good-natured acceptance of the gag won the fans over to his side, and the jeers that had greeted him the day before now turned to cheers. Although Ruth went hitless in five times up and struck out three times, once with the bases loaded, the Yankees rallied for four runs in the final three innings to beat the Athletics 4–1.

For the next two days, it rained. While the players milled around the hotel lobby or killed time by playing cards, Huggins brooded in his room. From all indications, he thought, it was going to be a tumultuous summer.

27

As he stepped onto the field in Fenway Park on the afternoon of April 19 to begin his warmup tosses, Mays was braced for another hostile reception from the Boston fans. They did not disappoint him. There were resounding boos and cries of "Traitor!" It was not a pleasant way to begin the season.

Mays had rejoined the club after it left Philadelphia, and it was his bad luck to make his first start against his former team. Worse, it was the annual Patriots Day doubleheader in Boston, adding to the size of the turnout. The Red Sox had won the morning game 6–0 before six thousand fans, and by the time the afternoon contest began the crowd had swollen to twenty-two thousand.

The inactivity of the past week had taken its toll on Mays. He struggled to get loose and he could not seem to find his rhythm. He gave up only six hits but they came when they did the most damage. The Red Sox scored four runs off him in seven innings en route to an 8–3 victory. As Mays left the field, he was subjected to more jeers and catcalls.

*   *   *

The Yankees continued to struggle even after returning home. In the home opener at the Polo Grounds, Ruth swung savagely at a pitch in batting practice and strained a muscle in his side. He insisted on starting the game, but after striking out in the first inning he hobbled back to the dugout and collapsed onto the bench holding his side. When the Yankees took the field, Frank Gleich trotted out to take over in center and the Babe, supported by catcher Truck Hannah, gingerly made his way to the locker room.

Ruth finally hit his first home run as a Yankee on May 1. It was a massive drive that carried all the way out of the Polo Grounds, over the right-field stands, and into the first-base coaching box of a nearby amateur game. New York won 6–0 over Boston, but in the process Mays, Ernie Shore, and Frank O'Doul managed to get themselves ejected from the bench for taunting umpire Will Dineen.

Three days later, umpire Dick Nallin responded to the harassment from the New York dugout by halting the game and ordering all of the Yankee substitutes off the premises. As the fans and Red Sox fielders watched, the Yankee reserves trooped across the field en route to the clubhouse. That left manager Huggins, coach Charley O'Leary, and trainer Doc Woods as the only inhabitants on the bench.

Not all of the Yankees' barbs were directed at the umpires. There also was discord among their own ranks. One day, outfielder Babe Pinelli, angered by some of Mays's remarks, lashed out bitterly at his teammate in front of the other players. At five foot nine and 165 pounds, Pinelli was not an imposing man, but he gave Mays a thorough dressing down and questioned the pitcher's bravery. Mays accepted the challenge to fight and agreed to meet Pinelli in the clubhouse after the game. Pinelli said he would be waiting.

When the time came, Pinelli showed up but Mays didn't.

28

Like the other Cleveland ballplayers, Chapman was road-weary and homesick as the team checked into the Hotel Ansonia at Seventy-third and Broadway in New York. It was May 14, a Friday, and the Indians had been away from home for all but five of the past twenty-four days.

In a typical baseball season, the Cleveland ballclub would cover in excess of thirteen thousand miles, all of it by rail. The Indians, at least, traveled in style. They always had two Pullman cars on the train, and no one had to sleep in an upper berth. When it got too hot in the summertime, the players would hang damp towels over the open windows to cool off the car. They got four dollars in meal money, sometimes seven dollars if they were staying in a more expensive hotel. "Open your mouth in some of them, and just that would cost you money," Charlie Jamieson used to grumble.

All in all, it added up to a lot of long hours to be killed on train cars or in hotel lobbies. The players passed the time in different ways. Jamieson and Wood used to play pool four or five hours a day and think nothing of it. Wood was widely regarded as the best pool player in baseball; Jamey liked to brag he was the second best. Pinochle and checkers also were favorite pastimes among the Indians, especially on the train. Others read cheap novels or slept away the boredom. Gardner, the scholar of the team, preferred "high-class" fiction.

Chapman's two most popular pastimes were singing and story-telling, and he was adept at both. He was the best storyteller on the team, and he could hold an audience's attention for hours by spinning yarns about baseball or some of the players he had known.

One of Chapman's favorite tales concerned his rookie year, 1913, when he roomed with Shoeless Joe Jackson at Cleveland's spring camp. As Chapman told the story, Jackson liked to slip out after curfew every night, and finally manager Joe Birmingham got wind of it. He threatened Jackson with a stiff fine if he ever caught him out of his room late.

"Well, Birmy waits until after bedtime. Then he creeps up to Joe's room and gets in. Joe wasn't there. He doesn't say anything but he does the same thing the next night. He peeked around. Joe couldn't be seen.

"But just as Birmy was backing out, Joe peeks out from under the bed. 'Here I am, Birmy,' he says, 'same as last night when you came in.' "

At other times, Chapman entertained his teammates with his singing. Through the years, he and Graney had been the standard-bearers of the Quartette, a singing group that at various times also included O'Neill, Johnston, or Joe Evans. They would get together in one of the coaches and belt out song after song while other travelers gathered around to listen, convinced that Cleveland must have won that day.

In past years, the nomadic lifestyle of a ballplayer had appealed to Chapman. He enjoyed the glamour of the Eastern cities and the camaraderie of the ballclub. Now, newly married, he found it difficult to be away from Kathleen for such long periods of time. The recent stretch of games had been especially trying.

It had started with a 548-mile journey to St. Louis. From there, it was back to Cleveland, where the Indians took two of three games from the defending champion White Sox. In one of those victories, Speaker had made what was hailed the greatest catch in history, racing full-speed toward the fence after a drive hit by Shoeless Joe Jackson and spearing the ball just as he crashed into the wall.

The next day, it was back on the road for the 171-mile trip to Detroit, where Chapman's two hits and two runs scored handed the Tigers their thirteenth consecutive defeat to open the season. From

Detroit, the Indians headed west to Chicago and four more victories over the White Sox in a five-game series.

After a stop in Cleveland for a single game with the Browns, there was a 680-mile haul to Boston. Then came the 248-mile trip back down the coast to New York. It rained all the way. The Indians were a tired ballclub, but they arrived in New York in first place in the standings with sixteen victories in twenty-two games.

*   *   *

The scene at the Polo Grounds on the Sunday afternoon of May 16 was chaotic. Thirty minutes before game time, 36,800 people already were inside the stadium and another 10,000 or so were outside clamoring to get in. The ticket sellers were unable to satisfy them, not only because there was no more space but also because there were no more admission tickets to distribute.

Mounted police moved up and down the street to keep the disappointed throng at bay, and inside the overflows were crowded even beyond World Series capacity. The fans standing behind the regular seats could have formed several regiments. Hundreds who could not get into the park rushed to Coogan's Bluff to stake out the grounds on the heights overlooking the big scoreboard, which they could use to follow the progress of the game below.

Newsmen arriving less than fifteen minutes before the three o'clock starting time had to gain entry by climbing a special fence once they received approval from club officials. There was no chance to open the gate, for the fans outside would have made a rush for it.

Although the atmosphere was more in keeping with a World Series contest, this was only the second of a four-game series between the Indians and Yankees. But the fans could sense the importance of this early-season showdown between the two contenders, and the recent surge by the Yankees had only added to the excitement.

Earlier in the week, New York had knocked Chicago out of first place with a pair of victories. On Saturday, the Yankees had opened the series with the Indians by handing Coveleskie his first loss of the season and in the process bumping Cleveland off the top of the standings.

Now, there were 36,800 people in the Polo Grounds anxious to see if the New Yorkers could extend their four-game winning streak, which had boosted their record to 12–10. They roared with anticipation as Mays completed his warm-up tosses and signaled that he was ready for play to begin. Graney stepped to the plate to lead off for Cleveland, while Chapman crouched in the on-deck area holding a pair of bats.

*   *   *

In previous years, just the presence of the underhand pitcher on the mound would have been enough to ensure defeat for the Indians. Two years earlier, Henry Edwards had written in the *Plain Dealer:* "Clevelanders know by this time that whenever Mays performs the Indians might just as well leave their bats in the clubhouse."

Mays's mastery of Cleveland had begun the first year he was in the league. Half of his six victories came against Cleveland, and in eighteen innings he allowed only one run and one walk. In his first three seasons in the league, Mays had a won-lost record of 12–2 against the Clevelanders.

The spell had not been broken until 1918. The turning point came that spring before a large crowd in Fenway Park, when Mays still was with the Red Sox. The game was scoreless until Mays hit a triple to touch off a seven-run rally by Boston in the fifth inning. Armed with a comfortable lead, he cruised into the eighth with things well under control. Then he threw an inside pitch right at Speaker's head. Speaker barely was able to duck, and the ball hit him on top of the skull with such force it ricocheted all the way into the grandstand. Speaker started to go to first base, then stopped and turned toward the mound.

"You're a dirty player to pull a trick like that!" he shouted.

"I didn't mean to do it!" yelled back Mays.

Speaker, who had disliked the pitcher when the two were teammates in Boston three years earlier, was not appeased.

"I worked on the same team long enough with you to know your methods, and I have half a mind to go right out there and give you some of your own medicine!"

With a fight imminent, about twenty players gathered around to cool off things.

Mays won that game, but the Indians beat him the next three times they faced him that season. In 1919, they beat him on four of five occasions. Where once the underhand pitcher had owned the Indians, now they felt as if they owned him.

Still, the hard feelings remained. The Cleveland ballplayers were convinced Mays liked to throw at batters. Even Chapman, who rarely spoke out against a fellow ballplayer, had expressed just such a view to his family. He was telling baseball stories one winter, and the topic turned to the top pitchers in the league. Chapman talked about how much he admired Walter Johnson, and he claimed his teammate, Coveleskie, was an outstanding hurler also, as well as a fine man. Then someone asked about Mays, and Chapman's sister, Margaret, saw a dark look come over her brother's face. "Carl Mays throws it so he'll dust you off the plate," said Chapman. "But I'll stand right up there. He doesn't bother me. He's not going to intimidate me."

*　　*　　*

Cleveland wasted no time jumping on its old adversary. Graney, who normally liked to wear out a pitcher by taking a few pitches, hit Mays's first offering on a line to center field for a single. Chapman followed with a looping drive that fell into right field for a hit, allowing Graney to race all the way around to third base. When Aaron Ward bobbled Speaker's slow roller to third base, Graney came home with the first run of the ballgame.

The next batter, Elmer Smith, pushed a bunt toward the third-base side of the mound and beat it out for a hit when Mays was slow getting to the ball. The bases were loaded. Mays bore down to retire Gardner, but Wamby hit a shot off the fence for a double, scoring two more runs. Johnston kept it up with a single to drive in Smith and Wamby, and suddenly it was 5–0.

Huggins had seen enough. He emerged from the Yankee dugout and headed toward the mound. Mays waited for him, then sullenly handed over the ball and made the long walk off the field in front of the huge crowd.

Even with a big lead and Sarge Bagby on the mound, the Indians showed no signs of letting up. In the seventh, they had two runners on base when Chapman lined his third hit of the day into right-center field. Ruth fielded the ball cleanly, but as he did he slipped and fell. Chapman immediately dashed toward second, where he slid into the base just ahead of Ruth's hurried throw. Two more runs scored on the play. The final score was 8–2, Cleveland.

The two teams traded victories the next two days, New York romping 11–0 on Monday and Cleveland coming back the next day to win 5–0 behind Coveleskie's six-hit pitching. That final game was interrupted when a man wandered out of the stands and walked over in front of the Indians' dugout. He stood there smiling and refused to leave until umpire Brick Owens halted play long enough to grab him and push him through a nearby exit. No one bothered to find out what the man wanted, but the *New York Times* ventured a guess: "The stranger was probably a diamond salesman who has read in the papers that Cleveland is likely to be in the World Series and he wanted to sign them up for some sparkers."

When they left town and headed for their next stop on the road trip, the Indians were right back where they had started the series—in first place.

29

George Hildebrand had all the traits necessary to survive as an umpire. He was brusque, defiant, self-assured, quick-tempered, and fearless. Most important, he knew how to handle himself in a brawl.

On May 27, Hildebrand and his partner, Billy Evans, arrived in Boston for the Yankee game there. It was the first time during the season they had been assigned to a Yankee game, but they were well aware of the escalating tensions between the New Yorkers and the umpiring team of Dineen and Nallin. The two umpires had ejected so many Yankees for their unruly behavior that one New York writer criticized Ban Johnson for assigning them to the team's games. The writer urged that Johnson use Hildebrand and Evans, a pair the Yankees "never had problems with." Johnson's only reply had been to send the New York club a terse telegram: "Can bench chatter." The New York fans had been quick to support their team in the feud, and when Nallin called Ping Bodie out on a close play at first on May 23 two pop bottles were hurled at him from the stands. Both fell short of their mark, and later Dineen could joke: "A bottle thrower never is dangerous in May, but some of them acquire control in July and August."

It soon became apparent that the New Yorkers' dissatisfaction was not confined to the one umpiring crew. When Hildebrand went behind the plate to work the Yankees against the Red Sox, he immediately became the focus of New York pitcher Bob Shawkey's displeasure. Through the first few innings, Shawkey complained constantly about Hildebrand's ball-and-strike calls.

In the fourth, Shawkey was protecting a 3–0 lead when the Red Sox loaded the bases with two outs. The next batter, Boston catcher Wally Schang, ran the count out full, then watched a curveball go past. Hildebrand signaled ball four, and Schang trotted down to first base to force in a run. Enraged at the call, Shawkey walked halfway to the plate shouting at the umpire. Several of the other New York players joined in, and Huggins rushed out of the dugout to take up the argument for his pitcher. Hildebrand calmly listened to the complaints for a few moments, then told Huggins he had heard enough.

The manager returned to the dugout and the umpire gave the signal for play to resume. Shawkey chose this moment to kneel and make an exaggerated production of meticulously tying his shoelaces. It took him almost five full minutes to complete the task. All the while, Hildebrand stood behind the plate fuming.

Finally, the New York pitcher went back to work. He ended the inning by throwing a called third strike past Harry Hooper. When Hildebrand made the call on the final pitch, Shawkey doffed his cap and bowed low in a mock show of appreciation. Hildebrand watched silently, but when Shawkey walked past him toward the dugout the umpire informed the pitcher he was ejected from the game.

That was all it took to set off Shawkey. He wheeled and charged Hildebrand, throwing a wild punch that the umpire barely was able to duck. Shawkey took another swing before the two men grabbed each other and began struggling. As they did, Hildebrand pulled off his mask and brought it down hard on the pitcher's head. When the two combatants finally were pulled apart, blood was flowing from a gash behind Shawkey's ear where he had been struck by the mask. The pitcher was escorted to the locker room, and it took two stitches to close his wound. Hildebrand, showing no ill effects of the fight, stayed on the field to continue his duties.

The players milled around the home-plate area for another five minutes, but the presence of a police lieutenant who was stationed inside the field discouraged any further mayhem.

When it came time for the Yankees to take the field again, Mays went out to the mound to replace Shawkey. He was greeted by what the *New York Times* reported as "a chorus of jeers and hoots that must have been heard in Worcester."

Ignoring the hostile reception, Mays allowed just three hits the rest of the way as the Yankees won 6–1. Ruth thrilled the crowd with two home runs, one of them hitting the top of the forty-foot fence in left-center and bounding onto a nearby garage.

Writing in the *New York Sun* afterward, Joe Vila delivered a stinging commentary on the Yankees' actions:

> The attack on Hildebrand was the culmination of disorderly behavior by the Yankees in previous games. At the Polo Grounds they wrangled with other American League umpires, particularly Dineen and Nallin. Evidently they were encouraged by Huggins, or by the club owners, together with leading members of the Kitchen Cabinet.
>
> But Shawkey's behavior spilled the beans and attracted the attention of the entire baseball world to the methods of the New York Americans. Clean baseball is wanted here, not tough mug stuff. The Yankees, hitherto, enjoyed a reputation for sportsmanship that helped to make thousands of good friends. They can win games without resorting to cheap umpire baiting and Huggins knows this to be a fact as well as anybody.

The Sporting News was even more vicious in its calls for punishment. The publication said the Yankees had several temperamental ballplayers "who would be much better off for themselves, their club and the game if they were taken out and beaten up with a stiff club."

The action by Ban Johnson's office was much more restrained. Shawkey received only a one-week suspension and a two-hundred-dollar fine.

30

The day before Shawkey's run-in with Hildebrand, a stir was created back in New York when third baseman Art Fletcher of the Giants was caught roughing up a baseball in a National League game. Fletcher not only was tossed out of the game, he received an automatic ten-day suspension.

It was a seemingly minor incident, but it had far-reaching implications. Fletcher was the first player to feel the hooks of baseball's controversial new rules designed to eliminate the so-called freak pitches.

The legislation had been passed at the winter meetings in Chicago in February in an effort to do away with such pitches as the spitball, shine ball, emery ball, and licorice ball, all of which required either adding a foreign substance to the ball or altering its surface.

Pitchers now were barred from using "any foreign substance on the ball, such as resin, saliva, talcum powder, paraffin, and like aids to the shine ball."

In an effort to appease those pitchers who were dependent on such deliveries as the spitter, each club was allowed to designate for the 1920 season two spitball pitchers who had been using the pitch in the past. Those pitchers would be exempt from the ban on spitballs.

No consideration was given to pitchers who relied on other freak deliveries.

Essentially, the rule meant a pitcher must keep the ball in his pitching hand after receiving it from the catcher. He could not rub it on his uniform, nor could he place his glove in the dirt and then put the ball in the glove.

The rule applied to fielders, also, as Fletcher learned when he was caught tampering with the ball on May 26.

In conjunction with the crackdown on freak pitches were new requirements for the number of baseballs that must be available at each game. Previously, the home club had been required to furnish only two balls before the beginning of play. Since all balls that had been disfigured would be thrown out of play, the league presidents now were empowered to specify what they deemed to be an appropriate number of balls to be available at each game.

Predictably, the changes brought about an outcry of protest from the pitching community.

One of the first to speak out was shine-ball pitcher Hod Eller, who had won twenty games for Cincinnati's world championship team in 1919. In the June 1920 issue of *Baseball Magazine,* Eller noted that Washington owner Clark Griffith, one of the proponents of the new rules, "used to scratch the ball with his spikes and do about everything else to it that the law allowed" when he was a hurler before the turn of the century.

Irving E. Sanborn of the *Chicago Tribune* supported these charges, claiming that Griffith "merely hacked each new ball against his heel spikes . . . while all the world wondered whether it was one of Griffith's superstitions or he was only peeved at having to pitch a new pill."

Yet when Eller confronted Griffith about the unfairness of taking away a man's livelihood, he said the owner responded that the public wanted more hitting.

"The whole baseball world has gone mad over freak deliveries," wrote Eller. "You would suppose by what you hear or read that the man who had perfected a freak delivery was in the same class with bank robbers and pickpockets."

Another Cincinnati pitcher hard hit by the new rules was Slim Sallee, a twenty-one-game winner in 1919. He would be among the first to be banished for rubbing the first two fingers of his pitching hand with resin to improve his grip on the ball.

Sallee, who perspired heavily on the mound, contended the new rules adversely affected his control. He said he would "get a reputation as a wild, young busher if I keep on. Besides, I have hit two batters and they were probably nice men and maybe had families to support. Before this season, I don't believe I hit two batters in six years."

Sallee claimed he never used any of the so-called freak deliveries. All he ever did was rub his fingers with resin "because I can't stop sweating on a hot day."

The outlawing of resin was perhaps the most controversial of the new pitching rules. There were many who agreed with Sallee when he claimed the primary effect of such a ban would be an increase in the number of hit batsmen.

Mays was one of the pitchers whose alleged practices had brought about a clamor for stiffer rules against "tricky" pitching.

According to Ed Bang of the *Cleveland News,* one of Mays's favorite tricks "was to rub the ball across the pitching rubber just prior to stepping into the box. . . . Mays always tried to do the stunt when no one was looking and very often got away with it. . . . Rubbing the ball across the rubber produced a roughened surface that made the old pill act like the emery ball."

Mays's critics were quick to point to the underhand pitcher's substandard performance in the early part of the 1920 season as proof that he had relied on tricky pitching for his previous successes.

Reporting that one backer of the Yankees bemoaned the team's struggles with the complaint, "If Carl Mays would pitch the kind of ball he did last year . . . ," *The Sporting News* offered the reply, "Well, probably he would if he could use the now banned tricks of the pitching trade but shiners are barred."

But Mays also had his defenders. One of them was F. C. Lane, who used his forum in *Baseball Magazine* to dwell on the pitcher's reputation:

> Mays uses his head at all times. As a pitcher, he has been called tricky. Most pitchers who use their heads are tricky. Mays has taken full advantage of all the law allows him and very possibly has been a bit unscrupulous. But the base stealer who slides into second with his spikes high in the air is also unscrupulous.

Baseball is not exactly a parlor game. It is a game indulged in by strong men, where give and take is not always defined within strict latitudes.

31

When the Indians returned home at last on May 28, they were dealt a tragic setback. Coveleskie reported to the ballpark at noon that Friday and, in keeping with Speaker's plan to pitch him in the opener of every series, was preparing to loosen up for his start against the White Sox. Before he finished putting on his uniform, he was summoned upstairs to the front office. A telegram had just arrived: Coveleskie's wife had died suddenly at the couple's home in Shamokin, Pennsylvania. She had been ill for nearly three years, but she had not been thought to be in critical condition and her death had been unexpected. Coveleskie, devastated by the news, left that afternoon for his home. The flags at League Park flew at half-mast as the Indians opened the home stand with a 13–6 victory over the White Sox.

The loss of his star pitcher left Speaker in a desperate situation. Already, his staff was short-handed. Caldwell had hurt his back and George Uhle had been ineffective because he somehow was tipping his pitches to the batters. Coveleskie and Bagby had done the bulk of the pitching, responding with eight consecutive victories each, but Covey's absence and a run of doubleheaders coming up would force Speaker to throw Myers, Joe Boehling, and rookie Dickie Niehaus into the breach.

*   *   *

Speaker had other personnel problems to deal with as May turned into June: the benching of left-fielder Jack Graney, a long-time favorite of the fans. Graney had been a fixture in Cleveland for more than a decade, as well known for his fun-loving ways as his skills on the ballfield. He had first reported to the club's training camp in Macon, Georgia, as a cocky twenty-one-year-old busher in the spring of 1908. A rookie was expected to treat the veterans with respect and a certain amount of awe back then, but by the end of his first trip with the team Graney was calling even the established stars by their first names. The older players didn't know quite what to make of this flamboyant newcomer. On the way to the ballpark one day, he commandeered a mule-drawn wagon that was loaded with scenery for a musical comedy. He called out for the other players to hop aboard, and he proceeded to drive them in style to their destination.

Graney was a pitcher at the time, but he was as wild as he was brash. Once, he accidentally dropped his stockings out of his third-floor hotel window. Spotting a porter below, he yelled down asking him to throw the footwear back up. The porter tried in vain, but the stockings weren't heavy enough to carry that far. Graney instructed the man to tie them around a rock and try again. The porter obliged and heaved the missile toward the window. Just as Graney was about to catch it, the socks came untied and the rock hit him square in the mouth. The cut on his lip would leave a scar for the rest of his life, but even with the blood pouring out of the wound, Graney was able to crack, "With your control added to my speed, I'd be the greatest pitcher in the world."

Eventually, not even Graney's breezy manner could overcome his wildness on the mound. During an intrasquad game one day, he hit Cleveland manager Nap Lajoie with a pitch. A few innings later, Graney uncorked another wild toss toward the manager. This time, the ball glanced off Lajoie's head. Nap stalked out to the mound cursing and told the young pitcher to get off the field.

The next morning, Lajoie called Graney to his room. "Here's a rail ticket to Portland. I figure anybody as wild as you belongs in the wild West."

Graney switched to the outfield in Portland and made his return to Cleveland the following season. He had been there ever since, becoming the team's all-time leader in games played, runs scored, and triples. But Graney never was much more than a .250 hitter, relying primarily on his ability to work the pitchers for walks to get on base. Twice, he had led the league in bases on balls, but this did not fit in with Speaker's more aggressive style of offense. The hard-hitting Jamieson was pushing for Graney's job.

The final straw turned out to be an attack of tonsilitis. Worn down by the long road trip, Graney was battling a severely sore throat when the Indians returned home in late May. On Memorial Day, he became so ill he had to be taken to the hospital, where an operation was performed on his tonsils. In his absence, Jamieson moved into the lineup for good. When Graney returned to action in the early part of June, he was relegated to bench duty. Jamieson's batting average was .380, third best in the league behind Speaker's .397 and Johnston's .382.

32

It was only a matter of time before the Yankees began to make their move. The inevitable winning streak began quietly enough, with a 4–3 victory over the Tigers on May 25 in the Polo Grounds. The difference was a two-run homer by Ruth, giving him seven for the season, breaking a tie with Chicago's Happy Felsch for the league lead. Not even the Shawkey incident in Boston could slow the Yankees' momentum. They swept four games from the Red Sox, then came home and took both ends of a Memorial Day doubleheader against Washington to run the streak to eight games.

On the first day of June, Ruth got his first pitching assignment of the year. He hurled four innings, then retired to the outfield after New York took a ten-run lead over the Senators. The Yankees won their ninth straight, 14–7, to move into second place behind the

Indians, but all anyone talked about was Ruth's pitching and a towering fly ball he hit. The drive had not cleared the fence, and had in fact been caught by right fielder Bobby Roth, but according to the *New York Times,* "it broke all altitude records in baseball. It was the greatest perpendicular crack that ever bounded off a bat."

The next day, Ruth hit two homers as New York beat Washington 8–1 in the first game of a doubleheader. The winning streak ended at ten when the Senators took a 7–6 victory in the second game, but the Babe hit another home run, his fourteenth of the season. The Yanks won four more in a row before dropping the final game of the home stand to the Athletics. Departing on their first western trip of the season, their record stood at 29–17, leaving them only percentage points behind the first-place Indians.

In Detroit, the Yankees pounded out forty-eight hits and scored thirty-six runs to sweep four more games. One of the victories went to Mays, his sixth of the year against five losses.

33

Clevelanders liked to believe their fans were the best in baseball, not only fiercely loyal to the home team but also true sportsmen of the highest class. Taunting the opposition was frowned upon, booing one of the Indians was strictly forbidden.

At one game, a man in the bleachers began heckling the team and Speaker's handling of it. After a couple of innings of such abuse, the center fielder walked over to the stands and ordered the ushers to reimburse the man for his ticket and remove him from the premises. The other fans applauded Speaker's action.

On another occasion, Barney Barnard overheard a member of the gate crew make a comment critical of the team's play. The employee was fired on the spot.

There was a host of rooters' organizations formed to root for the team, each of them vying to outdo the others in the extent of its allegiance to the team. The most prominent among these groups was the Stick-to-the-Finish Club, which, as its name implied, was pledged to remain firm in its commitment to the last out of every game and to the final game of the season.

The local sporting writers encouraged such loyalty and whenever necessary the scribes took it upon themselves to prevent the bugs from growing discouraged or from stepping too far over the bounds of good sportsmanship.

Such a lecture was called for in early June when the Yankees, accompanied by Ruppert and Huston along with a party of their friends as well as eight correspondents from the New York papers, arrived in Cleveland by boat for a crucial four-game series. With eighteen victories in their past twenty games, the New Yorkers had pulled into a virtual tie with the Indians atop the standings.

Worried that the importance of the series might lead to some uncalled-for displays by the local supporters, Ross Tenney of the *Press* offered the following words of advice:

> It's to be hoped that there'll be no repetition of ill-bred and uncalled-for booing in this series when Babe Ruth steps to the plate. A few fans did this without any excuse whatever when Joe Jackson was here early this season with the White Sox. Jackson merely answered them by pounding the ball all over the lot and making life miserable for Indian hurlers.
>
> So let's shut up anybody that tries to boo or jeer Babe Ruth. He's one of the greatest players in the history of baseball and as such should be greeted with cheers instead of jeers.

*   *   *

It rained until noon on Saturday, holding the turnout for the first game to only twenty thousand, but the bugs in attendance were in rare form. Ignoring Tenney's pleas, they derided the Yankees with cries of "bushers" from the moment they stepped onto the field and rooted loudly for the Indians at every turn. Some of Speaker's aviator friends even went so far as to fly over League Park, returning in the fifth inning to circle the field and watch some of the action.

"The community has the pennant bug in serious form and there was more commotion and hullabaloo than there is at most world's series carnivals," noted the *New York Times*.

In the bottom of the first, Jamieson led off with a single off Jack Quinn, the New York spitballer who entered the contest with a 9–1 record and an eight-game winning streak. Chapman followed with a base hit to right field, and there were runners at first and third with no outs.

Speaker rapped out the third consecutive hit, a single to left, and Jamieson jogged home with the game's first run. At the same time, Chapman tried to dash all the way to third base. He slid into the bag, catching it with the toe of his shoe just as Bob Meusel took Duffy Lewis's throw and slapped the tag on him. Umpire Billy Evans hesitated a split second, then emphatically signaled Chapman out.

Normally, Chapman was adverse to arguing an umpire's call. In fact, Evans had told friends he could recall only one instance of Chapman disputing a decision. Even then, Chappie had made it a point to come up to the umpire the next inning and good-naturedly tell him: "Well, Bill, I guess you win that one. Everybody else on the team saw the play as you did. Seems as though I must have been wrong." Evans had marveled, "It took a real fellow to do that."

But the tense atmosphere that surrounded the contest with the Yankees led to a rare show of anger by Chapman, who leaped up to express his surprise at the decision. Before he could say a word, Chet Thomas came running over from the third-base coaching box bellowing his protest. Thomas, known as "The Human Megaphone" for his loud and incessant chatter, could be heard all the way up in the press box. Evans quickly turned to face his tormentor and brought him to a halt by jerking his thumb in the air and yelling, "You're out of the game!" Thomas, startled by the umpire's quick and decisive response, left the field without further protest. His departure brought the dispute to an abrupt halt.

With the score tied 4–4 in the sixth, the tension between the two teams led to another blowup. It happened during a play at the plate, when Johnston slid hard into Hannah in a futile attempt to knock the ball out of the catcher's grasp. At the same time, one of Johnston's spikes nicked the toe of Hannah's foot. The burly catcher immediately threw down his mitt and squared off for a fight, while players from both teams rushed toward the plate. Before any blows were exchanged, O'Neill was able to act as a peacemaker with Hannah, and the game proceeded under an uneasy truce.

Indians pitcher Slim Caldwell also kept the Yankees agitated over his deliberate tactics on the mound. Time and again, the New York batters tired of waiting for Caldwell's delivery and stepped out of the box.

The score still was tied in the eighth when Chapman led off by working Quinn for a walk. Speaker hit a hard shot that looked like a hit, but shortstop Roger Peckinpaugh made a diving stop and got up in time to peg the ball to first for the out as Chapman moved to second. Smith was called out on strikes for the second out, but Gardner poked the ball past second base for a hit that allowed Chapman to race home with the go-ahead run.

The Yankees put up one final threat in the ninth. Bodie led off with a single, then Lewis hit a high pop foul that O'Neill was able to snare as he charged toward the screen. Whirling around, the Cleveland catcher fired the ball to second base in time to double up Bodie, who had attempted to advance on the play. Caldwell retired Hannah to nail down the 5–4 victory.

*   *   *

On Sunday, the gates were opened at 11:30 in the morning—3½ hours before game time. By one o'clock, the last of the general admission seats was taken, and from then on the overflow crowd spilled onto the fringe of the playing field.

The early arrivals were treated to an awesome batting practice display by the Yankees, with several balls being batted into the outfield crowd. Ruth hit a mighty shot that sailed clear over adjacent Lexington Avenue.

Altogether, there were more than thirty thousand fans in the park, and at one point during the game umpire Hildebrand would have to run interference through the crowd to allow Hannah to chase a pop foul.

The Yankees picked up where they left off in batting practice, scoring six runs in the first inning en route to a 14–0 rout. Ruth hit his seventeenth home run of the season, and it traveled farther than his pregame shot. When the game ended, the two teams were even in the standings once again.

In the subdued Cleveland locker room, pitcher Elmer Myers shook his head at Ruth's awesome display of power.

"I gave him only one fastball, and you saw what he did with it."

Across the way, Chapman called out, "We'll get them tomorrow. And the next day."

*　　　*　　　*

Steve O'Neill had matters other than baseball to concern him. Two days earlier, his wife had given birth at the couple's home in Scranton, Pennsylvania. A devout Catholic, the curly-haired O'Neill was known as one of the nicest men in baseball. Easygoing and congenial, he was always quick to step into the midst of an argument to try to help the two sides settle their differences peacefully. His good nature and earnestness also made him a popular target for his teammates' humor. When he received word on Friday that he had become a father, O'Neill endured plenty of good-natured kidding from his teammates. His wife had given birth to twins.

But two days after the babies were born, complications arose. Mrs. O'Neill began to lose strength. On Sunday afternoon, shortly after the twins were baptized, the mother's condition began to deteriorate rapidly. She was rushed to the hospital, where her condition was listed as serious.

O'Neill was at the home of Johnny Kilbane that evening when he received a telegram: "May worse. Nothing serious but come at once."

He departed immediately.

On Monday afternoon, Coveleskie, still recovering from his own personal tragedy, was forced to pitch to a new catcher, Leslie Nunamaker. It made little difference. Covey allowed just five hits, and on the three occasions when Ruth came to bat with runners on base he was given free passes to first. Even the partisan Cleveland fans booed the strategy and demanded that the Babe be given something to hit. When Covey did choose to pitch to Ruth, right fielder Joe Wood stationed himself with his back up against the fence. The strategy paid off, as the Babe was held in check without a hit during the Indians' 7–1 victory.

That evening, the Indians received another bit of good news. Word arrived from Pennsylvania that Mrs. O'Neill's condition had improved and her chances of recovery were good. The Cleveland catcher was due to return to the ballclub within two days.

*   *   *

On the morning of Tuesday, June 15, Mays was sitting in the lobby of a Cleveland hotel reading a newspaper when he came across a story that concerned his lack of effectiveness that season. The words almost jumped off the page at him: "A year ago, the disruption of the American League was threatened because of the suspension of Mays by Ban Johnson, and today we find the most-talked of pitcher in the country, whose release cost New York $50,000, acting merely as a relief hurler. They go quick sometimes."

It was an interesting conclusion, especially in light of the fact that Mays had won three of his past four decisions. Finally, he seemed to have put his early-season troubles—most notably the occasion in which he failed to last through the first inning against the Indians—behind him. Mays blamed those troubles on the Fewster beaning, which, he claimed, had left him reluctant to throw the ball on the inside part of the plate. "The horror of that accident made a deep impression on me," he would say later, "and I believe it was one of the reasons for my failure to pitch effectively earlier in the season. I was throwing the ball too far out from the batters where they could get the fat part of their bats on it."

Huggins had a different theory. He attributed the pitcher's ineffectiveness to the inactivity brought on by his inability to travel to Philadelphia for the opening series and a subsequent string of rainouts that idled the ballclub.

Whatever the cause of the problem, Mays set out that afternoon with renewed determination to atone for his previous poor showing against Cleveland.

For a while, it appeared he might. He made it through two innings without allowing a run. Then the roof caved in on him. His control suddenly deserted him in the third inning, and he walked Jamieson, Chapman, and Speaker in succession. By the time Huggins came out to pull him with two outs in the inning, he had given up five runs on three hits and four walks, two of them with the bases loaded. The Indians romped to a 10–2 victory.

The Yankees left town and headed to Chicago that evening, now two games behind the Indians. Their early departure spared Mays having to read Ross Tenney's latest assessment of his performance. Under the heading "Fatty Mays wasn't there at all," Tenney wrote:

> He's hog fat as compared with his pitching condition in former years. His speed is all gone. He only tried once to pitch at speed against the Tribe and that effort produced such a wild heave that it went behind the back of Wamby, who was at bat.
>
> He has only a pitiful slow curve. His control is gone and he can't go the route. It's doubtful if he'll ever get into anything like his old-time pitching form this season.

34

A week later, after a winning effort against the White Sox, an old problem reared its head to confront Mays. He was accused of throwing a bean ball.

The charges stemmed from an incident June 22 in St. Louis, where an overflow crowd of twenty-seven thousand was on hand at Sportsman Park to see two of the hottest teams in the league. The Yankees had recovered from the setbacks in Cleveland to win four of six in Chicago, giving them twenty-three victories in their past twenty-nine games. The Browns had won ten in a row before being beaten by the New Yorkers the day before.

From the beginning of the game, Mays was bothered by the condition of the field, which had been left muddy and sloppy by a series of thunderstorms that had hit the area. At one point he slipped and fell while fielding a bunt.

In the third inning, the Browns already had pushed across three runs when catcher Hank Severeid, a lean but muscular six-footer, stepped to the plate. Severeid was of Norwegian descent, and he prided himself on his toughness and durability. Once, a baserunner's spikes had caught him above the knee, severing an artery. Severeid was taken to the clubhouse, where he sat and watched as a doctor tied the two ends of the artery together. A week later, he was back behind the plate. Everyone in the league agreed, the big Norwegian was as tough as they come.

Though slow to anger, Severeid presented a frightening sight once he did lose his temper. He demonstrated this when one of Mays's pitches sailed inside and plunked him in the ribs. Convinced that the pitcher was throwing at him, Severeid went into a rage. He flung his bat at Mays, then sprinted toward the mound ready for a fight. Mays threw down his glove and waited. Before Severeid got close enough for the two men to start swinging, several other players rushed between them. Severeid, still shaking with anger, was led away until he could cool off.

In the following inning, Mays loaded the bases with nobody out and then walked St. Louis's Baby Doll Jacobsen to force in another run. Once again, Huggins was forced to pull his star pitcher. For the day, Mays had surrendered eight runs on nine hits and three walks. His won-lost record now stood at a mediocre 7–7.

Around the league, his critics waited for another blowup similar to the one the previous season. In Boston, Paul Shannon wrote: "Just as long as the team goes along at a winning gait no one will work harder for New York than will Mays. But let adversity overtake the outfit, let the Yankees get a few of the tough breaks they have suffered for years, and then Carl is pretty apt to sulk."

35

The pennant race had become a three-team affair, with Cleveland and New York taking turns in first place and Chicago hanging close behind.

On July 1, the Yankees beat the Athletics 9–6 to move ahead of the Indians and into first place by the narrowest of margins. New York was 45–23 for a .6617 percentage, while Cleveland was 43–22 for a .6615 mark. In the clubhouse, the New York players celebrated their ascension to the top of the standings by giving three cheers and a couple of hip-hips.

"They were a jubilant troupe," reported the *New York Times*. "They exuded almost as much joy as if they had clinched the championship and were assured of a place in the world's series sun."

A day later, the Indians pulled even again. The Yankees reclaimed the lead the following day. On Independence Day, the Tribe bounced back into first place with an 11–3 rout of the Tigers in Detroit, coupled with the Yankees' 5–2 loss to the Nationals in Washington.

Chapman was the hero of the Fourth of July game, triggering the assault with a line-drive home run into the center-field bleachers in the first inning. It was his second home run of the season. In all, he had three hits to lead the Indians' sixteen-hit attack.

It was shaping up to be his finest season ever. His batting average stood at .306, and again he was leading the league in sacrifice hits, with thirty. He had picked up five hits in the three games in Detroit, starting him on what would become a sixteen-game hitting streak.

*   *   *

Chapman's success came as no surprise to those who had followed his career throughout the years. In the estimation of one respected authority, veteran baseball writer John B. Sheridan, the Cleveland shortstop was a model batter. In describing Chapman, Sheridan noted he "held the bat away back of him, motionless, without the preliminary movement or 'waggle' as golfers properly call it, so common to all batters. Thus Chapman did not disturb his eye—all motion at the bat disturbs the eye—and he always had the bat back there ready to hit."

Chapman's only weakness was a lack of power, but Sheridan claimed he made up for this "by bases on balls, sacrifices, stolen bases and runs."

The writer also maintained Chapman had few equals in the field. "He was not so strong on his right hand nor was his arm as good as some I have seen, but, all in all, he was a great shortstop. He had fine hands, was a good judge of play and could go miles on fly balls."

Added to all this was Chapman's speed. In 1917, a team of baseball all-stars had been selected to play the Red Sox in a charity game in Boston to raise money for the widow of Tim Murnane, who had been one of the city's most popular ballplayers and, later, one of its most respected sports writers. In addition to the game, there were a number of other events scheduled, such as batting and throwing contests and even a roping competition. In the baserunning contest, Chapman won a large loving cup by circling the diamond in the then-incredible time of fourteen seconds. "That is a record few will ever attempt to lower," predicted F. C. Lane in *Baseball Magazine.*

To take advantage of Chapman's speed, Speaker liked to hit-and-run with him on base. But even with no predetermined play called, Chapman's aggressive baserunning kept the fielders off balance. He frequently went from first to third on singles to left field. And if he was on first base when a batter grounded out, he often caught the defenders napping by racing all the way to third, usually beating the first baseman's hurried throw across the diamond.

Bobby Quinn, the business manager of the Browns, said it was these often-overlooked qualities that made Chapman such a valuable player.

"He was the hardest of hard-working ballplayers, always in the game, thinking up plays both on and off the field," said Quinn.

On June 28, Chapman played in his one thousandth game in the big leagues, yet he was only twenty-nine years old and showing no signs of slowing down. Still, he harbored a fear of hanging on too long in the game. He had seen it happen to others, and he was determined he would not meet a similar fate. Perhaps it was this thought that had helped lead him to consider making this his final season.

"A baseball career is a very short career," Chapman once told his family. "I will never play ball until I can't do my best."

The way he was playing that summer, there seemed to be little chance of that ever happening.

36

Because of his legal problems in Philadelphia, Mays once again was unable to accompany the team there in early July. This time, however, things would be different. Connie Mack, who both owned and managed the Athletics, was able to persuade Bryan Hayes to drop his charges against the ballplayer if an apology was forthcoming. Word was sent to Mays, who caught the next train to Philadelphia.

There, at a meeting in Mack's office on July 3, he delivered a personal apology to Hayes, who responded by withdrawing the warrant for the pitcher's arrest. Mays also made a public apology to the sixteen thousand fans at the ballpark that day. He celebrated with a 5–0 shutout over Mack's last-place team, which had a 17–53 record and had been derisively dubbed the "Apathetics."

*　　　*　　　*

Ruth was on everyone's mind that summer. The season was not yet half completed, and already the Yankee colossus had swatted twenty-four home runs, leaving him just five shy of the major-league record he had established the previous year. For good measure, he was keeping his batting average around the .370 mark.

Even when he wasn't hitting the ball out of the park, the Babe put on a good show. In St. Louis, there was a memorable confrontation between Ruth and pitcher Urban Shocker. When the Yankee slugger stepped to the plate against Shocker, the Browns pitcher cockily signaled for his outfielders to move in. The startled Ruth gripped his bat all the tighter, determined to teach the brash hurler a lesson. Shocker's first pitch sailed in, and Babe took a mighty swing and missed. Shocker turned and waved for the outfielders to move in even closer. Ruth gritted his teeth, flailed angrily at the next pitch, and once again missed. Once more, Shocker signaled his outfielders to move up. By now, the Babe was so furious, he couldn't see straight. He took a roundhouse swing for strike three and stormed back to the dugout, with Shocker's laughter ringing in his ears.

The next day, Ruth struck out two more times. He reacted by smashing his bat on the concrete of the dugout.

"I'll never strike out with that bat again!" he shouted.

On the bases, the Babe was such a reckless runner that Huggins placed him under orders not to slide for fear he would injure himself. On July 5 in Washington, Ruth did just that. He carelessly slid into second base and jammed his wrist in the process.

There would be more headaches stemming from that trip to Washington. Babe had taken his four-door touring sedan on the road with the club, and when the series against the Nationals ended, he loaded the automobile and prepared to head back to New York. With him were his wife, Helen; outfielder Frank Gleich; catcher Fred Hofmann; and coach Charley O'Leary.

It was a raucous drive, with much singing and laughter, and there were several stops along the way for bootleg liquor. Around 3:00 A.M., outside Philadelphia near a small town named Wawa, Ruth took a curve too fast and ran the car into a ditch. The vehicle rolled onto its side, pitching the passengers onto the ground nearby. Miraculously, the Babe emerged from the accident unhurt. Crawling out of the wreckage, he looked around for the others. He found Helen and the other two ballplayers nearby, all of them unharmed. Then he spotted O'Leary lying motionless on his back in the road. A few feet away was the coach's new straw hat. Ruth was frantic as he rushed over and knelt by his friend.

"Oh, my God! Oh, my God!" Babe cried out. "Oh, God, bring Charley back! Don't take him! I didn't mean it!"

As if in answer to Ruth's prayers, O'Leary suddenly opened his eyes.

"Speak to me, Charley, speak to me!" Babe yelled excitedly.

O'Leary blinked a few times and looked around.

"What the hell happened?" he growled. "Where's my hat?"

Ruth was the most seriously injured of the group, having banged up his knee. He limped as the five set out walking to a nearby farmhouse to summon help.

By the time they were able to get another car and continue their journey into New York, it was daybreak. They arrived to see a newspaper headline proclaiming, "RUTH REPORTED KILLED IN CAR CRASH."

News of the accident had spread rapidly, and many New Yorkers had taken off work to hang around bulletin boards waiting for more news. It was around noon before it was reported that Babe was not seriously hurt, and the relieved fans were able to return to their jobs.

The Sporting News seized the opportunity to take another jab at Ruth and the Yankee followers.

> A ball player, in whom his club has invested $135,000, to whom it is paying $20,000 a year in salary, and upon whose daily appearance in the lineup the success of the club depends, with all that success means to the New York Yankees—this player with several of his fellows embarking on a more or less wild all-night ride over strange country roads for a distance of a couple of hundred miles!
>
> Hitting 'er up on high over the hills of Pennsylvania, the automobile overturns in the ditch, its occupants are caught underneath—and Babe Ruth escapes without any apparent injury.
>
> . . . And then the followers of the Yankees moan that the club is be-Jinxed because Lewis has a lame leg, Ward is out with a spike wound, Peckinpaugh has indigestion or something, Mogridge has a sore ankle and Shawkey a sprained back.
>
> Jinxed? Well, we would say that ball club is a foul for luck, that's all.

The fans were not nearly so harsh in their assessment of Ruth's actions. Soon after the accident, there was talk of building a commemorative granite marker on the site of the wreck.

37

On July 8, the day after Ruth's famous auto accident, the Indians arrived in Washington to open a nineteen-game swing through the East. Speaker, still searching for more pitching, decided to give Guy Morton a starting assignment against the Griffmen.

Morton was only twenty-six-years-old but already he had endured years of arm problems and poor health. Tall and gangly, his nickname was the "Alabama Blossom," and when he had arrived in the big leagues six years earlier he threw the ball so hard his pitches could be heard all the way in the dugout. He appeared destined to become Cleveland's answer to the great Walter Johnson.

Morton had been discovered in 1913 by the manager of the Columbus, Georgia, team in the Cotton States League. According to the story, the manager was driving down a country road one day when he came upon Morton, who had a string of squirrels slung over his shoulder. Seeing the youngster had no gun, the manager asked how he had managed to kill all the squirrels. "By throwin' rocks at 'em," came the reply. The manager signed Morton on the spot.

Following a year in the Eastern League, where he struck out 122 batters in eighty-one innings, Morton joined Cleveland in 1914. He pitched well but lost his first nine decisions and finished the season 1–13. Undaunted by such an inauspicious debut, he returned in 1915 to win sixteen games, including one outing in which he struck out fifteen batters. The next year, he won nine of his first eleven decisions, once fanning four men in one inning. Then his arm suddenly went bad, and from then on he was an erratic performer.

In 1919, his effectiveness was further reduced by a stomach ailment. With his arm sore and his confidence shaken, the Alabama Blossom barely was able to keep his spot on the team in the spring of 1920. He had pitched sparingly throughout the campaign but on the sidelines he was beginning to show flashes of his old self.

Given a chance to show his stuff in a game, Morton turned out to be every bit as good as Speaker had hoped. In the opener of a doubleheader, he pitched a five-hitter to beat Washington 4–2. When the Indians won the second game 9–6, they moved back past the Yankees and into first place. Over the two games, Speaker hit seven consecutive singles.

The next day, Speaker had three hits, a walk, and a sacrifice in an 8–4 victory. On Sunday afternoon, July 11, he doubled in his first at-bat to run his string to eleven consecutive hits and push his batting average over the .400 mark. Spoke flew out his next time up to end the streak, but the Indians won 7–2 before losing the second game of the twin bill 2–1.

On Monday, Morton closed out the series in Washington with a seven-hit shutout for a 4–0 victory. The Tribe had won five of the six games, and Speaker had found a fourth starter. His rotation now was Coveleskie, Bagby, Caldwell, and Morton, with Uhle the number-one man in relief.

38

As he had throughout his career, Mays proved his critics wrong. He was not washed up. Just as he had maintained, he began to round into form as the weather heated up. After the debacle in St. Louis, he began to put together a string of victories. He won his next three starts, then came on in relief to gain credit for a win against Detroit. He beat the Tigers again the next day, escaped without a loss in a poor showing against the Browns, and then bounced back to defeat the White Sox.

He now had won his past six decisions, four of them with complete games, raising his record to 13–7. The resurgence could not have come at a better time for the Yankees as it enabled them to stay close to the red-hot Indians. On July 21, the Clevelanders arrived in New York having won twelve of fifteen games on their road trip to open a two-game lead over the Yankees. Huggins chose Mays to pitch the opener of the series in the hope of slowing down the Indians.

This time, the underhand pitcher was up to the challenge. For eight innings, he set down the Clevelanders without a run. There was barely a hint of trouble as he allowed only five hits through the first eight innings. Another batter, Jamieson, reached base when he was hit by a pitch, but he failed to advance. Heading into the ninth, Mays had a 4–0 lead. Not even a lead-off double by Speaker was cause for concern. When Smith grounded to first baseman Wally Pipp for the first out, the twenty-five thousand fans were fully confident of victory.

Then Gardner lined a shot off the right-field fence for a double to score Speaker and spoil the shutout. Wamby followed with a roller to Peckinpaugh, who picked up the ball and threw it past first for an error, allowing Gardner to score. Johnston promptly lined a single to center to score Wamby, and suddenly it was 4–3. O'Neill's single to left moved Johnston to second base.

On the bench, Huggins couldn't believe what he was seeing. Once again, Mays mysteriously had lapsed into a spell where he couldn't get anyone out. The New York manager had no choice but to call on reliever Rip Collins to try to save the game.

Speaker allowed Caldwell to bat for himself, and the Cleveland pitcher responded by lining the ball into center field for yet another base hit. Johnston never slowed down as he rounded third and headed toward home. In the outfield, Ping Bodie, the "Wonderful Wop," fielded the ball cleanly on one hop and fired it toward the plate. The throw was right on the money, and the sliding Johnston was out. Now, there were two down, but Joe Wood, who was running for O'Neill, was on third with the tying run and Caldwell on second with the go-ahead run. The Yankees elected to give Jamieson an intentional walk to load the bases and bring up Chapman.

The count went to three and two, then Collins threw a curveball. Chapman swung and missed for the final out, and the fans swarmed onto the field to mob the pitcher. The Yankees had hung on for a 4–3 victory.

*　　　*　　　*

New York pounded out two more victories to move back into first place heading into the final game of the series. That contest proved to be typical of the way the two teams would battle each other all season.

Desperate to figure out some way to slow down Ruth, Speaker devised a special shift to use against the slugger. When the Babe came to bat, the Indians placed three men in right field. Ruth responded by blasting the ball off the flagpole on top of the right-field grandstand. It was his thirty-fourth home run, already five more than the standard he had set the previous season, and it gave New York a 2–1 lead.

The Indians fought back to tie the score, then in the eighth inning Pipp was ejected for arguing with umpire Ollie Chill. Huggins was forced to switch Ruth to first base, a move that proved to be costly. With one out in the eleventh, Chapman hit a grounder to first. Ruth fielded the ball cleanly, but he threw high to pitcher George Mogridge, who was racing over to cover the bag, and Chapman was safe. Speaker fouled out for the second out, but Wood was hit by a pitch to put runners on first and second. Gardner followed with a triple to right field to drive in two runs. Sarge Bagby retired the Yankees in the bottom of the inning and Cleveland salvaged the series finale 4–2.

The Indians managed to return home still in first place, although by the barest of margins—just seven-tenths of a percentage point.

*　　　*　　　*

The next day, July 25, Mays beat Boston 8–2 for his eighth consecutive victory. His record now stood at 15–7.

Afterward he was in a hurry to get home. Freddie was pregnant, and the baby was expected any day now. In his haste, Mays was motoring down St. Nicholas Avenue just over the speed limit. He was pulled over by a motorcycle policeman, George F. Dailey, who wrote the Yankee pitcher a ticket for traveling twenty-seven miles per hour over three blocks. Mays would have to appear in court to enter a plea on the charge. His court date was set for August 20, an off-date in the Yankees' schedule.

39

Ruth's phenomenal slugging focused attention on yet another burden the pitchers were forced to bear that summer. Not only were they laboring under new restrictions on trick pitches, they also were forced to serve up a baseball that many observers believed to be significantly livelier than those in the past.

The evidence that the ball had been tampered with lay in the dramatic increase in home runs being hit. Not only was Ruth slamming the ball out of the ballpark at an alarming rate, lesser figures also were getting in on the act. In 1919, there had been 448 home runs hit in the major leagues. In 1920, that number would jump to 630.

"They fixed up a ball that if you don't miss it entirely it will clear the fence," wrote Ring Lardner, "and the result is that ball players which used to specialize in hump back line drives to the pitcher is now amongst our leading sluggers."

Eddie Collins, the White Sox second baseman, claimed he had been "whirled around by hard hit grounders more often this year than ever before.

"Mediocre batters have handcuffed me with their fierce drives," added Collins. "For a time I was willing to charge it up to fast grounds, but when the grounders kept coming to me as if fired out of a cannon, I changed my mind and began to believe there was some other reason for the increased batting."

The A. J. Reach Company of Philadelphia, which supplied the American League baseballs, denied there had been any changes, and the baseball owners issued similar statements.

"They're simply furnishing us good baseballs in place of the bum ones we have had to put up with for the past couple of seasons when the war was on," said Washington owner Clark Griffith. "For these two years, the balls were of such poor material and so badly made that they got lopsided the instant they hit anything, but the balls this season are being made of good material like they were before the war."

Nonetheless, as talk of a lively ball persisted, even the owners were compelled to take some action. On July 14, sports writer Ross Tenney reported that "Moguls of both leagues have inserted special detectives into the Reach factory to run down this widespread rumor about the livelier balls."

*   *   *

There was one other matter making life miserable for the pitchers. The umpires, in an effort to comply with the recently adopted pitching rules that prohibited trick pitches, were throwing more balls out of play than ever before. As a result, claimed the pitchers, they weren't being afforded the opportunity to break in a baseball properly.

Detroit pitcher Howard Ehmke complained this—not a livelier ball—was the cause of the increased batting in the game. For a pitcher to get a good enough grip on the ball to throw a curve, said Ehmke, the ball should be in play long enough for the cover to be loosened.

"As it is now," he said, "a ball no sooner gets so a pitcher can use it effectively than the umpire throws it out. As a result, the pitchers cannot get their curveballs working right and the batters slam them."

On this issue, the penurious owners sided with the pitchers. The price of baseballs had increased 100 percent in the past three years to a whopping $2.50 per ball. The magnates couldn't help but wince every time an umpire tossed a relatively fresh ball out of the game.

The guidelines on when to place a new ball in play had been the object of periodic revisions since the establishment of the first major league in 1871.

Before 1883, umpires had to wait until the end of an even inning to introduce a new ball, and as late as 1886, umpires had to wait five minutes after a ball had been knocked out of the park or lost before putting a new ball in play.

In 1887, it was determined that the home team must furnish two new balls at the start of the game and additional balls as needed. The winning team was awarded only the last ball in play. Nine years later, the number of balls the home team needed to have available was raised to one dozen.

Still, the owners parted with the baseballs reluctantly. Often, special police would go into the stands to retrieve foul balls, and in 1910, an unidentified newspaper clipping noted, "The practice of concealing balls fouled into grandstand or bleachers has reached disgusting proportions in New York." Six years later, in that same city, three fans were arrested at the Polo Grounds and charged with petty larceny for refusing to return baseballs hit into the stands.

By 1920, the owners were so concerned with the matter that at the league meetings in Chicago in February, they decided to increase the cost of bleacher seats from twenty-five cents to fifty cents to cover the rising cost of the baseballs. Not even those additional revenues appeased the magnates. As the season progressed and the umpires liberally tossed out more and more balls in compliance with the new pitching rules, the owners grumbled louder and louder.

Finally, even *The Sporting News* felt compelled to take the umpires to task for their excesses. In its August 5 issue, the periodical carried an editorial titled, "A Waste That Should Be Checked." It read:

> We are going after the umpires again, and without apologies, because it seems to us this criticism is warranted. This time, they are called to account for their waste of perfectly good baseballs, which cost $2.50 per ball and are hard to get at that or any price in these days of shortage of material and labor.
>
> In a recent game to which attention has been called, 36 baseballs—three dozen, count 'em—were used in the first three innings, and as we remember it not more than two or three of the balls were lost over the park boundaries or in the crowd. They were just thrown out by the umpire behind the plate because they did not suit his fancy or that of some finicky batter.
>
> It seems to have reached the point where a ball is thrown out if it gets as much as a fly speck on it. This should not be. It's not patriotic, for true patriotism still demands economy and conservation. Balls cost money, and as stated above, they are scarce and going to be scarcer. Also, this constant inspections of balls and discarding and demanding of new ones takes time, interrupts play and wearies the fan.

Ban Johnson, ever mindful of the owners' concerns, needed no further convincing. In an effort to curb the complaints, he issued a directive to his umpires "to keep the balls in the games as much as possible, except those which [are] dangerous."

40

Jim Dunn was enjoying the most spectacular summer of his life. The turnstiles at his ballpark were clicking at a record rate and as July turned to August his ballclub was beginning to open a little distance on its two nearest competitors in the tight AL pennant race. When he walked down the streets of Cleveland, people recognized him. They would call out to him and stop to talk baseball with him. He always took the time to chat with them. Baseball, and especially his Indians, was a subject he never grew weary of discussing.

Monday, August 9, was starting out as an especially memorable day. The Indians, armed with a 4½-game lead on the second-place Yankees and a five-game margin on the third-place White Sox, were opening a four-game home series against the New Yorkers. The showdown in League Park was being billed as the "Little World's Series." Demand for tickets at the game was so great that all the reserved seats were sold days in advance, and it had been necessary to put the circus seats along the foul lines. This time, Dunn had chosen not to stretch ropes across the outfield to accommodate the anticipated overflow crowds. He remembered that when that had been done in the last series between the two teams, the Yankees had slammed several balls into the crowd for extra-base hits on drives that ordinarily would have been caught. Not even the lure of additional revenue was enough to make him jeopardize his team's chances in such an important series.

Dunn also could afford to enjoy the irony of a Cleveland fan, Max

Rosenblum, presenting Babe Ruth with a twelve-foot floral bat as a tribute to the Yankee slugger's record home-run total. "Babe Ruth—41 home runs," read the inscription.

Handing over the massive bat, Rosenblum echoed the sentiments of all Cleveland fans. "I hope you hit one hundred home runs—if none of them are against Cleveland." Ruth grinned as he took hold of the bat and posed for photographers.

In the stands, Dunn circulated among a group of seventy old-time ballplayers who were his special guests that day. The owner had dubbed this "Golden Year of Baseball Day" in honor of the first game ever played at League Park fifty years before. To show their appreciation to the owner, the veteran ballplayers, many of whom were old college men, stood in unison and gave him "three cheers and a tiger." As Dunn made his way back to his private box, there were tears in his eyes.

Less than two hours later, Dunn left the ballpark in a much less cheerful mood. The Yankees had taken the crucial first game by a score of 6–3. No sooner had the last out been recorded than several fans swarmed onto the field to strip the posies from the floral bat, which Ruth had left behind. The Babe, frustrated by going hitless in two at-bats and being walked three times, had not even bothered to take the gift with him.

"It was too heavy," he explained. "I couldn't swing it."

*   *   *

More than twenty-one thousand fans showed up for the Tuesday game, but a downpour in the second inning forced the umpires to call a halt to the proceedings.

The next day, another twenty-seven thousand packed the tiny ballpark. It was a record turnout for a weekday game in the city. The fans hooted and jeered when Mays was announced as the Yankees' starting pitcher, then they sat back to watch Sarge Bagby face the New Yorkers. They barely had a chance to settle in their seats when Ruth slashed a single to center with two outs in the top of the first. Seeing Speaker bobble the ball, the Babe made a mad dash for second base. He slid in safely as the throw came in high, but when the play was over the big fellow remained on the ground clutching his right leg. He had twisted his knee, and in his frustration Ruth banged the joint with his fist in a futile attempt to force it back into its proper position. As he did, he looked up to see his friend Ping Bodie racing to his aid.

"Bring me a ball bat!" Ruth shouted to Bodie. "Maybe we can hammer this thing back into place!"

It was a futile plea. The Babe was helped off the field, and Huggins was forced to replace him with Bob Meusel, who recently had been benched because of his indifferent play.

The outlook soon worsened for the Yankees. Mays, who had won ten of his past eleven decisions, breezed through the first two innings but ran into trouble in the third. O'Neill led off with a little pop fly that fell into shallow left field just out of Peckinpaugh's reach for a base hit. Mays fanned Bagby, but then he issued a walk to Jamieson. Bearing down, he forced Chapman to hit an easy fly to Meusel in right field. There were two outs, but Mays pitched too carefully to Speaker and ended up walking him to load the bases. That brought up Smith, Cleveland's cleanup hitter.

With the crowd on its feet yelling, Mays sensed the batter might be too anxious for a hit. He took a little something off his first pitch, and sure enough Smith swung with such force he spun all the way around while fouling the ball harmlessly back into the stands.

Mays came back with another underhand shoot, but this time Smith timed his swing perfectly. He hit the ball squarely, with all his strength, and it shot off the bat like a rocket, still rising as it sailed high over the right-field screen and onto Lexington Avenue. It was a grand slam, touching off one of the wildest celebrations ever seen at the ballpark.

Every one of the twenty-seven thousand rooters stood and cheered, and many of them tossed straw hats onto the field. The Indians charged from their dugout to greet Smith at the plate, where they alternately pounded him on the back, hugged him, and attempted to lift him to their shoulders.

Outside, Harry L. Davis was preparing to enter the ballpark when he heard the commotion. Davis recently had resigned his post as mayor and was just returning to town after winning the Republican nomination for governor of Ohio. He and his aides hurried into the park to see what was happening. Davis could not have hoped for a more dramatic entrance. When the fans spotted him, they renewed their cheers, and the Cleveland players, led by Speaker, rushed back out of their dugout to extend their congratulations to the former mayor. One by one, the Indians leaned into the stands to shake the hand of the Republican gubernatorial candidate.

In the midst of the hoopla, Mays stood on the mound, a solitary and dejected figure. To the Clevelanders, he appeared a beaten man. The Indians had a 4–0 lead, and Bagby, who had defeated New York three times already during the season, had been sharp through the first three innings, allowing just one hit.

But the euphoria did not last long. In the next inning, the Yankees struck for three runs, two of them scoring on a single by Mays. Suddenly, the Cleveland lead was down to one run. In the bottom of the inning, Mays served up another reminder that the battle had just begun. He threw a pitch that was headed straight at Johnston, forcing the Indians' first baseman to throw up his arm to shield himself. The ball glanced off Johnston's shoulder, sending him sprawling in the dirt. In the Cleveland dugout, Graney and several of the other Indians grumbled loudly that the pitch had been aimed at Doc's head. It was Mays's fifth hit batsman of the season, raising his career total to fifty-four.

The Yankee pulled even with a run in the sixth, and the game settled into a tense duel between Mays and Bagby. It stayed that way through the ninth and headed into extra innings.

Mays led off the tenth for New York, and again he used his bat to hurt the Clevelanders, slicing a double into deep left-center. Aaron Ward followed with a bunt toward first and Johnston, in his haste to make a play on Mays at third, overran the ball and both men were safe. Meusel promptly singled to left field to score Mays and break the tie.

Rattled by the turn of events, the Indians continued to self-destruct. An error by Wamby led to two more runs, making it 7–4.

156

It was Cleveland's eighth error in the two games. Mays easily retired the Indians in the bottom of the inning to complete the victory. When the final out was recorded, the Cleveland ballplayers sat in their dugout staring out at the field, still shocked by the sudden turn of events. They had blown a game that seemingly was theirs. Their lead was down to two games and, worse, their confidence was shaken.

*   *   *

On Thursday, Coveleskie arrived at the ballpark tense and irritable. It would be his job to reverse the Indians' fortunes. Normally a friendly man with a good sense of humor, he became sullen and uncommunicative on days he was scheduled to pitch.

Covey was the ace of the Cleveland staff, a two-time twenty-game winner, but his climb to the top hadn't been easy. Born in the middle of coal country in Pennsylvania, he started working in the mines by the time he was twelve years old. He worked from seven in the morning until seven in the evening, six days a week, and for his seventy-two hours he earned $3.75. There was no time to play baseball, but when he got home after dark he would entertain himself by throwing stones at tin cans in his yard. That was where he developed his amazing control. He got where he could hit a can from forty to fifty feet away with consistency. He was eighteen years old when the local semipro team heard about his prowess and asked him to pitch for them. Before long, Coveleskie signed a contract with the nearby team from Lancaster, and he was out of the mines for good.

An older brother, Harry, preceded him to the big leagues, joining the Philadelphia Phillies in 1907 and later becoming a three-time, twenty-game winner with the Detroit Tigers. Following in Harry's footsteps, Stanley broke into the big time in 1912 with the Athletics. Failing to earn a spot in their powerful rotation, he was shipped out to Portland, where he learned to throw the spitter. In 1916, he made it back to the American League with Cleveland, and over the next thirteen seasons he would win more than two hundred games.

Covey got off to a shaky start against the Yankees when leadoff batter Aaron Ward singled. One out later, Covey issued a walk to Ruth, and Pratt followed with a triple into the right-field corner to score two runs. With two outs, Pipp singled to center to drive home Pratt, and Bodie followed with a run-scoring double off the right-field wall to make it 4–0.

Covey settled down after that, allowing just one hit over the next six innings, but it was too late. The damage had been done. The Yankees breezed to a 5–1 victory to close to within 1½ games. The hard-charging White Sox were only one game back of the Indians.

In their frustration, the Cleveland rooters began to cast about for a scapegoat for their team's rapidly deteriorating situation. They settled on Wambsganss, the scholarly second baseman who had been battling a slump both at the plate and in the field. When he failed to handle O'Neill's low throw to second on a steal by Ward, the fans jeered him. When he cleanly fielded a grounder on the next play, Wamby could hear the sarcastic applause from the stands.

Speaker was livid over the crowd's behavior. The next day he blasted the abusive fans in a by-lined articled in the *News:* "We haven't quit, as some few fans may have surmised. My boys don't know the meaning of that word. . . . We want the fans to show the same spirit—stick to the finish and never say die."

*　　　*　　　*

The final game of the series was on Friday the 13th, not a good omen for a team desperate to change its luck. In the bottom of the first, the Indians loaded the bases with two outs and Wamby due up. Now was the time for the Cleveland second baseman to redeem himself. Instead, he hit an easy grounder to Pratt, and again the fans shouted their unhappiness at him.

In the second, the Yanks had a man on first with two outs when Shawkey hit a drive that appeared headed into left field for a hit. Instinctively, Chapman made a desperate dive to his right and, while stretched out in the air, he somehow got his mitt on the ball. When he landed, the ball popped back in the air. Still lying on his stomach, Chapman reached up and grabbed the ball with his bare hand for the out.

An inning later, Ruth walked with two outs and Pratt scored him with a double off the right-field wall.

The Yankees pushed across two more runs in the fifth for a 3–0 advantage. Meanwhile, the Indians' batting slump continued. In the sixth, Graney made an exaggerated show of rearranging the team's bats, always a potent jinx-breaker. For a moment, it appeared the ploy might work as Smith led off with a walk. Then came a fielder's choice and two easy fly balls, and the drought continued.

The Indians finally scored off Shawkey in the seventh, with Chapman's deep fly ball bringing Caldwell home from third, but the Yankees countered with a run in the eighth.

Mays had been sitting quietly at the end of the New York bench watching the action when Huggins called out to him in the bottom of the eighth. The manager wanted to know if he would be ready to pitch if Shawkey got into trouble. Mays, who had thrown ten innings only two days earlier, nodded his assent. Huggins told him to stay ready. The words were no sooner out of his mouth than Smith hit a hard shot into right center for a single. Gardner followed with a long drive that appeared headed for extra bases before Ruth raced over and made a sensational running grab. That was all Huggins needed to see. He sent Mays running down to the bullpen area to loosen up.

Wamby was up next, and he drove the ball down the left-field line, where it landed on the chalk stripe and rolled into the corner. By the time it could be relayed back to the infield, Smith was standing on third and Wamby was perched on second. The Yankees screamed that the drive was foul, and Huggins as well as nearly every other member of the team surrounded Nallin to argue the call. The debate raged for nearly five minutes, and Mays took advantage of the break to continue throwing on the sidelines.

When play finally resumed, Johnston hit a single to center to score both runners. New York's lead was down to 4–3, and there still was only one out. Huggins wasted no more time. He called time and signaled Mays into the game. The first man to face the Yankee ace was O'Neill. With two strikes on him, the Cleveland catcher swung and missed as Johnston broke for second base. Muddy Ruel pegged the ball down to second in time to catch Johnston for a double play, and the inning was over.

The Indians had one last chance in the ninth. Graney batted for Caldwell and led off with a walk. But Mays fanned Jamieson and got Chapman to ground out to Pratt as Graney advanced to second. With the tying run in scoring position, Mays threw a third strike past Speaker to end the game and complete the Yankees' sweep.

In the four-game series, Mays had won one game and saved another, and he had hurt the Indians with his hitting as well as his pitching. As he left the field, he looked in the direction of the Cleveland writers, who earlier in the summer had been so quick to gloat over his demise. Mays seemed to be mocking his tormentors as he smiled briefly before disappearing from sight.

41

The Indians' collapse had raised the specter of past failures. Their once-commanding lead in the race had evaporated within a matter of days, and now both the White Sox and Yankees were just one-half game back in the standings. Worse, the collapse had occurred in Cleveland's own ballpark.

Speaker knew there was little time to dwell on what went wrong. In just three days, the Indians and Yankees would meet again, this time in New York. It loomed as the most important series of the season, and the Cleveland manager felt it was imperative to have his best pitchers ready to throw. That meant he would have to rest Coveleskie, Bagby, and Caldwell over the weekend.

It was a dangerous gamble, especially after the Indians lost to the Browns 5–3 on Saturday to extend their losing streak to five games. The Tribe was desperate for a victory Sunday, and Speaker was forced to give untested rookie Bob Clark his first major-league start.

Clark was a giant of a man, six foot four and two hundred pounds with huge legs. He had started his career as a first baseman, but in 1919 the Lowell, Massachusetts, team in the New England League came up short a pitcher and Clark was pressed into service. He responded with a shutout, and from that day on was a pitcher.

The league folded in late July, so Clark went down to Boston for a tryout. The Indians were in town that day, and Speaker liked what he saw of the big pitcher. Clark was invited to Cleveland's spring camp in 1920, and his fastball and hustle earned him a spot on the team. The Indians also were intrigued by his underhand motion, which was a dead ringer for Mays's style, only from the opposite side.

A cheerful fellow, Clark spent most of the season as a batting practice pitcher. Despite Clark's limited experience, Speaker was sending him out to face one of the hardest-hitting teams in the league. To boost the rookie's confidence, Speaker told him, "You have as much stuff as any pitcher on my staff. I don't feel as if I'm experimenting."

Clark came through brilliantly, throwing a four-hitter for a 5–0 victory. The big blow for the Indians was provided by Johnston. With two men on base in the eighth inning, he hit a drive that rolled all the way to the scoreboard in center field. He never slowed down rounding the bases, and slid home ahead of the relay throw for an inside-the-park homer. Chapman was the first player off the bench to rush out and hug Johnston.

That same afternoon, the White Sox beat the Tigers 10–3 while the Yankees lost to the Senators 6–4. The day ended with Cleveland four percentage points ahead of Chicago, with New York only one-half game and ten percentage points back in third place.

*   *   *

Late that afternoon, an automobile pulled up in front of a partially constructed house on Alvason Road in East Cleveland. The four occupants got out noisily, laughing and talking excitedly as they paused on the lawn to survey the structure.

Jack Graney would long remember that brief visit to the home that Mr. Daly was having built for Ray and Kathleen. The Indians would be departing for New York shortly, and Graney was riding to the train station with Chapman and his wife. The fourth member in the group that day was Dan Daly, Kathleen's sixteen-year-old brother. Mr. Daly, believing it was time for his son to do some traveling, had made arrangements for Dan to accompany the ballclub on its trip to the East.

They all were in a jovial mood as they marched into the house to survey the builders' progress. Graney had never seen Ray and Kathleen happier. They had brought him by the house before, but this time Ray was particularly buoyant as he took his friend from room to room pointing out the various features.

"What are you going to do with all these rooms?" Graney asked.

Chapman smiled broadly as he gave his answer. "Fill them up."

Graney shook his head and laughed. Only recently, Ray had told him that Kathleen was pregnant. It was no secret Chapman wanted a big family.

When it came time to leave, the others almost had to drag Chappie out to the car. Graney kidded him about how much time he had spent at the house, checking out every detail of its construction.

"You must be counting the bricks in this place," said Graney.

By the time the group arrived at the depot, there were storm clouds overhead. Ignoring the threat of rain, thousands of well-wishers had gathered near the depot to cheer the Indians on their departure for New York. Estimates of the crowd size ranged as high as twenty thousand. The fans cried out to each of the ballplayers they saw and gathered around them to shake their hands and wish them good luck.

Even Kathleen's brother Dan, already six feet tall, was able to bask in the attention. Two boys, believing him to be a new pitcher just up from the minors, rushed up to talk to him.

Finally, it came time to board, and Dan hopped on the steps to one of the two Pullman cars reserved for the Indians' traveling party. He looked back to see Ray lingering by his automobile, still telling Kathleen good-bye. For a moment, Dan feared his brother-in-law might be left behind. But the flagman also saw the couple, and he waited for Chapman to race over and jump aboard the Pullman car before he gave his signal to the engineer.

As the train slowly pulled away from the platform, the people in the crowd shouted and waved and honked their auto horns. Just as the last car disappeared into the distance, the first drops of rain began to fall, scattering the crowd. A few mintues later, a thunderstorm hit, knocking out electricity in many parts of the city.

IV

The Beaning

Tomorrow we ought to win pretty easily. I can't hit this man Mays, but the rest of the team sure can.

Ray Chapman
August 15, 1920

The Prelude

42

The heat was the prime topic of conversation in New York on Monday, August 16. It was muggy and oppressive, and all around town people were fighting a losing battle to keep cool. By midday, the temperature was in the eighties and still climbing, but the 94 percent humidity and lack of a breeze made conditions almost unbearable. Before the day was over, four people in the city would collapse from the heat and humidity.

Shortly before noon, Carl Mays emerged from his apartment in the Roger Morris Hotel atop Coogan's Bluff and paused on the sidewalk outside. He had other things on his mind besides the weather. His thoughts were on that afternoon's ballgame against Cleveland. A victory by the Yankees would move them past the Indians and into first place. With so much at stake, Mays had drawn the starting assignment in the game, although his turn in the rotation was not due to come up for another day.

Mays felt rested and confident. He had gone to bed early the night before and risen at 8:30 in the morning. Following his game-day routine, he had eaten a large breakfast of ham and eggs. He spent some time with Freddie and his three-week-old baby, then prepared to head to the ballpark. Before leaving, he had taken a chicken neck out of the icebox and stuck it in his pocket. As was his custom, he would chew on it during the game to keep his mouth moist.

It was only a short walk to the garage where he kept his automobile, but Mays already had worked up a sweat by the time he began his drive to the ballpark. He took his customary route down

the bluff, across the 155th Street viaduct, and into the back of the
Polo Grounds. Around 12:30, he walked into the clubhouse, one of
the first players to arrive.

Before putting on his uniform, Mays went to the office to remind
one of the secretaries to have a ticket available for Freddie. She
would take a taxi to the ballpark later and Mays, anticipating a large
crowd for the game, wanted to make sure she would have no trouble
getting seated.

This was one game Mays did not want his wife to miss. Today,
he was going for the one-hundredth victory of his career.

*　　　*　　　*

Graney was lost in his thoughts while the Indians were riding the
elevated train en route from the Hotel Ansonia to the Polo Grounds.
He was brought back to reality by the cheerful sound of Chapman's
voice.

"Say, fellows, I know why we haven't been winning," called out
Chappie. "We haven't been singing lately. That's the trouble."

As Graney listened, Chapman began to sing "Dear Old Pal o'
Mine" in the beautiful tenor voice his teammates had come to know
so well. After a few moments, Graney began to sing, also. So did
Johnston and O'Neill. Soon, everyone on the ballclub had joined in
the song.

They arrived at the ballpark as relaxed as they had been in weeks.
Entering the locker room, Chapman said loudly, "Mays is pitching
for the Yankees today, so I'll do the fielding and you fellows do the
hitting."

Graney laughed along with the rest of the players.

*　　　*　　　*

In Cleveland, a construction crew from the Osborn Engineering
Company arrived at League Park in the morning to begin work on
a new press box. The project was yet another sign of Dunn's
boundless optimism. The Indians owner wanted the press box
erected on top of the grandstand in order to seat the 480 baseball
writers and telegraph operators he anticipated at the World Series.

Dunn also gave in to public demand and announced the Indians would begin accepting mail applications for World Series tickets.

All that remained now was for Cleveland to win the pennant.

*   *   *

This also was a landmark day for John B. Sheridan. His instructional booklet, "Baseball for Beginners," was scheduled for release by the American Sports Publishing Company of A. G. Spalding & Bro. In the book, Sheridan had used various star players to illustrate his guidelines for youngsters.

The section on the proper batting stance featured Chapman, who was, according to Sheridan, "the perfect model for all baseball players in his position at the bat."

*   *   *

Despite the stifling heat, the crowd at the Polo Grounds numbered twenty-three thousand, including players from six other major-league teams who had taken advantage of a day off in their schedules to come out for the showdown.

There also were several residents of Paterson, New Jersey, who had turned out to honor one of their hometown boys, Indians left fielder Charlie Jamieson. Early in his professional baseball career, Jamey would return home to Paterson in the offseason and pass himself off as a fireman in order to play in the Fireman's League. Whenever he was asked his name, he would claim it was O'Reilly.

"And what precinct are you out of?" they would ask.

"The second," Jamieson would tell them.

"Oh? Do you know Callahan?"

"Of course I do."

"Well, that's funny," they would say, "because he died five years ago."

But "O'Reilly" always donated his pay from the league to the firemen's Widows Fund, so for two years they let him get by with his charade. To express their gratitude to Jamieson, the firemen traveled to the Polo Grounds to stage a "day" for the ballplayer. They brought Jamey's mother and sister with them to the game.

43

A light rain had started to fall across the Polo Grounds as umpire Tommy Connolly stood behind home plate and waited for Mays to complete his warm-up pitches. The temperature had climbed above eighty degrees, and not even the overcast skies or the rain seemed to offer much relief from the muggy conditions. Connolly feared it was going to be an uncomfortable afternoon, but otherwise there was little to make him think this game would be any different from the thousands of others he had umpired.

Connolly was five foot seven and forty-nine years old, a soft-spoken Englishman who made his calls in an Irish brogue with a broad "a" used by New Englanders. He had been born in Manchester, England, but his family had moved to Natick, Massachusetts, when he was thirteen. Connolly became interested in the American game of baseball, and although he never was much of a player, he read every book on the sport he could find and soon became an expert on the rules.

He began umpiring and was working in a YMCA league in Natick when he caught the interest of Tim Hurst, a famous National League umpire. Hurst helped Connolly get a job in the New England League in 1894. Four years later, Connolly was promoted to the National League.

When the American League was formed in 1901, Ban Johnson was looking for experienced umpires, and Connolly quickly signed up. On Opening Day, he was scheduled to work the Cleveland at Chicago game. As it turned out, the other three games that day were rained out, giving Connolly the honor of umpiring the first American League game ever played.

He also had the distinction of umpiring the first World Series, teaming up with Hank O'Day of the National League for the 1903 showdown between the Boston Pilgrims and Pittsburgh Pirates.

Connolly was a firm but fair umpire and early in his career he established a reputation for helping young ballplayers. In 1901, a young pitcher named Eddie Plank was making his first major-league start for the Philadelphia Athletics. Plank was being harassed unmercifully by the opposing players, who were trying to rattle him by claiming he was not toeing the pitching rubber properly.

Finally, Connolly called time and walked out to the mound.

"Son," he told Plank, "there are right ways and wrong ways to pitch in this league. Let me show you the right way. I'll take care of that wrecking crew in the dugout. And from what you have shown me today, you'll be up here for a long time."

Plank went on to become one of the greatest pitchers in the game, winning 327 games in a seventeen-year career.

No umpire commanded more respect than Connolly. He worked alone in those early years, and the players towered over him. Often, an angry player would charge him following a close play, and Connolly would calmly stand his ground and let the man have his say. Then he would look up at his adversary and impatiently ask, "Well, are you through? Officially, he's safe, and you better go back to your position."

Even the feared Ty Cobb said of him, "You can go so far with Connolly, but when you see his neck get red, it's time to lay off him."

Connolly's philosophy was a simple one, and it served as an apt description of his career: "Maybe I called it wrong, but it's official."

*   *   *

The Indians, still smarting from the sweep by the Yankees the week before, went right after Mays. Jamieson was the first batter up, and with his friends and family cheering him on, he slashed a single to left field.

Chapman stepped in next, and Ward crept in from third base in anticipation of a bunt. Mays looked in for his signal from catcher Muddy Ruel, then aimed the ball at the inside edge of the plate. Chapman was the best bunter in the league, and Mays wanted to keep the ball high and tight to make it more difficult for the batter to get down the sacrifice hit.

The pitch sailed in high for ball one.

Mays came back with another inside pitch as Chapman crouched over the plate. This time, the pitcher got the ball out in the strike zone, and Chapman quickly squared around and pushed a bunt in front of the plate. Ruel sprang forward and pounced on the ball. He looked toward second and saw Jamieson already sliding into the bag, so the catcher took the only play available, throwing to first base for the out. It was Chapman's thirty-fourth sacrifice hit, the most in the league.

Speaker was applauded as he stepped to the plate, but Mays easily disposed of him on a fly ball to Bodie in center field. Smith also flew out to Bodie to retire the side.

In the second inning, the Indians took a 1–0 lead when O'Neill, who had been moved up to sixth in the batting order ahead of Johnston, hit a one-out homer into the left-field bleachers.

In the third, Jamieson led off with his second single of the game. Again, Chapman was called on to bunt. This time, he was unable to get his bat squarely on Mays's underhand offering, and he popped the ball in the air toward first base. Pipp quickly made the catch and whirled around to double Jamieson off first, ending the rally.

As the fourth inning began, the rainfall stopped. Mays retired the first batter, then issued a walk to Larry Gardner. O'Neill followed with a single to center to put runners at first and third.

That brought up Johnston, and he hit a sharp grounder to Peckinpaugh at shortstop. Peck threw home ahead of the runner, but Gardner crashed into Ruel and knocked the ball loose to score the Indians' second run.

Ward then fumbled Wamby's grounder to third to load the bases, and Coveleskie helped his own cause by hitting a sacrifice fly to Bodie in center field to score O'Neill. Cleveland led 3–0.

Chapman was waiting in the on-deck circle when Mays fielded Jamieson's grounder and threw to first to retire the side.

The Yankees went out quickly in the bottom of the fourth. Peckinpaugh, who had hit two homers in two at-bats the last time he faced Coveleskie in the Polo Grounds, hit a high pop-up to Gardner for the first out. Ruth grounded out to Johnston, and Pratt fouled out to O'Neill, who almost fell into the dugout making the catch.

The skies were overcast and gray, but no rain was falling as Mays walked to the mound to begin the fifth inning.

44

Chapman carried two bats with him to the plate, swinging them loosely over his shoulder. He tossed one toward the Indians' dugout, then stepped into the batter's box and pulled his cap down as he took his stance. Speaker kneeled in the on-deck area, idly waiting his turn at bat. Connolly gave the signal for play to begin, then leaned into position behind Ruel.

On the mound, Mays stared in toward the plate, covered the ball in his gloved hand, and began his windup for his first pitch of the inning. He brought the ball chest high, raised his hands high over his head, and swung his right arm back as he stepped forward. His arm was at the farthest point of his backswing when he detected a slight shift in the batter's back foot as if Chapman was preparing to push a bunt down the first-base line. In that split second, Mays made the decision to switch to a high-and-tight pitch. The knuckles on his right hand almost scraped the ground as he whipped his arm forward and shot the ball toward home.

Squatting behind the plate, catcher Muddy Ruel followed the path of the ball. Ruel always had difficulty handling Mays's pitches, as the pitcher's underhand motion caused the ball to take unexpected twists and turns. That was especially so on days such as this when Mays was throwing with greater speed than usual. But this pitch did not fool Ruel. It was a fastball and it took a noticeable although not extraordinary shoot as it approached the inside part of the plate. The catcher raised his glove in anticipation of catching the ball. From his vantage point, the pitch was in the strike zone.

The ball sailed directly toward Chapman's head, but he made no effort to move. He remained poised in his crouch, apparently transfixed as the ball flew in and crashed against his left temple with a resounding crack that was audible throughout the ballpark.

Mays heard the noise, then saw the ball bouncing toward him. Thinking it had struck the bat handle, he grabbed it and threw to first base. He watched as Wally Pipp made the catch and turned to toss the ball around the infield. It was a routine Mays had seen thousands of times before. But suddenly, Pipp froze, his arm still cocked behind his ear. Mays wondered what was happening, then he saw Pipp staring toward home plate with a look of shock on his face. Only then did the pitcher realize something was wrong.

At the plate, Chapman, who had stood motionless for a brief moment after being struck, was sinking slowly to the ground, his face twisted in agony. Ruel stepped forward to grab him, but he slumped to his knees, never uttering a sound.

Umpire Connolly took one look at the stricken ballplayer, blood rushing from his left ear, and immediately pulled off his mask and sprinted toward the grandstands.

"We need a doctor!" he shouted to the crowd. "Is there a doctor in the house!?"

Seeing Chapman fall, Speaker raced over from the on-deck area. He arrived just as Chapman was struggling to a sitting position, dazed but still conscious. As he knelt and reached for his friend, it appeared to Speaker that Chapman was trying to get up to charge at Mays.

The other Cleveland players, led by Graney, rushed from the dugout to lend their assistance. So did several of the Yankees, and as the ballplayers crowded around, Speaker ordered them to move back and give Chapman some air.

Among the Indians, only Larry Gardner stayed behind. He had been mopping his face with a sponge and had his back turned to the plate when Chapman was struck. It was a moment he would never forget.

"I heard that sound when the ball crushed his skull, and I saw him fall," Gardner later recalled. "I didn't want any closer view than that."

Cleveland coach Jack MacCallister ran to the injured player fearing the worst. MacCallister had heard what he described as an "explosive sound" when the ball struck Chapman, and he had the awful conviction Ray would be dead within seconds.

As the players gathered around him, Chapman tried to speak. His lips moved but no words came out. A moment later, Dr. Stewart, the club physician of the Yankees, and Dr. Joseph Cascio of St. Lawrence Hospital rushed to the scene in answer to Connolly's pleas for medical assistance. They called for some ice to be applied to the injured player.

After several minutes, Chapman was revived sufficiently to be helped to his feet. When he stood, there was an outburst of applause from the relieved fans.

Chapman shrugged off all efforts at assistance and began to walk across the infield toward the clubhouse in center field. He was flanked by Graney on one side and another Cleveland player on the other. As Chapman approached second base, his knees began to buckle and the two players quickly grabbed him. They draped his arms around their shoulders and carried him the remainder of the distance to the clubhouse.

*   *   *

While attention was focused on Chapman, Mays chose to remain on the infield near the mound. His main concern seemed to be the baseball that had struck the batter. Regaining possession of it, he called for umpire Connolly. Mays pointed out a rough spot on the surface of the ball. That, he claimed, had caused the pitch to sail farther inside than he had intended.

Connolly examined the ball and removed it from play. Just how scuffed the ball was would remain a matter of dispute. No one bothered to keep track of it, and it soon became mixed in with the other baseballs removed from play that day, forever lost as a piece of evidence.*

*   *   *

D. L. Webster of New York witnessed the beaning from the upper deck of the stands at the Polo Grounds. As the ball approached the plate, Webster screamed out, "A wild pitch!" Then he heard a resounding crack, which he assumed was the ball striking Chapman's bat. "I thought Chapman fell because his spikes caught and twisted his ankle as he tried to dodge."

Even after it became obvious Chapman had been struck by the pitch, neither Webster nor many of the other spectators imagined the severity of the injury. They applauded as the ballplayer was helped off the field, then they turned their attention back to the ballgame.

*   *   *

Harry Lunte jogged out to first base to run for Chapman, and Speaker stepped in as the next batter. Spoke hit a grounder to second baseman Del Pratt, who forced Lunte at second base. After Smith struck out, Gardner hit the ball off the right-field wall for a single, sending Speaker around to third.

O'Neill followed with a line drive to right. Pratt leaped high in the air, but the ball grazed the top of his glove and went into right

---

* Whatever his intentions, Mays's actions drew the wrath of several Cleveland players. In an unverified account of events given in 1945, MacCallister claimed that as Chapman lay on the ground in agony Mays was protesting to Connolly that the ball had struck the wrist of the bat and that Chapman was feigning an injury.

"One look at Chapman was enough to prove to anyone he was no more than a called strike from death," MacCallister remembered. "I think it was Pipp who finally made Mays pipe down and led him away, while I did what I could to hold Graney and O'Neill, Chapman's greatest pals, in check."

field for a single. Speaker scored easily, giving Cleveland a 4–0 lead. The inning finally ended when Johnston hit a routine grounder to Pratt for a forceout.

45

Inside the clubhouse, there was nothing to do but wait. The two doctors who had tended him on the field had determined Chapman should undergo an immediate operation to relieve the pressure on his brain. An ambulance was en route from St. Lawrence Hospital, which was less than one-half mile away. Dr. Cascio assured those in the room that although the injuries were serious, he did not believe they would be fatal.

Chapman lay on a table as the others stood around nervously. He looked up at Graney and tried to speak, but he could only mumble incoherently.

"Get me a pencil and some paper," yelled out Graney. "I need something to write with."

Someone handed him a tablet and a pencil, and he placed them in his friend's hands. Chapman started to write, but he was too weak and the pencil fell to the floor.

Trainer Percy Smallwood stood across the room watching. When Chapman spotted him, he motioned for Smallwood to come over. He began mumbling again, and the trainer strained to make out the words.

"Katy's ring, Percy, Katy's ring," he kept repeating.

Finally, Smallwood understood. Before the game, he had been given Chapman's wedding ring for safekeeping. The trainer retrieved the ring and slipped it on the ballplayer's finger. A look of relief came over Chapman's face. To Smallwood, the look in Chappie's eyes spoke volumes.

Nearby, Dan Daly tried to sort out his thoughts. He had witnessed the beaning from his box seat, yet at the time had not realized what had happened. Like many others in the stands, he thought the ball had struck Chapman's bat. It wasn't until later, when someone came over and said, "Ray is in the clubhouse, do you want to go see him?" that Daly realized the gravity of the situation.

He watched as one of the Yankees arrived to see how Chapman was. Daly was not sure who the player was, but the sight of the New York uniform seemed to anger Ray. The ballplayer was visibly shaken as he turned to leave.

Another of those in the room was John Henry, a former catcher with Washington and Boston and one of Chapman's closest friends. He had come down from his home in Boston to watch the game that day, and after the beaning had rushed to the clubhouse to see his friend. When the ambulance finally arrived, it was Henry who climbed into the back with Chapman. He held an ice pack to Ray's head on the drive to the hospital.

When they arrived, Chapman complained there was not enough air in the elevator that was transporting him upstairs. Henry stood beside his friend and fanned him.

"John, for God's sake, don't call Kate," Ray said softly. "But if you do, tell her I'm all right."

Those were the last words Chapman spoke before he lapsed into unconsciousness.

46

If Mays was unnerved by the beaning, he did not show it. He retired the Indians in order in the sixth, seventh, and eighth innings.

But the Yankees were having no luck against Coveleskie, who had allowed only three singles and one walk through the first seven innings. The score remained 4–0 heading into the bottom of the eighth.

With one out and no one on base, Huggins decided it was time to go to his bench. He called on Sammy Vick to pinch-hit for Mays, and Vick responded with a hard-hit single to right field. The rally ended quickly when Coveleskie retired the next two batters.

Mays sat on the bench to watch as the final inning began with Hank Thormahlen on the mound for New York.

*   *   *

F. C. Lane elected not to wait for the conclusion of the ballgame, instead heading to the clubhouse to check on the severity of Chapman's injury. Lane was not allowed inside the room, but as he stood outside he spotted Colonel Huston of the Yankees coming out the door.

Approaching the Colonel, Lane asked for an update on Chapman's condition. Huston frowned and shook his head.

"It looks bad, very bad. I hope he will pull through, but his chances are not encouraging. I've seen hundreds of men die on the battlefield, but death is a thing you never get used to."

Rather than return to the press box, Lane went to the Yankees' clubhouse to await the arrival of Mays. As he did, he could hear the New York fans cheering loudly.

Outside, the Yankees had mounted a ninth-inning rally. Ruth led off with a double and Pratt followed with a walk. Coveleskie retired the next two batters, but Bodie hit a double down the right-field line to score two runs. Ruel singled past third to drive home Bodie, and suddenly New York trailed by only a run.

A nervous Speaker ran in from center field to confer with his pitcher, but finally decided to leave Coveleskie in the game. The batter was pinch-hitter Lefty O'Doul, a seldom-used twenty-three-year-old second-year player who later would attain greatness with the Giants.

O'Doul hit a sharp grounder to Lunte at shortstop. Chapman's replacement fielded the ball cleanly and flipped it to Wamby at second base for the final out. The Indians had won 4–3 to hang on to first place, one-half game ahead of the idle White Sox and 1½ in front of the Yankees.

Moments later, Lane spotted Mays approaching the clubhouse. To Lane, the pitcher was a lonely and dejected figure as he walked through the shadows of the bleachers amid the discarded scorecards, old cigar butts, and wadded-up candy wrappers. Mays did not want to talk at first, but once inside the clubhouse he agreed to give his version of the events.

"I was wild as a hawk," said Mays, sitting on a stool in front of his locker. "I always am when I am saved up for a special game. I never was effective under such circumstances, and I used to tell Barrow so, just as I have told Huggins. But when a manager calls on you to pitch, you have to do the best you can."

The pitcher paused, reviewing the incident in his mind.

"The ball was wet, which didn't make it any easier to control," he added.

Across the room, one of the Yankees was kidding Ping Bodie about his surprisingly strong fielding.

"They'll be calling you Tris Bodie pretty soon if you keep it up," the player shouted.

"Hah!" replied Bodie. "They'll be calling him Ping Speaker if he ever gets anywhere near as good a fielder as I am."

Mays seemed far removed from the locker-room banter. Looking up at Lane, he said, "I don't know whether Chapman was seriously hurt or not. Have you seen him?"

Lane replied that he hadn't. All he knew was that the ambulance had taken Chapman to the hospital a few minutes earlier.

Mays did not answer. He sat with his head resting in his hands, apparently lost in his thoughts. Not wishing to disturb him, Lane turned and quietly left the room.

47

When he released his statement to the press at the hospital that evening, Speaker spoke optimistically about Chapman's condition.

"I was hit on the head in 1916 in a manner similar to this, and I am hopeful that Chappie will be back again as soon as I was. I was out of the game for ten days.

"The blow laid me out much as this one laid out Chappie, and for a time a severe fracture was feared, but it turned out that it was the other way. I was badly scared when I saw Ray try to talk this afternoon, but he was able to talk tonight, so that worry is over. I am inclined to believe that if there is a fracture, it is not a severe one."

Speaker and Indians business manager Walter McNichols had been at the hospital since the conclusion of the ballgame. A short while later, they had been joined by the Cleveland players and Yankees secretary Charles McManus. By nightfall, the players had been sent back to the Ansonia Hotel to await further word, while Speaker and McNichols continued the vigil at the hospital. Earlier, Speaker had talked with Kathleen by telephone to inform her of Chapman's condition, and she departed immediately for New York.

At 9:30 that night, the doctors summoned Speaker and McNichols to a room for an update on Chapman's condition. X rays had confirmed the ballplayer had sustained a two-armed fracture extending 3½ inches to the base of his skull on the left side. It was a depressed fracture, and one piece of bone was pressing down on the brain. Worse, Chapman's pulse was dropping at an alarming rate, and was down to forty.

With the patient's condition worsening, the doctors believed it would be unwise to postpone surgery until Kathleen arrived the following morning. Speaker and McNichols talked it over, and at ten o'clock the Cleveland manager gave approval for the operation.

The operating team would consist of Dr. M. J. Horan and Dr. T. D. Merrigan of the St. Lawrence staff, with Drs. Joseph Cascio, A. A. White, and J. E. Quinn as attendants.

Before surgery could begin, Chapman suffered spasms on both sides, indicating to the surgeons that the brain on both sides had been injured by the force of the blow. Dr. Merrigan said there probably was a laceration on the right side of the skull, opposite the side that had been struck.

At 12:29 A.M., Chapman was placed on the operating table. The surgeons made an incision 3½ inches long through the base of the skull on the left side and found a rupture of the lateral sinus and a quantity of clotted blood. Dr. Merrigan removed a piece of skull about 1½ inches square and found the brain had been so severely jarred that blood clots had occurred.

The shock of the blow had damaged the brain not only on the left side of the head, where the ball had struck, but also on the right side, where the shock of the blow had forced the brain against the skull. The surgeons noted there were symptoms of paralysis.

The operation lasted one hour, fifteen minutes. Afterward, Chapman began breathing easier and his pulse climbed back to ninety. The physicians believed the chances of his recovery were fair, but they said it would take forty-eight hours to know for sure.

Encouraged by this news, Speaker and McNichols returned to the hotel to inform the players that Chapman was showing signs of improvement.

48

The overnight train from Cleveland arrived at ten o'clock in the morning. When Kathleen stepped onto the platform, she was met by Father Connors, a friend of the Chapman's who had come to New York from his home in Philadelphia upon learning of the accident.

"I feared that something must happen," Kathleen told the priest. "We had been too happy together, and it couldn't last."

Father Connors said little as he accompanied Kathleen from the station to the Ansonia Hotel. They went immediately to Speaker's room, where the Cleveland manager was waiting. McNichols and a couple of the players also were in the room. When she walked through the door and saw the men standing there awkwardly, Kathleen looked over at Speaker expectantly. Spoke stared back at her, unable to speak.

"He's dead, isn't he?" she said.

When Speaker nodded his head, Kathleen fainted.

*   *   *

Chapman had died at 4:40 in the morning, Tuesday, August 17. He was twenty-nine years old, the first casualty on a major-league diamond.

The news had been relayed immediately to the Ansonia, where the players had been hanging out in the lobby or sitting around in their rooms talking, unable to go to sleep while their friend's life hung in the balance. When the announcement was made, several of them broke down sobbing while others sat there numbly, too shocked to react. Speaker went to his room to be alone in his grief, leaving McNichols to handle all calls from reporters.

After a while, a few members of the team wandered the hallways dazedly. Some gathered in small groups and spoke in hushed tones, trying to come to grips with their friend's death.

Les Nunamaker, the big catcher, sat with his head buried in his hands. "Aw, gee, Ray was so full of pep. I remember before the game Monday, he looked up at me and said, 'Say, fellows, I know why we haven't been winning. We haven't been singing lately. That's the trouble.' "

"Sure," added Smoky Joe Wood, his voice cracking, "and do you remember when he . . . when he . . . " Wood swallowed hard, then walked away from the group, unable to continue talking.

Larry Gardner, his face unshaven and his eyes reddened, stared ahead vacantly. "I can't realize that Chappie has gone. I can see him now coming up behind me with that smile he always wore, and saying, 'You're not mad, are you?' "

In his room, Graney wept openly and bitterly. Tom Raftery, one of Chapman's friends who had come down from Boston after learning of the beaning, tried to comfort him. Later that morning, when Graney had regained his composure, he would lash out angrily at Mays.

"We don't think Mays tried to dust Chappie off. Neither did he try to dust any of the boys off yesterday, but we think he has in the past. Anyway, we don't think he ever should be allowed to pitch against us again.

"A batter has a chance to dodge the fastball thrown by an ordinary pitcher, but Mays has a freak delivery and his fastball has a sudden dip to it that never gives a batter a chance to dodge."

Others on the team spoke more harshly of the pitcher and his motives. Doc Johnston was not alone when he said, "Mays should be strung up."

*   *   *

Across town, the bell at Mays's apartment rang just after ten o'clock that morning. Mays had just finished eating breakfast.

Freddie was in the kitchen washing dishes. The baby was asleep in the other room.

"I'll answer it," Mays told his wife.

When he opened the door, he saw a man standing nervously in the hallway, clutching his hat in front of him. Mays recognized the man as an employee from the Yankees' front office, but he could not recall his name.

Mark Roth, one of the ballclub's secretaries, did not bother to identify himself.

"Carl, I've got some bad news for you. Ray Chapman died at five o'clock this morning."

The words hit Mays like a sledgehammer. He stood there stunned, then slowly shut the door in Roth's face.

The next few hours were a blur to Mays. He did not know how long he sat in his apartment in a daze. Finally, he was jarred back to reality by the ringing of the telephone. It was a police inspector, offering his sympathy and a police guard if Mays felt one was necessary to ensure his privacy. Mays accepted.

Soon, a police captain and patrolman arrived from the local police precinct. Minutes later, Frederick Grant, a lawyer from the Yankees' counsel, arrived and advised Mays to make a formal statement on the beaning. Mays, accompanied by Grant, went to the local precinct station, where he was directed to report to the district attorney of Manhattan.

When he arrived at the DA's office, Mays was taken to see Assistant District Attorney Joyce, who was in charge of the Homicide Bureau. To those present, the pitcher was visibly depressed.

Joyce asked Mays a few questions, then told him to describe the incident. When Mays began to speak, his eyes filled with tears but he delivered his statement in a straightforward manner.

"It was a straight fast ball and not a curved one. When Chapman came to bat, I got the signal for a straight fast ball, which I delivered.

"It was a little too close, and I saw Chapman duck his head in an effort to get out of the path of the ball. He was too late, however, and a second later he fell to the grounds.

"It was the most regrettable incident of my career, and I would give anything if I could undo what has happened."

Joyce did not feel it necessary to deliberate the matter. Even if he had chosen to do so, he would have found little precedent to guide him.

Previously, the most noteworthy ballplayer to have died as the result of a beaning had been Johnny Dodge, who had played for the Philadelphia Phillies from 1912 to 1913 and the Cincinnati Red Legs in 1913. Dodge was with Mobile, Alabama, of the Southern League when he was struck and killed by a pitch from Tom "Shotgun" Rogers in Nashville, Tennessee, on June 18, 1916. Rogers apparently was undaunted by the fatal beaning, for he went on to win five consecutive shutouts after the accident. He was purchased by the St. Louis Browns the following season. In 1919, he joined the Philadelphia Athletics and compiled a 4–12 won-lost record. On the day of Chapman's death, Rogers was back in the minors trying to earn a chance with another big-league club.

Another fatal beaning had occurred on August 9, 1906, in the New England League. Joseph Yeager of Fall River, Massachusetts, threw a pitch that fractured the skull of outfielder Tom Burke of Lynn, Massachusetts. Two days later, Burke died.

Yeager attended Burke's funeral on August 14 and then returned to the mound to pitch a game four days later. When he did, he was arrested by Inspector John Fitzgerald of the Lynn police on a formal charge of manslaughter. The order had been issued by police chief Thomas Burckes. Yeager posted a five-hundred-dollar bail and was ordered to appear before Judge John Berry in two days. At that time, the charges were dropped by Berry.

In the Mays case, Joyce saw no reason to believe the beaning was anything other than a tragic but unavoidable mishap in a potentially dangerous sport. After listening to Mays's statement, he declined to so much as call in any witnesses to the incident. He ruled that Chapman's death was accidental and there would be no further investigation by the district attorney or the police. The pitcher was released from custody and allowed to return home.

When he arrived at his apartment, Mays learned that Freddie

already had received two threatening phone calls. One caller had vowed to shoot her husband the next time he drove across the 155th Street viaduct.

49

News of Chapman's death had spread quickly across the country. The late editions of the *Cleveland Plain Dealer* reported the tragedy on page one with a seventy-two point headline that shouted out, "RAY CHAPMAN IS DEAD." Across the top of the page was a letter from Mayor FitzGerald to the people of the city:

> Thru a singularly unfortunate circumstance, Cleveland has lost by death one of its most able ball players, at a time when his services made him invaluable in the team's fight for the American League championship.
>
> Ray Chapman, I believe, represented the American ideal of a baseball player. He was a clean, high-principled sportsman, typical of those who have kept the game of baseball on a high plane, and made it worthy to be the national game of the United States.

The widespread sorrow of Clevelanders was evident throughout the city. In the words of a writer for the *Plain Dealer*, "Lawyers forgot to talk of cases, ministers found it hard to concentrate on their work, politicians neglected their interests for the time being, workmen stood at their tools, and all thought of Chapman and his loss."

Later that day, one of the newspaper's reporters stopped at the corner of East Sixth Street and Superior Avenue Northeast, where a young paperboy known only as "Izzy" recorded the scores of all the ballgames on a poster for his customers. Today, there were no scores posted. "Aw, what's the use?" said Izzy. "I don't feel like it with Chappie gone. He was the best of the whole Cleveland bunch."

Jim Dunn was in Cincinnati, where his niece was seriously ill, when he heard the news. He immediately contacted Speaker and said he would meet him in Cleveland the following day. Among other things, he wanted to discuss the team's shortstop situation.

At the American League offices, Ban Johnson issued a statement expressing his regret and praising Chapman for his service to the Cleveland ballclub and to baseball.

President John Heydler of the National League ordered all NL clubs to fly their flags at half-staff for the remainder of the week as a sign of respect to Chapman.

The Yankees immediately announced the game with the Indians scheduled for that afternoon was being postponed indefinitely. However, Colonel Huston said the club would make no official statement on Chapman's death.

"I am terribly sorry that Chapman was killed," said Huston. "I'm sorry such an accident had to happen in our park or that any of our team had any connection with it. It is unfortunate that it should have been Mays who pitched the ball, too, because of the tremendous publicity he has already had. I can't say anymore than that."

*　　　*　　　*

Later in the morning, Huston met with Speaker to personally extend his sympathy to the Cleveland ballclub. During the brief conversation, the Yankee colonel also stressed that he wanted no hostility between the two teams. It is not known exactly how Speaker replied to Huston's plea.

Initially, Huston said the Cleveland manager gave him the following assurance: "On the part of two or three of our players, there is some bitterness toward Mays, but I am going to do all I can to suppress it and any bitterness that might arise. For the good of baseball, for the good of the players themselves, and especially out of regard for the poor fellow that's dead, it is our duty to do that. I am going to do all I can to see there is no bitterness."

Huston's answer to Speaker supposedly was, "And you can depend on it that we'll do all we can."

However, the day after the alleged conversation was reported,

Huston was forced to amend his remarks. Speaker claimed he had made no such statement while in New York. The Yankee colonel issued the following clarification: "I have been quoted as saying that Speaker exonerated Mays of all blame and possibly it was my fault that I was misquoted. What Speaker did say to me was this, 'Nobody has a right to think it was other than an accident.' Speaker's attitude in the matter was splendid, and I would not misquote him for the world. He is a fine fellow, and I think too much of him."

*   *   *

Still shaken by events, Mays chose not to leave his apartment for the remainder of the day. He had considered trying to contact Chapman's widow to express his condolences to her, but Huston advised him against such action.

Mays gladly took the Colonel's advice, as he admitted weeks later. "I could not, under the circumstances, bring myself to undergo this ordeal, though I would have done so if any good would have come of it."

Similarly, Mays declined to pay a personal visit to the funeral home where Chapman's body lay—a gesture of respect many expected him to perform. Again, he was guided by a simple motive. "I knew that the sight of his silent form would haunt me as long as I live."

*   *   *

Thousands of fans, many of them unaware that Chapman had died, gathered at the Polo Grounds that afternoon to see the scheduled game. They were met by league officials and a force of detectives, who told them the game had been postponed because of the ballplayer's death.

After hearing the news, hundreds of the fans went to the undertaking establishment of James F. McGowan at 153rd Street and Amsterdam Avenue, where Chapman's body had been taken. In all, three thousand fans visited the undertaking establishment to pay their respects to the deceased ballplayer.

That evening, Chapman's body, accompanied by Speaker, Wood, Jane McMahon, Dan Daly, and Kathleen, was taken to Grand

Central Terminal. The casket was enclosed in a white pine box. On top was a bouquet of flowers bearing a white card that read, "For the one we both loved, John and Dorothy Henry."

As the casket was carried through the terminal, hundreds of spectators gathered. The men removed their hats and stood bareheaded while many of the women wept.

At 6:30, Chapman's body was placed aboard the Lake Shore Limited, and the ballplayer began his final journey home to Cleveland. Watching the train pull out of the station, F. C. Lane, the baseball writer, could not help but think, "Chapman at least is freed from further care and worry. But there are many who would not like to face Carl Mays' future."

V

The Boycott

It is terrible to consider the case at all, but when any man, however ignorant, illiterate or malicious, even hints that a white man in his normal mind would stand out there on the field of sport and try to kill another, the man making that assertion is inhuman, uncivilized, bestial.

Carl Mays

50

Among the players around the league, it had not taken long for sorrow to turn to anger. The first signs appeared at a clubhouse meeting in Boston at midday Tuesday, with members of both the Boston and Detroit teams present.

The joint meeting was called by Red Sox first baseman Stuffy McInnis, whose dislike of Mays had been evident during the internal turmoil that had wracked the Boston club the previous season. McInnis had been at his seaside home in Manchester, Massachusetts, that morning when he learned of Chapman's fate. He wasted no time in rushing to the ballpark to round up players from the two teams to discuss possible retaliation against Mays.

The atmosphere in the room was bitter and acrimonious, fueled by all the old hatreds and charges of dirty tactics aimed at Mays, and there would be conflicting reports of what actually was said. According to Boston outfielder Mike Menoskey, the Red Sox agreed to send a petition to Ban Johnson demanding that Mays be thrown out of baseball. To accentuate their demands, the players would agree to refuse to bat against Mays. Menoskey was left with the impression the Detroit players would join in such action. Ty Cobb also was quoted as saying summary measures should be taken against Mays immediately, and Tigers catcher Oscar Stanage confirmed that the players had discussed such action. Other reports said that while the Detroit players were sympathetic to such a move, they were not ready to commit themselves. The only thing agreed upon by those present was that some sort of action was justified. At the suggestion of some of the more moderate voices in the room, it was decided the players should contact Speaker and get his version of the beaning before any further steps were taken.

In reporting the Tigers' action in *The Sporting News,* writer H. G. Salsinger was convinced the boycott threat was real. "The members of the team declared they would not bat against Mays and an interesting baseball episode will take place if they go through with their threat, providing Miller Huggins decides to pitch Mays against the Detroit team."

When the meeting ended, Detroit shortstop Donie Bush announced to the press he was offering his services to the Indians for the remainder of the season if sanction for such action could be obtained from league offices. Bush said his teammates had no objection to such an arrangement. On the surface, the gesture seemed to be as self-serving as it was magnanimous. After all, it would take Bush from a seventh-place ballclub to one with a shot at World Series money. But the feeling among the Detroit players seemed to be that giving up their shortstop to Cleveland was the best way for them to express their sympathy over Chapman's untimely death.

Meanwhile, similar meetings were taking place elsewhere around the league.

In Washington, the Browns met before a game with the Senators and unanimously agreed that Mays "must be removed from baseball." They voted to write every player in the circuit, asking their cooperation in bringing about Mays's expulsion. The St. Louis players believed rival teams should refuse to play against the New York pitcher if need be.

Despite proposing this action, the Browns backed down from charging Mays with deliberately beaning Chapman. They would say only that "his record is against him." The St. Louis players also pointed to alleged instances of Mays's attempts to "dust off" players and to his previous declarations that he would do so.

The deep-seated anger toward the pitcher was evident by the tone of the players' words. The *St. Louis Globe-Democrat* reported that many of the Browns denounced Mays "in no uncertain terms and their language would not look well in print."

The feeling of the St. Louis players was summed up by a report in *The Sporting News*: "If the news had come over the wire that a ball player had been killed by a pitched ball, without naming who pitched the ball, the Browns to a man would have guessed who did the pitching. That was the way they felt about it, and that was the conviction they had regarding Mays' style of delivery. They are mighty earnest about their stand that Mays and his ilk belong to a past age, and they don't care who knows it."

The Washington players were not ready to take action, but they were in agreement with the views presented by the Browns. Adding credence to the sentiment against Mays, Nationals captain George McBride recited an incident of Mays's intentionally hitting him with the ball. McBride claimed he had been tipped off beforehand that Mays had vowed to "dust him off."

The White Sox also reacted angrily to Chapman's death, and some wanted to run Mays out of baseball. They quickly backed down, realizing that such action would mean they were charging Mays with intentionally trying to harm Chapman.

Speaker had not yet left New York that afternoon when he was told of the action proposed by the Boston players and by others in the league. He chose not to comment on the matter.

"I am all broken up over Chappie's death," he said. "I can't talk. I can't do anything now, but I am convinced it was an accident. I will reply to the Boston players later."

Later in the day, Johnson received a telegram informing him of the threatened players' boycott against Mays. When asked by the writers how he would react to such a movement, Johnson was noncommittal.

"I will make no definite statement regarding Mays' future status until I have more complete and definite reports," he said.

When asked if there was any merit in the players' position, the league president was conspicuously silent.

51

That afternoon, Mays spoke with reporters for the first time since Chapman's death. Sitting in the living room of his apartment playing with his infant daughter, he appeared to have recovered from the initial shock of the news. He showed no signs of having suffered a breakdown, as had been rumored.

"If I were not absolutely sure in my own heart that it was an accident pure and simple I do not think that I could stand it," he said. "I always have had a horror of hitting a player ever since the accident to Chick Fewster. I chummed with him in the spring and I liked him very much. When he was hurt by a pitched ball it affected me so that I was afraid to pitch close to a batter.

"This fear affected my work. In the early part of the season I could not do my best. I kept them on the outside because whenever I felt that the ball was going close to a batter's head I saw a picture of poor Fewster lying beside the plate. I had to fight that down. I had to play the game."

Mays held his daughter in his lap and she "wrassled with his fingers." Like any proud father, he proclaimed his baby to be "the cutest kid in the world."

"Just like its mother," he added proudly.

He turned his thoughts back to baseball.

"As to my pitching in the future, I do not think that this thing will unnerve me. My conscience is absolutely clear. If it was not, I could not think of ever going near a baseball park again. It was an accident for which I am absolutely blameless."

If anyone was to blame for what happened, Mays noted, it was

umpire Connolly. Reiterating his charge that the ball was disfigured, Mays concluded: "It was the umpire's fault. A roughened spot
on the ball, sometimes even a scratch, will make a ball do queer
things. Umpires are instructed to throw out balls that have been
roughed."

52

On Wednesday morning, hundreds of people gathered
at Union Station in Cleveland to await the arrival of Chapman's
body. Across the city, flags hung limply at half-mast. It was ten
o'clock when the Lake Shore Limited finally pulled into the station,
more than an hour late. The crowd watched silently as Kathleen
stepped off the train and went directly to an automobile that was
waiting to take her to the Daly home. She was accompanied by her
father, who had joined the group at Utica, New York. The body
would be removed to an undertaker's morgue and in the afternoon
taken to the Daly house.

Speaker, who had been unable to sleep on the overnight train
ride, tried to hurry through the crowd, but he was surrounded by
reporters who wanted to know his reaction to the proposed boycott.

"I do not care to comment about any phase of the move against
Mays," he said as he continued walking. "I have left Jack MacCallister in charge of the team. I don't know when I will get back into
the game."

That afternoon, at the apartment he once had shared with
Chapman in the Hotel Winton, Speaker met with Dunn and Joe
Wood to discuss the ballclub's plight. Although he was overcome
with grief, Speaker knew it was imperative he help make plans to fill
the void on the team left by Chapman's loss.

Throughout the meeting, Speaker's eyes were red and moist, and there was a catch in his voice whenever he spoke. Much of the time, he sat disconsolate, with his head buried in his hands.

Bush's offer was dismissed out of hand because it was too far past the trading deadline to get approval for such a transfer. There was little choice but to hope that smooth-fielding, light-hitting reserve Harry Lunte could do the job at shortstop. The only other man on the team capable of playing the middle infield was outfielder Joe Evans, and he was suffering from an illness that threatened to keep him out of action for the remainder of the season.

There was one other possibility for help. Earlier in the summer, Cleveland had purchased an option on a young shortstop at New Orleans of the Southern Association. Although he was fresh out of college, the youngster was batting over .300 and fielding magnificently to spark the Pelicans to the top of the league standings. The player's name was Joe Sewell, although he still was being misidentified in most publications as "Sewall."

There was one catch. Pelicans manager Johnny Dobbs claimed his prized prospect was not subject to optional recall and would remain with New Orleans until the conclusion of the Southern Association season on September 18. Dunn would take steps to settle the dispute, but no one in the room was overly concerned with Sewell's status. Speaker was convinced the young ballplayer was too inexperienced to be of any immediate value to the Indians.

53

Mays's charges that umpire Tommy Connolly was to blame for the fatal beaning drew a swift and heated reaction from fellow umpires Billy Evans and Will Dineen. From Boston, where they were working the Red Sox–Tigers series, they issued a statement refuting the allegations. They even went so far as to place much of the blame for the revised pitching rules squarely on Mays's shoulders.

"No pitcher in the American League resorted to trickery more than Carl Mays in attempting to rough a ball to get a break on it which would make it more difficult to hit. Until the new pitching rules came into force which put a severe penalty on a pitcher roughing the ball, Mays constantly used to drag the ball across the pitching rubber to roughen the surface. Hundreds of balls were thrown out every year because of this act."

The two umpires pulled no punches in their statement. If a disfigured ball was in play at the time of the beaning, Evans and Dineen wanted it known where the fault lay.

"A short time ago, the club owners complained to President Johnson that too many balls were being thrown out. President Johnson sent out a bulletin telling the umpires to keep the balls in the games as much as possible except those which were dangerous."

Johnson had no response to the statement by the two umpires. Members of the Yankees' front office said they would have no reply to the umpires' charges that Mays roughed up the ball because "that has nothing to do with the present case."

*   *   *

The allegations by the two umpires only added fuel to the already raging debate over Mays's role in the unfortunate affair.

The New York papers were solidly behind the Yankee pitcher, echoing the sentiments of the *New York Tribune*'s W. O. McGeehan: "The splendid young man's death dwarfs considerations of pennant races and matters of that sort, but there is no reason why this other young man whose ill luck made him the innocent instrument of Ray Chapman's death should be a victim of the jealousies, intrigues and cruel short-sightedness of baseball politics.

"It is unfortunate for Mays that he has not been as popular as the dead player," added McGeehan, "but he must not be sacrificed because of his unpopularity."

But elsewhere, there were calls that Mays, as well as his underhand style of pitching, should be banned from the game.

Under the heading "Carl Mays Should Go!" the *Cleveland Press* claimed the Chapman beaning was proof "that Mays' pitching is dangerous to the safety of other players in the league. His control is so poor that it is a menace to the welfare of baseball."

The newspaper called upon Mays to voluntarily retire for the good of the game. "Unless he does this, he faces the slow soul-wringing process of being driven from it by public opinion and the resentment of fellow players."

H. C. Walker of the *Detroit Times* also condemned Mays and his methods. "This pitcher . . . has been accused of using the so-called bean ball. Players have distrusted him and many have grown to hate him because they feared him."

54

In the wake of the fatal beaning, baseball executives were forced to take a look at the safety of the game. Several club owners mentioned the possibility of equipping their players with headgear to be worn while batting. Magistrate F. X. McQuade, the treasurer of the New York Giants, said that sporting goods companies had been requested to offer various models, and the most suitable type would be adopted.

The headgear most likely would resemble the leather helmets first popularized by aviators and recently in vogue among football players.

Although the idea seemed to be far-fetched, the use of headgear did receive the endorsement of the *New York Times*.

Though the idea of headgear in baseball will sound strange to the fans, the adoption of such a form of protection will be following the trend of the sport to bring out at intervals protective devices that lessen the tendency to injury on the part of the player. When introduced the various devices invariably meet with some ridicule on the part of players who had gone through years of service without the protecting equipment, and from the fans as well, but in turn each additional bit of armor has come to be regarded as an essential.

When the big glove now in general use behind the bat was introduced it was ridiculed as a pillow. Up to the time of its adoption the catcher wore a skin tight glove with little padding in the palm, and some without fingers. The breast pad got a similar reception and the shin guards, when introduced at the Polo Grounds by Roger Bresnahan less than fifteen years ago, were ridiculed from one end of the major league circuit to the other.

The wisdom of all these appliances has been proved beyond question, and today no catcher would think of going into a game without all the equipment, since each plays its protective part against injury by a pitched or tipped ball. A headgear for batsmen, in view of the fatal accident of a few days ago, probably would not be ridiculed to the extent of the devices mentioned, though it would seem odd at first to the fan.

55

The twenty-four flags atop the grandstand at the Polo Grounds were flying at half-mast when the Indians, wearing mourning bands of black crepe on their left sleeves, dejectedly took the field Wednesday afternoon. The fans greeted them with polite but restrained applause.

The Yankees also wore mourning bands on their sleeves. Noticeably absent was Carl Mays.

During batting practice, Ruth hit a drive far over the outfield fence. The fans began to cheer loudly but quickly stopped themselves, as if such an outburst was not proper under the circumstances.

"There won't be any yelling here today," said one writer. "The gloom is thick enough to keep them quiet for once."

Lunte played shortstop, Jamieson was switched to center field to replace Speaker, and Graney started in left field for Cleveland. Wamby was moved up to second in the batting order.

Jack Quinn struck out Graney to start the game, bringing up Wamby, who was batting in Chapman's customary spot. The seventeen thousand fans grew silent, then clapped politely.

"The crowd vaguely tried to express the wish that the Cleveland team would not suffer by the loss of the dead player," wrote McGeehan in the *New York Tribune.*

Wamby grounded out to Pratt at second base.

The fans finally began to show some signs of spirit in the third inning when Lunte stepped to the plate and was greeted with loud applause.

In the fourth inning, with the Indians trailing 1–0, Wamby drove a single to center and came around to score the tying run on a single by Gardner.

One inning later, Bagby hit a one-out double. He went to third on Graney's groundout and scored on Wamby's triple off the right-field wall. Smith added a homer in the sixth, and the Indians led 3–1. The Yankees closed within a run in the seventh when Pipp singled in Lewis.

Bagby seemed to have matters well in hand as he nursed the one-run lead into the bottom of the ninth inning, prompting many of the fans to begin moving toward the exits.

"Glad to see them get it," said one spectator. "They deserve to win."

As he spoke, Lewis poked a one-out single to left field. Fewster was sent in as a pinch-runner and the hard-hitting Pipp stepped up to hit.

"Give us a hit, kid!" yelled one of the rooters, and the crowd began to come alive with excitement.

Pipp wasted no time responding to the pleas. He jumped on Bagby's first offering and sent the ball on a line toward the right-field corner. Smith got a good jump on the ball, but as he raced toward the foul line he realized he would not be able to catch up with it. He saw it hit the right-field gate and take a crazy bounce into the corner. As the crowd roared, Smith frantically chased the ball. Finally, he caught up with it and turned to peg it toward the infield. By now, Fewster had scored the tying run and Pipp was barreling around second base. Smith quickly fired the ball to Jamieson, who had come over from center field to relay the throw home. It was a good, hard throw and for a moment Smith thought they might be able to prevent Pipp from scoring. But in his haste to make the relay, Jamieson let the ball get away from him and Pipp, who had not slowed down in his mad dash around the bases, crossed the plate standing up. It was an inside-the-park homer, giving the Yankees a dramatic 4–3 victory.

Hats were tossed in the air and the fans joyously hugged one another in ecstasy. Recording the moment for the *Plain Dealer,* William Slavens McNutt wrote: "A savage roar of triumph, untempered by any remembrance of the dead, went up from the crowd." As far as the New York fans were concerned, the mourning officially had ended.

*   *   *

The return to normalcy at the Polo Grounds was re-emphasized on Thursday when Huggins was ejected from the premises by Connolly. The New York manager had become upset in the second inning when Shawkey was unable to field a ground ball back to the mound because O'Neill's bat slipped from his hands and flew onto the field after he hit the ball. Huggins wanted interference called on the play, and when he persisted in arguing his case Connolly tossed him out of the game.

In the fourth inning, Ruth hit a shot over the top of the right-field stands and into Manhattan Field for his forty-third home run of the season. Amid the celebrating touched off by the homer, Theodore Sturm, who was sitting in the box back of third base, collapsed and died of heart failure. Most of those in attendance at the game were not even aware of the commotion in the stands surrounding the stricken man.

Despite Ruth's home run, the Indians hung on for a 3–2 victory behind the five-hit pitching of Slim Caldwell. In addition to Caldwell's strong showing, the Clevelanders were boosted by the play of Lunte. Chapman's replacement not only was impressive in the field, he also contributed two hits to the cause.

But the Indians were in no mood to celebrate the victory. Following the game, they immediately boarded a train to return to Cleveland for Chapman's funeral the next day. The unscheduled trip home at Dunn's expense had been made possible by Red Sox owner Harry Frazee, who had agreed to postpone the Indians' game in Boston on Friday, rescheduling it as part of a doubleheader on Monday.

56

No one had been more devastated by Chapman's death than Graney. On Wednesday, upon viewing his friend's body at the hospital, he had broken down sobbing and had to be forcibly removed from the room.

On Friday, Graney and the other ballplayers arrived at the Daly residence before the funeral. As the players filed past the casket to pay their respects to their deceased teammate, Graney fainted. So, too, did O'Neill. The emotions of the past days were taking their toll on the Indians. Secretary Walter McNichols had collapsed from grief and exhaustion the night before as the team was preparing to leave New York.

That morning, as thousands gathered at St. John's Roman Catholic Cathedral for the funeral services, Graney and Speaker were conspicuously absent. It was reported that Graney was too distraught to attend, and that former Cleveland star Nap Lajoie had driven him out into the countryside in an effort to calm him. Speaker remained in bed at the Daly residence, reportedly under the care of a physician after suffering a nervous breakdown.

But among themselves, the Cleveland ballplayers were telling a far different story. There had been a disagreement over where Chapman's funeral services should be held. Kathleen, a Catholic, had wanted a Catholic ceremony. She indicated that before his death, Chapman had made plans to join the Catholic church. And at the funeral services the Reverend Scullen would refer to the ballplayer's dramatic deathbed conversion. However, Chapman's parents, who were Protestants, were unaware of such plans. They preferred a Protestant service. The Cleveland players had taken sides in the dispute, leading to hard feelings. Significantly, Chapman would be buried at Lake View Cemetery in Cleveland, not in the Daly family plot at Calvary Cemetery.

Graney and O'Neill, both Catholics, and Speaker, a Protestant, apparently were the most outspoken in the dispute over the services. It was the common belief among the other players that these feelings led to a fight pitting Speaker against Graney or O'Neill or possibly both players. That alleged fight, the players believed, was the cause for the absence of Speaker and Graney from the funeral. And although O'Neill was able to attend the funeral, his playing status for the next few days was affected by what was reported in the newspapers as "a slightly bruised right hand."

Bob McDermott, who lived in the boarding house where many of the players stayed, claimed to have witnessed the confrontation between Speaker and O'Neill. Later, he stated: "I saw the fight. Speaker picked O'Neill to pieces. With all the facial punishment Steve took, I was surprised he could catch the next day."

Years later, Wambsganss added credence to McDermott's claim. Although none of the players involved would talk about the incident, Wamby said it was common knowledge on the team that Speaker fought with Graney and O'Neill over the funeral arrangements.

"Speaker was a very bigoted man at the time," Wamby recalled. "He was a 32nd degree Mason of the South. And he couldn't see the idea of Chapman being buried in the Cathedral.

"I think there was quite an argument about it between him and Graney and O'Neill. And they really knocked the hell out of him. He couldn't see to play ball—didn't show up for one day on account of the marks on his face.

"I asked Jack Graney about it point blank one time. He looked at me, and he kind of laughed and said, 'No, Bill, that never happened.' But I knew damn well it did."

57

Much to his displeasure, Ban Johnson once again found himself being swept into a controversy centered on Carl Mays. On Thursday, August 19, he had publicly stated that in his opinion Mays "is greatly affected and may never be capable temperamentally of pitching again." At the very least, he felt, because of the bitterness directed at Mays by rival players "it would be inadvisable for him to attempt to pitch this year at any rate."

Boston's Frazee, one of Johnson's antagonists, had been quick to denounce the league president.

"If Mr. Johnson is quoted correctly, I consider his statement ill advised regarding the Mays-Chapman unfortunate tragedy without first ascertaining the facts and consulting the owners of the American League, whose interests if any are involved."

Johnson also was under attack by New York's Ruppert and Huston, who disputed his notion that Mays was either incapable of pitching or poorly advised to do so.

"Mays, while bowed down with grief, is not a broken reed," said the Yankee colonels in a statement. "He will go along and follow his regular means of livelihood as a strong man should. He will take his regular turn in the pitcher's box and we expect him to win games as usual. If he requires protection he will receive it from us to the extreme limit, no matter where that may lead."

On Saturday, Frazee called for a special league meeting to discuss the matter. Johnson had no choice but to grant the request. He announced he would meet with the owners in Philadelphia in three days.

58

After their second all-night train ride in two days, the Indians arrived in Boston at 1:30 Saturday afternoon. The events of the past few days, plus the exhausting travel schedule, had left the players drained, both mentally and physically.

Within an hour of their arrival, the Clevelanders were in uniform for a doubleheader at Fenway Park. When they walked onto the field for their warm-ups, they were given an extended ovation by the seventeen thousand fans on hand. Speaker still was not with the team, and Joe Wood had been appointed to serve as manager.

Graney, who had recovered sufficiently to make the trip, was cheered loudly as he stepped in to lead off the game. Like many of the Indians, he performed as if he were in a daze. He went hitless in four at-bats and committed an error in the field before he finally was removed by Wood, who put himself in left field.

Lunte also was cheered each time he batted, but he too was ineffective. He was hitless in six tries.

After dominating the Red Sox all season, the spiritless Indians managed a total of only six hits in the two games. They lost by scores of 12–0 and 4–0.

The White Sox, who had moved into first place by percentage points on the afternoon of Chapman's funeral, won in Washington

5–2 to increase their lead to 1½ games over the Indians. While Cleveland was showing signs of collapsing, Chicago had won eleven of its past thirteen games.

59

Mays had dropped out of public sight, choosing to remain secluded in his home with Freddie and the baby. He did not go to the ballpark, nor did he appear in traffic court on Friday to pay his fine for the speeding ticket he had received a month earlier.

Yet he was not isolated from the outside world and what others were saying about him. He was aware of the conspiracy against him among the other players, and he read Johnson's statement questioning his well-being. He also received an abundance of letters. Most, he claimed, were supportive. Others were vicious in their condemnation of him. Mays would never forget those letters: they "were malicious, even threatening in tone, from people whom I never saw or even heard of.

"It is no doubt a very courageous thing to write such a letter," he added sarcastically, "and I admire the manhood of the person who could do it."

On Saturday, Mays finally ended his seclusion. He chose to do so before the Yankees' game with the Detroit Tigers. He arrived at the Polo Grounds early and put on his uniform for the first time since the beaning. When he went onto the field, there already were several thousand fans in the stands. They cheered him loudly while he warmed up near the center-field fence. Afterward, well before it was time for the game to start, Mays retired to the clubhouse. He quickly changed clothes and left the stadium to await his next scheduled pitching assignment. Huggins had informed him he would start on Monday.

*   *   *

Ty Cobb spent Saturday morning lying in his room at the Commodore Hotel in New York, weak and dizzy from a bout with the flu. His temperature had climbed to 102 degrees, and newspaperman Grantland Rice, who had come to visit the ballplayer, urged him to call a doctor. Cobb refused. As sick as he was, he was more concerned with newspaper reports quoting him as saying Mays should be run out of the league. The stories had put Cobb squarely in the center of the Mays controversy, and he wasn't happy about it. It was no secret that Cobb disliked Mays, and he would write in his autobiography in 1961, "I dodged a lot of them from him which gave me dark suspicions." Nonetheless, Cobb was adamant in his insistence he had made no statements against Mays following the Chapman beaning.

According to Cobb, he had received a telephone call in Boston from a man identifying himself as a reporter.

"Did you hear what happened in the Yankee-Cleveland game today?" asked the caller.

"No, I didn't," replied Cobb.

"Ray Chapman was hit on the head by Carl Mays, and he may not live. There's a lot of feeling over this. The Washington club has stated that it won't play the Yankees again while Mays is pitching. They claim he throws at batters deliberately. Cleveland says it'll boycott Mays, too. I'd like to ask you—what about Detroit?"

"Just who are you?" Cobb asked warily. "Who do you represent?"

The man repeated his name and claimed to be a reporter with the United Press Association. Only then did Cobb agree to talk.

"Well, I'm only a member of the Detroit team. I don't own the club and I don't set the policy."

"What about Mays?" insisted the reporter. "What do you think of his beaning Chapman?"

"I'm here in Boston. I didn't see the accident. I know nothing of how it happened and under no circumstances would I comment on it. Even if I'd been there, I doubt that I could have commented."

Cobb claimed that was the end of the conversation. Only when he arrived in New York did he learn that he had been accused of calling for retaliation against Mays. Whether the stories were true or not did not matter at the moment. They had made Cobb the focal point for New Yorkers' resentment against the anti-Mays sentiment sweeping baseball. Consequently, he knew if he did not show up at the Polo Grounds that afternoon to face the New York fans, it would look as if he were backing down from a confrontation. For Cobb, that would be unthinkable. No matter how ill he might be, he knew he could not afford to miss this ballgame.

When Detroit's Hughie Jennings came to the room to check on him, Cobb assured the manager he would be able to play. His only concession to his weakened condition would be to skip pregame practice.

"Let them think I've done a run-out if they want to," he told Jennings.

The atmosphere in the Polo Grounds that afternoon was highly charged. The brief appearance by Mays during warm-ups only added to the emotions. The Yankees were just finishing infield drills and the stands were almost full when Cobb finally made his entrance. He did so in typically dramatic style. He came through the big gate in right field and stepped onto the field in full view of the thirty thousand fans. They recognized him immediately and greeted him with angry boos and hisses, which rose in intensity as he slowly and defiantly walked toward the infield. Before joining his teammates in the dugout, Cobb chose to openly confront the fans. He walked past second base, pushed aside the Yankee pitcher, and made his way to home plate as the curses and jeers rained down on him. Facing the crowd, he swept his hand from the first-base stands all the way around the park. Then he motioned toward the press area to signal that the newspapermen sitting there were the ones to blame for all the hostility aimed at him. Taking a few steps forward, Cobb doffed his cap and bowed majestically to the writers. The fans were unappeased by the gesture. They screamed even louder. According to the newspapermen present, it was the most hostile demonstration ever witnessed at the ballpark.

The crowd's anger was not yet spent. For the rest of the afternoon, the fans booed and hissed whenever Cobb stepped to the plate, took his position in the field, or caught a fly ball. He responded with one hit and one run in four at-bats as the Tigers pounded out a 10–3 victory.

The hostility of the crowd had shaken even the hard-bitten Cobb. He called it the most fearful riding he ever had received. He also reiterated his assertion that he had made no statements critical of Mays and claimed that he had been used as "a smoke screen" by those who had a grudge against the pitcher.

"I won't make any alibis," said Cobb. "No crowds can frighten me, but this is all untrue."

60

Speaker was a robust man, with broad shoulders and a solid 193 pounds spread over his five-foot, eleven-inch frame. But as he left the Daly house on Sunday evening to catch an overnight train to Boston, the effects of Chapman's death and the resulting turmoil had taken their toll on him. His shoulders sagged and he had lost around fifteen pounds. The lines in his face appeared deeper and his pace had slowed considerably. Nonetheless, he felt it was time to rejoin his team.

The Indians had been off that afternoon, but were scheduled to play a doubleheader in Boston on Monday. Meanwhile, the Yankees had dropped an 11–9 decision to the Tigers, who had been sparked by Cobb's five hits, two runs batted in, and two runs scored.

By the time Speaker arrived in Boston on Monday, it was midday and the first game of a doubleheader between the Indians and Red Sox already had begun. A crowd of twelve thousand, boosted by the Shriners and their band, was on hand at Fenway Park.

The Red Sox were batting in the bottom of the second inning

when Speaker, clad in his civilian clothes, emerged from the clubhouse door and began walking toward the Indians' dugout. Speaker still was a favorite in Boston, and the fans who saw him cheered loudly. Just as he arrived at the dugout, Speaker looked up to see Stuffy McInnis hit a high fly toward Graney, who circled unsteadily and was unable to draw a bead on the ball. At the last moment, Jamieson raced over from center field to make the catch. Speaker immediately sent Joe Wood into left field for Graney, who trotted off the field with his head down.

During the game, Spoke went back to the dressing room and put on his uniform, but when he returned he remained on the bench. In the ninth inning, with Cleveland clinging to a 2–1 lead, he finally put himself in the game as a pinch-hitter for O'Neill, who was hampered by his sore right hand. After a rousing reception from the fans, Speaker lofted an easy pop-up to McInnis at first base.

In the bottom of the inning, Slim Caldwell retired the Red Sox to complete a five-hitter and give the Indians a much-needed victory. Curiously, in his first game back with the team, Speaker removed from the lineup both Graney and O'Neill—the two players he allegedly had fought.

O'Neill was back behind the plate for the second game, but Graney remained on the bench. Speaker also stayed on the sidelines, leaving Jamieson in center field. Spoke finally replaced Wood late in the contest, but he failed to get a hit in two times up and then removed himself for Joe Evans. Cleveland lost 4–3 in thirteen innings. Surprisingly, one of the few players who had hit the ball well in the two games was Lunte. He had three hits in eight at-bats.

61

Before leaving for the Polo Grounds the morning of Monday, August 23, Mays paused to reread a letter he had received from his uncle Pierce in Portland. The letter concluded with the following statement: "Carl, you are on the toughest spot of your life right now. If you can pitch your way off this one, you're good."

As he prepared to make his return to the pitching mound, Mays was determined to let the baseball world know just how good he really was. It had been exactly one week since the fatal beaning when he put on his uniform and walked onto the field to begin warming up for his return to action. The support of the New York fans was evident by the vocal reception Mays received when he appeared in front of the grandstand for his initial warm-up pitches.

After loosening up, Mays returned to the clubhouse for the final time before the start of the game. He was lacing his shoes when the clubhouse boy approached him.

"I've got a note for you," the boy said.

Mays took the piece of paper and glanced at it. On it was a crudely printed message.

"You say Cobb gave this to you?"

"Yes, sir. I was on the dugout steps watching batting practice when he came over, handed the note to me, and asked me to pin it on your locker door."

Mays looked back at the note and reread the words:

> If it was within my power, I would have inscribed on Ray Chapman's tombstone these words: "Here lies a victim of arrogance, viciousness and greed."

Mays slowly tore up the paper and let the pieces fall to the floor. Then he bent down and continued tying his shoes.

When he walked to the mound and was announced as the starting pitcher, Mays received another loud ovation from the fans. The cheering soon gave way to nervous anticipation as the spectators waited to see whether the Detroit ballplayers would follow through on their boycott threats. The answer was provided by Tigers leadoff hitter Ralph Young, who stepped to the plate without the hint of a protest. Mays immediately whipped a strike past him, touching off a wild round of cheers.

Although he did not give up any runs in those early innings, Mays's nervousness was evident. Twice, he threw curveballs he was afraid weren't going to break properly. Both times, he shouted to the batter, "Look out!" He was in trouble throughout the game, and in all the Tigers would rough him up for ten hits and three walks. Somehow, he managed to escape every jam.

Meanwhile, the Yankees were piling up the runs. At the end of six innings, they led 9–0 and the fans turned their complete attention to Mays's pitching. Supported by cries of "Shut them out!" he struggled through those final three innings without allowing a Detroit runner to cross the plate. The final score was 10–0, and after the last out the fans rushed onto the field to congratulate Mays.

As he made his way off the field, the smiling Mays shook every hand that was offered him. It was perhaps his greatest moment of triumph. He had served notice he still was capable of pitching, no matter what Ban Johnson or others might think.

62

Rather than put an end to the talk of a boycott, Mays's return to the mound only served to rekindle the movement. Once again, the impetus came from Boston, where the Indians were headquartered when they received word of Mays's victory over the Tigers. The Cleveland ballplayers wasted no time in reacting to the news.

Already, they had been upset that Mays had been on the field warming up so soon after Chapman's funeral. They pointed to that as evidence the pitcher was "hardboiled." Mays's failure to offer his condolences to Chapman's widow also was proof to them the pitcher had not shown sufficient remorse over the beaning.

A story reported by Melville E. Webb, Jr., in the Monday-morning edition of the *Boston Globe* further fanned the flames. According to Webb, Mays and Chapman had exchanged heated words in a game "some time ago, and it has been said that Chapman told Mays in a recent game that he intended to bunt and suggested that Carl cover first base."

Whether the Indians believed Mays intentionally threw at Chapman was difficult to ascertain. Immediately after the beaning, most of their complaints against Mays had been directed at his style of pitching rather than his motives. Now, however, their feelings had hardened. Joe Williams of the *Cleveland News* polled the team and reported, "The players' verdict was unanimous: Mays had deliberately fired at Chapman's head."

On Monday evening, spurred by the news of Mays's shutout of Detroit, the Cleveland players took the first step toward driving the pitcher from the league. They drafted a "round-robin" letter to be circulated to the other American League teams, excluding New York. The letter was a plea to the players in the league "to refuse to participate in any games where Mays was assigned to pitch."

One by one, the Cleveland players signed their names to the petition. Every member of the team except Speaker placed his signature on the document.

*   *   *

Speaker still was showing no signs of emerging from his deep depression. When he was not at the ballfield, he spent most of his time alone in his hotel room. Those around him made efforts to talk to him and to cheer him up, all to no avail. His closest friends on the team, Wood and Gardner, were having increasing worries about his health.

Before the game on Tuesday, Speaker took only a few token swings at the ball in batting practice and then walked off the field complaining of dizzy spells. "I'm having trouble seeing the ball," he told Wood.

Once again, Speaker kept himself out of the lineup for most of the game. It was not until the ninth inning that he pinch-hit for Lunte, and he singled for his first hit since rejoining the team. It was to no avail. The Indians lost 7–2 as Bob Clark was rocked for thirteen hits by the Red Sox. One of the two Cleveland runs was scored by Graney, who had returned to the lineup and showed signs of coming around with one hit in four at-bats.

Watching the halfhearted effort, the *Globe*'s Webb noted sadly, "Without Speaker going in the lineup, the club surely is all at sea."

On Wednesday, Speaker put himself back in the lineup in Philadelphia. Hitless in two at-bats, he walked to lead off the ninth inning with the Indians trailing the lowly Athletics 2–1. The next batter, Smith, attempted a bunt in order to move Speaker into scoring position. The ball skidded down the third-base line a few feet from the plate, and Smith, thinking it was foul, remained standing in the batter's box. But catcher Cy Perkins, hearing no call from umpire Hildebrand, quickly grabbed the ball and pegged it to second base for the forceout on the sliding Speaker. With Smith still standing at the plate, the Athletics needed only to lob the ball over to first to complete the double play.

That was all it took to set off Speaker. He leaped up from second and raced toward the plate screaming at Hildebrand. For a full ten minutes he shouted at the umpire in a violent fit of rage. Wood rushed to Speaker's side to join in if a fight broke out, but Hildebrand refused to react to the outburst. Knowing the strain Speaker had been under since Chapman's death, he stood by patiently while fellow umpire George Moriarty attempted to calm the Cleveland manager. Finally, Speaker returned to the bench and sat down, still shaking from anger and frustration as Gardner was retired for the final out, sending the Indians to their sixth loss in the past eight games. The other players in the dugout sat there awkwardly, too afraid to speak. They had never seen their manager come so close to snapping before.

*   *   *

Ban Johnson had concluded the league meeting in Philadelphia on Tuesday confident that he had weathered another crisis. The owners had spent most of their time discussing the possibility of the Yankees building their own stadium in New York. Colonel Ruppert stated that his team had been told by the Giants it no longer would be a welcome tenant in the Polo Grounds following the 1921 season. It was agreed the Yankees would begin making plans for a home of their own. During the meeting, the only official mention of the Chapman beaning was the naming of a committee of three to draft a suitable resolution to be presented to Chapman's widow commemorating the ballplayer's service to the league.

Johnson still was in Philadelphia on Thursday, August 26, clearing up some business when he was given a document to read. It was a copy of the petition being circulated by the Indians calling for a boycott against Mays. For more than a week, the league president had refused to react to any talk of retaliation against the New York pitcher. Now, Johnson had no choice but to take action to head off the movement. He immediately got on the telephone to find out just how far the proposed boycott had progressed. Over the next few hours, he was able to piece together the following information.

At least two teams, the Browns and the Senators, had agreed to support the Indians in the movement. The Tigers and Red Sox also were bitterly antagonistic toward Mays but were waiting to see signs the boycott was in effect before they joined. Connie Mack had prevented any retaliation by the Athletics, and he was steadfast in his conviction that the fatal beaning of Chapman was an accident. The White Sox, who were in New York to play the Yankees, were taking a similar stance.

As much as he disliked Mays, Johnson could not allow the boycott to go into effect. He met with Speaker before the Indians' game in Philadelphia and was assured the Cleveland manager knew nothing of the petition being circulated by his players. Johnson emphasized that regardless of how the players might feel toward Mays, they could not attempt to take any action against him. Speaker agreed to do what was necessary to head off the boycott.

Cleveland secretary Walter McNichols confirmed that neither Speaker nor any team officials were aware of the movement under way on the ballclub.

"This action was taken unknown to me," said McNichols. "I knew nothing about it until this morning. Then I was told by some of the players that they had decided never to play in any game against Mays.

"I want you to understand that Tris Speaker had nothing to do with this. He, too, knew nothing of the meeting of the players nor their action. This thing was born in the midst of the players and developed by them alone."

While the Indians were in the process of dropping a 3–2 decision to Philadelphia pitcher Three-Finger Keefe that afternoon—marking their seventh loss in nine games—Johnson sent word throughout the league that any team refusing to bat against Mays would face a forfeit of the game and a thousand-dollar fine.

James Isaminger of the *Philadelphia North American* was among the first newsmen to get wind of the petition and Johnson's reaction to it. While admitting the prospects were remote that such a boycott would be enacted, Isaminger did not believe Mays was off the hook yet. "The feeling against Mays will exist and he may find himself 'a man without a country' from a baseball standpoint. Certainly no such action has ever before been taken by players against a brother player."

63

Kid Gleason, Chicago's pugnacious little manager, had little sympathy for those who talked of boycotts and Mays's unfair pitching tactics. Gleason had spent eight years of his twenty-two-year playing career in the big leagues as a pitcher, winning 134 games. He played the infield the rest of the time, so he had been on both sides of the battle. He knew what it took to survive as a pitcher and as a hitter.

When the first-place White Sox arrived in New York to open a three-game series on Thursday, Gleason wanted it known his players would face Mays or any other pitcher the Yankees chose to throw against them.

"The ballclub that determines not to play against Mays lacks courage," he said contemptuously. "To me it appears as if they are afraid to oppose him. My ballclub does not look at it in that light. We will face Mays any and every time he pitches.

"We have never had any trouble with him. He has attempted to drive some of my players back from the plate when he thought they were getting a toehold. That is part of the game. I used to do it when I was pitching, and every good pitcher does it. Therefore, I contend Mays hitting Chapman was accidental pure and simple, and there is no reason why any move should be made to boycott him."

The White Sox did not have to wait long before backing up their manager's words. Mays started the second game of the series Friday afternoon before more than fifteen thousand fans. Gleason, anxious to improve on his team's 3½-game lead over the Indians and four-game advantage on the Yankees, countered with his ace, Eddie

Cicotte. As the game was about to begin, a reporter asked Colonel Ruppert for his reaction to the proposed boycott. The Yankee owner defiantly pointed to the mound, where Mays was completing his final warm-up tosses.

"There is our answer. Mays is pitching and will continue to pitch in his regular turn."

In the first few innings, it was difficult to determine who was more nervous, Mays or the White Sox. Mays was so fearful of hitting a batter, he did not dare throw a pitch above a batter's waist until he had gained complete confidence in his control. For their part, the Chicago players appeared tentative at the plate. Finally, Gleason called them together in the dugout.

"Just go in there and hit," he said. "You know one thing is certain—Mays isn't going to hit anybody."

Meanwhile, the Yankees' cause was not being helped by the absence of Ruth. The young slugger recently had signed to star in a movie titled *Safe at Home,* and during breaks in the Yankees' schedule he had been traveling to Haverstraw, New York, for filming of the picture. A few days earlier, something had bitten Ruth on the arm, causing it to swell. "The chiggers nipped me on the left arm," explained Babe, who was forced to sit out at this crucial stage of the pennant race. Midway through the game, Ruth decided he needed to seek medical attention for his sore arm. Honoring the Babe's request, the public-address announcer pointed his megaphone at the left-field stands, where Ruth's chauffeur was sitting. The PA man called out that the Babe wanted his car to take him to the doctor, and the fans greeted the announcement with cheers and laughter.

Even without Ruth's bat in the lineup, the Yankees took a 4–3 lead heading into the ninth inning. Then the White Sox pushed across a run against Mays to send the game into extra innings. They scored again in the tenth, and Huggins finally lifted his pitcher. Mays sat on the bench and watched as New York tied the score in the bottom of the tenth and went on to win 6–5 in twelve innings.

*   *   *

In Philadelphia, the Indians' batting attack finally came to life with twenty-one hits in a 15–3 victory over the Athletics. Harry Lunte got the rout started with a two-run single, and he finished the day with three hits.

"Our slump has come to an end," proclaimed Speaker, who also had three hits. "It had to end some time and now that we have it out of our system, watch us go. The boys have recovered their spirit and are playing smart baseball."

64

Mays now had successfully pitched against two teams, the Tigers and White Sox, without incident. On Sunday, August 29, he would face his toughest test to date. The St. Louis Browns, who had been among the most outspoken critics of Mays and his methods, were scheduled to play the Yankees in the Polo Grounds.

Before leaving their hotel for the ballpark, the St. Louis players met to determine their course of action should Mays be brought in to pitch. The Browns' dislike of Mays was so intense that almost to a man they were ready to defy Johnson's edict and refuse to face the submarine pitcher. Then someone—either one of the players or a team official—stood up and argued for a less militant stand.

"This is Cleveland's fight," he said. "Let them take the lead."

Reluctantly, the St. Louis players agreed.

It would be more than a week later before one of the Browns revealed to reporter Ross Tenney just how close the team had come to enacting the boycott before choosing to back down. At the time, neither the overflow crowd of thirty-five thousand on hand at the Polo Grounds nor the New York players knew just what course of action the Browns would follow. The mood of the New Yorkers was angry, and the appearance of the Browns had created so much interest another fifteen thousand fans had to be turned away at the gates.

Huggins started Jack Quinn, who, with the help of some outstanding fielding support, carried a 2–0 lead into the sixth inning. Then the rain began falling. Although he was one of the licensed spitball pitchers in the league, Quinn lost his effectiveness when the ball became too soggy in wet weather. With one out, a triple and three consecutive singles tied the score and forced Huggins to pull his starter. As the crowd roared with anticipation, Mays was signaled in from the bullpen.

Everyone in the ballpark stood to see what the reaction of the Browns would be. The next scheduled batter was St. Louis pitcher Urban Shocker, who returned to the dugout to watch as Mays completed his warm-up tosses. When the umpire signaled for play to resume, Shocker glanced back at his teammates before walking slowly to the plate. Seeing him do so, the fans shouted their approval and in the New York dugout even Huggins couldn't help but smile as he looked across the field to see the sullen looks on the faces of the St. Louis players. They had been forced to back down. The boycott was dead. There could be no doubt of that now.

Mays, however, had no time to celebrate. Shocker chopped the ball toward shortstop and Peckinpaugh bobbled it for an error. There still was only one out, and the bases were loaded for leadoff hitter Wally Gerber. He promptly hit a line shot into left field. It looked like a sure single, but Duffy Lewis charged the ball, grabbed it on one hop, and quickly fired it home. Jack Tobin, who had gotten a late jump starting from third base, was startled to look up and see catcher Muddy Ruel field the throw in time for the forceout. The bases still were loaded, but now there were two outs.

The next batter was Joe Gedeon, a pesky hitter who was tough with men on base. He rapped a sharp grounder to third base, right at Aaron Ward. It should have been the final out of the inning, but Ward misjudged the last hop, letting the ball bounce off his shoe and into left field. Hank Severeid easily scored the go-ahead run and Shocker charged around third and tried to follow him home. But Lewis alertly backed up the play and made another strong throw to the plate. Ruel caught the ball and slammed it hard into the sliding Shocker for the out, pinning him in the mud in the process. The Browns led 3–2, but the crowd cheered Mays's pitching and Lewis's outstanding defensive play.

It was raining hard now, but hardly anyone moved for cover. In the seventh, Bodie led off with a double. One out later, the rain got so bad play had to be halted. Forty-five minutes later, the teams were back at it. Ruel grounded out, moving Bodie, who represented the tying run, to third base. Mays received a sustained ovation when he stepped in to bat for himself. He responded to the cheers by slicing a wicked shot toward first base, where the ball bounced up and struck George Sisler on the cheek, knocking him to the ground as Bodie scored to tie the game 3–3.

It stayed that way until the bottom of the ninth, when Lewis led off with an infield hit and moved to second on Bodie's sacrifice. Ward then atoned for his earlier error by doubling off the right-field wall to score Lewis with the game winner. Mays not only had backed down the Browns, he had beaten them for his twentieth victory of the season.

*   *   *

That same afternoon, the Indians were in Washington. When they walked into their dressing quarters, there was a chalk-written message crudely scribbled in foot-high letters across the lockers: "Mays the Murderer."

When he heard about the sign, Senators owner Clark Griffith had it erased. On the field, the Indians lost 3–2 to fall below the Yankees into third place.

The next day, the same words were written across the lockers. Again, Griffith had them removed. Months later, the Cleveland players learned that the message had been written by the clubhouse boy.

65

Speaker watched as a hard-throwing rookie southpaw pitched on the sidelines in Washington on Wednesday. The newcomer's name was Walter Mails, an eccentric character who had been purchased from the Sacramento club of the Pacific Coast League for the stiff price of thirty-five thousand dollars.

Mails's nickname was "Duster," a reference to his tendency to dust off the batters at the plate. He claimed it was an unfair tag because it was his wildness and not his meanness that caused him to knock down hitters. Mails's brief stint with the Brooklyn Dodgers in 1916 seemed to verify this.

"Anybody who stood up to the plate when I was pitching at Brooklyn was in danger, I will admit that," he said. "I was very apt to hit him if he didn't move and move quickly. But I was just as apt to put the ball ten feet away from him where he couldn't reach it with a broomstick.

"I didn't deliberately try to dust them off. I simply couldn't make the ball go where I wanted it to go. Any batter who faced me then did so at his own risk. But I was wild, not from choice, but because I couldn't help myself."

Mails was a cocky, unpredictable fellow who preferred to be called "The Great Mails." To him, the ball was an "apple" and the plate was the "pan." He had been born at San Quentin, California, the site of the notorious prison, and he liked to boast of the times he ventured inside the prison yards to play against a team of inmates. "It must be a tough life in one of those big prisons, and a baseball game is about the best thing they have," he mused. "They would put a pretty tolerable team on the field, too, all things considered, although we usually had no trouble in defeating them."

The Great Mails broke into organized ball with Seattle in 1915, and five months later he was signed by Brooklyn. When the Robins gave up on him, he was picked up by the Pittsburgh Pirates, who sent him out to Portland, Oregon. After spending two years in the service during the Great War, he refused to return to Portland and his contract was sold to Seattle. There, he used to tell the manager how to run the team, a trait that prompted the newspapermen to refer to him as the "chesty southpaw." Mails was big and good-looking, and at a Ladies Day game once, he caught the eye of a group of women. "Yoo-hoo, Walter!" they called out in an effort to gain his attention. Looking over at the ladies, he shouted back: "Why don't you girls go home and wash the dirty dishes you left in the sink? And another thing! Stop feeding your husbands from tin cans!"

In 1920, Mails ended up in Sacramento, where he finally displayed some control to go with his overpowering fastball and his wicked curve. The day after Chapman's funeral, the Indians purchased him in the hope he would be the front-line left-hander they had been seeking for so long.

His first test would come in Washington, where he warmed up under Speaker's watchful eye. When Mails finished loosening up, he asked his manager to go over the weaknesses of the Washington batters.

"Forget the hitters," answered Speaker. "Just throw the ball over the plate, and you'll never lose a game."

It was good advice, but Mails was unable to put it into effect. Despite all his cockiness and bluster, he turned out to be so high-strung and nervous that day he couldn't gain control of his pitches. He never made it out of the second inning before Speaker had to replace him with Guy Morton. Mails at least could take some solace in the fact the Indians rallied to win the game 9–5. He also received a pat on the back from Ross Tenney, who reminded his readers, "Give this bird Mails a real chance and he's likely to prove all that his advance notices from the Pacific shore would indicate."

Despite the inauspicious debut of their prize recruit, the Cleve-landers still had reason to celebrate that night. That same afternoon, the White Sox lost for the sixth time in their past seven games to fall out of the lead. For the first time in twelve days, the Indians were back in first place as they prepared to return to Cleveland for a twenty-one-game home stand. Even the news that Mays had beaten the Browns 3–0 on a four-hit shutout that afternoon could not spoil the mood.

Speaker, who was showing signs of regaining his spirit, was convinced his team had turned the corner in its effort to recover from the terrible shock of Chapman's death. The next day, a by-lined article by the manager appeared in the *Cleveland News*. In it, Speaker repeated his vow that the Indians would win the pennant.

> The boys had a tough time of it getting squared away following Chapman's death. It was the hardest battle I ever had in my life to overcome my grief and all of the boys felt the same way about it. But we realized that all our tears and heartaches couldn't bring dear Ray back, and we just pulled ourselves together with that which was ever uppermost in Chappie's mind—the pennant and world's championship—as our goal.

66

On Friday, September 3, a lone bugler walked to the infield at League Park. In the stands, fifteen thousand fans watched silently, their heads bared. On the playing field, the members of the Cleveland and Detroit ballclubs stood at attention. The sailor lifted the bugle to his lips and began to play taps. He was a member of the Cleveland naval reserves, which was Chapman's old unit, and he stood at shortstop, which was Chapman's old position. The strains of the bugle echoed throughout the ballpark, and several of the men in the crowd could be seen crying. Many of Chapman's teammates wiped tears from their eyes. Inside the Indians' clubhouse, a Cleveland uniform with faint black stripes on a white background hung loosely in a locker. At the bottom of the stall was a muddy pair of shoes. On the top shelf was a hat with "Chappie" written across the sweatband. No one had bothered to remove Chapman's uniform, and his teammates had left the locker untouched as a memorial to their friend.

This was the Indians' first game in their home park since the beaning, and it had been declared Ray Chapman Memorial Day in Cleveland. Jim Dunn had commemorated the occasion by distributing a twelve-page booklet in memory of the ballplayer. Included were tributes written by Chapman's widow and his newspaper friend, Ed Bang. In her testimonial to her husband, Kathleen had closed with these words: "To me, the greatest praise that can be given is that he so lived as to cause only happiness and smiles. Therefore let us remember him as he would wish, without tears. Let us think of him, with a laugh at the memory of some joy, a smile at all times, and a deep prayer of thanksgiving that it was given us to have known him—to have his memory to lighten the gray days—and let us keep that memory fresh and sweet with a brave heart and a smile, for 'Chappie' loved both."

There also had been a hundred-member choir, which sang "Lead Kindly Light," one of Chapman's favorite songs.

When the Indians ran onto the field to begin the game, the fans created a huge din by shouting and banging their miniature "Tris Speaker" bats, which had been handed out by the Stick-to-the-Finish Club as noisemakers. The bugs continued to applaud the players at every opportunity, and each Indian received a loud ovation when he came to bat. But no one was greeted more enthusiastically than Harry Lunte. Following an extended ovation, Chapman's replacement set off a wild celebration when he drove a single up the middle to start the third inning, and even when he was thrown out attempting to steal second on the next pitch the bugs shouted encouragement to him.

Detroit's Bush, who had offered his services to Cleveland following Chapman's death, also was cheered loudly.

The game still was scoreless in the eighth inning when Detroit's Oscar Stanage hit a grounder to the left of third baseman Larry Gardner for an apparent hit. But Lunte ranged far to his right to grab the ball and, as Gardner threw himself to the ground to get out of the way, the shortstop fired the ball across the diamond just in time to retire Stanage. The spectacular fielding play prompted another loud ovation from the fans.

Meanwhile, Coveleskie was pitching what his teammates called his best game of the season. Through eight innings, he had allowed only six hits and no runs. But Detroit pitcher Dutch Leonard also was at his best, setting down the Indians without a run.

In the ninth, Ralph Young led off for the Tigers with a smash up the middle. Wamby dived and made a miraculous stop, but after he scrambled to his feet he made a hurried snap throw to first and the ball bounced in the dirt. It took a high hop past Doc Johnston and rolled into the dugout for a two-base error. After Bush walked, Cobb singled between Wamby and Johnston to score Young with the first run of the game.

The Indians threatened in the bottom of the inning, putting runners on first and second with one out. But Leslie Nunamaker struck out and Johnston, seeing the catcher bobble the ball, broke for third. Halfway there, Johnston realized he couldn't make it safely, so he scrambled back toward second. Stanage easily threw him out to end the game.

Discouraged by the 1–0 setback, many of the Cleveland fans left the park without bothering to take their booklets or their miniature "Tris Speaker" bats.

67

Although the boycott had failed to materialize, Mays was well aware his ordeal had just begun. So far, he had enjoyed the support of the New York fans in all four of his pitching assignments since the beaning. Now, it was time for the Yankees to go on the road. Mays could only guess how he would be received in other cities.

It was his bad luck that the team's first stop was in Boston, where there already was a deep-seated resentment against him stemming from his defection from the Red Sox in 1919.

In anticipation of Mays's visit to the city, *Boston Globe* writer "Uncle Jim" O'Leary voiced the opinion, "It would have been better if the New York club had given Mays leave of absence after the accident for the remainder of the season.

"Granted the players cease their agitation," added O'Leary, "if when the Yankees go on the road, partisan fans cause disturbances, discreditable to themselves and to the game, who is going to be held responsible?"

To head off any trouble, an extra detail of police was on hand at Fenway Park on Thursday, September 2, for the opener of the four-game series. Mays fielded grounders at second base during batting practice, but he returned to the dugout before most of the fans arrived. He remained there watching unobtrusively as Boston continued its recent domination of the three contenders with a 6–2 victory. In the past nine games, the Red Sox had beaten the Indians four out of five, the White Sox three straight, and now the Yankees once. Ruth still did not play, but he drew cheers from the fans when he went out to work the coaching box at first base with his arm bandaged.

The next day, the two teams had battled into the eighth inning tied 3–3 when Huggins lifted Quinn. Again, the New York manager called on Mays, who had been loosening up in the bullpen without attracting much attention. When the Boston fans realized who the new pitcher was, they began to boo loudly, the volume rising with each step Mays took toward the mound. After a few moments, from the grandstand came scattered cheers and applause mixed in with the boos.

Mays paid the crowd no mind as he prepared to pitch to Wally Schang, who stepped up without a hint of the protest the Red Sox had proposed almost three weeks earlier. Mays set Boston down in order, then was handed a two-run lead by his teammates in the top of the ninth. He finished off the Red Sox in the bottom of the inning for a 5–3 victory, his fourth straight since the beaning.

Afterward, in the Boston locker room, several of the players angrily denounced the fans for receiving Mays so cordially. Others lashed out again at the underhand hurler and reiterated the claim that his style of pitching was unsafe and gave him an unfair advantage.

Schang, who had caught Mays when he was a member of the team, dismissed such allegations.

"I don't mind that underhand ball, for that it is in fine control, but I know from experience that when Mays pitches overhand the ball is likely to go most any place. There is always a lot on the ball, but the direction of its flight is mighty uncertain."

Melville E. Webb, Jr., who a week earlier had written in the *Globe,* "It will take all kinds of nerve on Mays part to pitch ball at Fenway Park," also tempered his views on the Yankee pitcher. Referring to the mild crowd reaction, he surmised: "The fans aren't making a hero out of Mays by any means. Their attitude simply is 'On with the dance.'"

When the series ended on Saturday with a doubleheader, the fans had advance knowledge that Mays would be pitching. He was scheduled to start the second game, and that plus the return to the lineup of Ruth attracted an overflow crowd of 33,027 to Fenway

Park. The gates opened at noon, but long before that the fans had begun to gather outside the park. Part of the crowd was seated in roped-off sections of the field, and extra police were on hand to provide security.

Ruth did not disappoint his followers, as he hit his forty-fifth home run of the season in the first game to give the Yankees a 5–3 victory.

When the batteries were announced for the second game, Mays's name prompted some booing but that was soon drowned out by applause. More and more, the Boston fans seemed to be throwing their support behind the pitcher. The crowd reaction to Mays remained mixed once play began. For every person who booed him, there seemed to be another who called out his support. At one point in the contest, this tendency to line up on one side or the other in regard to Mays was carried to an absurd extreme. Mays hit Oscar Vitt with a pitched ball, and some of his supporters actually cheered.

Meanwhile, Ruth hit another homer, and New York appeared to have the game in hand when it scored two runs with two outs in the top of the ninth to take a 5–3 lead. All Mays had to do was get through one more inning and he would have yet another victory to his credit. But the Red Sox refused to make it easy for him. They pushed across one run and put the tying run on second and the winning run on first with two outs. The next batter was Harry Hooper, a right-hander, and Huggins elected to let Mays try to pitch out of the jam. The gamble backfired when Hooper lined a hit over second base. Bodie charged the ball, fielded it on one hop, and threw home in an effort to cut off the tying run. The ball and Gene Bailey arrived at the same time, so the runner lowered his shoulder and bowled into Muddy Ruel. When the catcher hit the ground, the ball shot out of his mitt and back toward the screen. Bailey was safe and Joe Bush rounded third and sprinted for the plate. Had Mays backed up the play, he could have nailed the second runner. Instead, he stood watching on the mound as the ball rolled all the way to the backstop, allowing Bush to score the winning run. It was a bush-league mistake on Mays's part, and it had cost his team the game.

The loss prevented the Yankees from moving into first place.

They left the field with a record of 79–50, leaving them percentage points behind the Indians at 78–49. In five more days, the two teams would have another showdown in Cleveland. It was one of those late-season series between contenders with the league championship riding in the balance. But this time there was an extra twist to the series that provided more drama than any pennant race. Everyone in baseball was waiting to see what would happen if Mays dared to venture into Cleveland.

68

The bugs no longer laughed at Harry Lunte as they once had. When he had made his major-league debut with Cleveland early in the 1919 season, the box score sent out by the Associated Press incorrectly listed his name as "Bunte." *The Sporting News* duly reported the mistake, along with the comment: "Maybe they thought he was sent up to sacrifice."

It was a prophetic misspelling, as well as the first of many jokes about Lunte's hitting. He proved to be the classic example of a good-field, no-hit ballplayer. At the end of that first season, his batting average was an anemic .195. In seventy-seven at-bats, he had managed only fifteen hits, thirteen of them singles. Although he was an outstanding fielder, Lunte was such an inept batter that Speaker spent much of the winter before the 1920 season in a futile search for a more capable reserve infielder.

Realizing his job was in jeopardy, Lunte reported to training camp with renewed determination. To the surprise of his teammates, he suddenly began hitting the ball with more authority. Even his fielding seemed more spectacular than before.

"I've seen Lajoie, Wagner and all the great infielders," proclaimed Speaker, "but never have I seen a better pair of hands than Lunte's."

Once he had reclaimed his spot on the team, Lunte faded back into anonymity. With Chapman at shortstop and Wamby at second base, Lunte was little more than a practice player and an occasional pinch-runner. It was a difficult role for a young ballplayer to accept.

"That riding the bench is the toughest job of all," Lunte told Ed Bang one day that spring. "I want to get in and play. It's so much easier to be doing something you like to do than to be always wishing for a chance."

While he was not satisfied with such an assignment, Lunte's temperament at least made him well suited for it. He was an easygoing fellow who took each day as it came. Occasionally, he would lean back on the bench, look over at his roommate, Wamby, and say with a smile, "You know, you can't make money any easier than this."

Three weeks after Chapman's death, all that had changed. Now, Lunte was one of the most visible figures in baseball. Wherever he went, he was accorded enthusiastic greetings by fans who had no way to pay their respects to Chapman other than to offer encouragement to his replacement. Rather than fade from the pressure, Lunte discovered he enjoyed his turn in the spotlight.

Though his hitting remained undistinguished, his fielding was brilliant. Lunte covered so much ground in the field it did not seem possible to get the ball through the left side of the Cleveland infield. He ranged far to his right or left to rob batters of base hits on sharply hit grounders. He made leaping catches of line drives. His hands were becoming so legendary in baseball circles that *The Sporting News* ran a front-page picture of them above the caption, "Harry Lunte and His Great Hands." Even with a batting average below .200, Lunte appeared to be at least a capable replacement for Chapman.

On Sunday, September 5, he received three standing ovations from the Cleveland rooters for his fielding plays in the Indians' 4–3 victory over the Tigers at League Park. And if Lunte could not hit, at least the Cleveland pitchers could. Sarge Bagby banged out a double and a sacrifice fly—giving him eight hits in his past eleven at-bats—while notching his twenty-sixth victory of the season.

The following day, Labor Day, Cleveland was in a virtual three-way tie for first with Chicago and New York. With the White

Sox and Yankees idle, the Indians had a chance to move into the lead in a doubleheader against the Browns.

Cleveland led the morning game 2–1 in the bottom of the fifth when Lunte hit a grounder past third baseman Earl Smith. Rounding first base with a single, Lunte suddenly felt a sharp pain in his left thigh. Immediately, he pulled up lame and hobbled back to the bag. With the help of Percy Smallwood, he attempted to walk out the soreness in the leg but to no avail. After a few moments, Lunte had to be helped off the field. Jamieson was sent in as a pinch-runner, and when the Indians went back into the field, outfielder Joey Evans, a former third baseman, was stationed at shortstop.

Evans filled in capably for the remainder of the two games, handling seven chances without an error as the Indians opened up a one-game lead with 7–2 and 6–5 victories. Mails pitched brilliantly in the opener to redeem himself for his poor showing in Washington, and Cleveland won the afternoon game with a dramatic two-run rally in the bottom of the ninth inning. When the winning run crossed the plate on Gardner's base hit, the overflow crowd of twenty-three thousand surged onto the field in celebration— shouting, dancing, hurling their hats into the air and even doing handsprings across the diamond.

In the clubhouse, Lunte did not share in the mood of triumph. His injury had been diagnosed as a pulled muscle. For him, the season, as well as his shot at glory, was over.

*　　　*　　　*

There was a sense of desperation when Speaker, Jim Dunn, and Barney Barnard met in Dunn's office to discuss the infield situation. Lunte's injury had left the Indians without a shortstop. Evans was only a temporary solution to the problem, and behind him only outfielder and former pitcher Joe Wood was capable of playing in the infield. Even the eternally optimistic Dunn seemed dejected.

"Now what?" asked Speaker.

"What about that Joe Sewell we've got at New Orleans?" Barnard replied.

Speaker was familiar with the reports on Sewell. The young

shortstop, who was only five foot six, was the sensation of the Southern Association. Already, he was being compared to Detroit's Bush, who had overcome a similar size handicap to establish himself as one of the premier shortstops in baseball. But Sewell was just twenty-one years old and woefully short of experience. Just four months earlier, he had been playing college ball.

"He's not ready for this league," said Speaker. "I feel certain of that."

Barnard and Dunn remained silent. Reluctantly, Speaker realized there was no alternative.

"What's he hitting down there?"

Barnard recited Sewell's statistics: In 92 games, he had a .289 batting average (seventeenth in the league), 58 runs, 19 doubles, 8 triples, 2 home runs, 7 stolen bases, and a .938 fielding percentage (fourth in the league) with 27 errors.

"Let's gamble on anything now," said Speaker. "We've got to have some help to win this race, and anyone is better than no shortstop at all."

The Indians' fortunes now rested in the hands of an undersized and untested rookie, who was being called upon to play one of the most important positions on the field in the midst of a tight pennant race. Speaker feared it was too much to ask of any youngster. As he left Dunn's office, Spoke could feel the championship slipping away from his ballclub.

69

That same Tuesday, Mays pitched a three-hitter to beat the Athletics 2–0. When the game ended, Colonel Huston made his way to the locker room to offer his congratulations to the pitcher. He also had some news to deliver. He had decided that

Mays would not accompany the Yankees on their trip to Cleveland and instead would rejoin the team in Detroit. Already, Huston's statement was being handed out to the press: "We are not taking Mays to Cleveland, not because we think there is danger of any trouble, but out of respect to the feelings of the people there. We don't want to offend them. It is largely a matter of sentiment."

The news would be greeted with relief in Cleveland, where the bitterness against Mays had prompted several threatening letters to the pitcher. But Mays showed little emotion as Huston informed him of the decision. He would do whatever was best for the ballclub, he assured the Colonel.

Huston left the room with mixed emotions. He regretted that the team would be deprived of the services of its best pitcher for such a crucial series. At the same time, he wanted to spare Mays any further trouble. The Colonel had developed a special affection for Mays over the past year. He admired the pitcher's toughness on the field and the way he stood up to his critics and continued to perform in the face of incredible hardships. In Huston's estimation, Mays had more guts than any other man in baseball. He knew the pitcher could handle anything thrown his way in Cleveland. But Mays's ordeal had lasted long enough. It was time, Huston believed, for baseball to turn its attention back to the pennant race.

VI

Joe Sewell

I was more frightened than pleased, but as I traveled north I made up my mind that when I took the field in a Cleveland uniform I would forget that I was Joe Sewell and imagine I was Chapman, fighting to bring honor and glory to Cleveland.

Joe Sewell

70

Joe Sewell was a confused young man on the morning of Tuesday, September 7. When he had received word to report to Jules Heinemann, he thought the owner of the New Orleans Pelicans wanted to discuss his contract for the following season.

It was a logical assumption. After all, in his four months with the Southern Association ballclub, Sewell had performed admirably. His batting average was pushing .300 and he had proven himself to be a flashy though erratic fielder at shortstop. If the owner wanted to go ahead and discuss his terms for next year, that was fine with Sewell.

But when he arrived at the front office to be greeted by Heinemann and manager Johnny Dobbs, the ballplayer was hit with an unexpected question from the owner.

"Joe, how would you like to go to Cleveland and play shortstop for the Indians?"

When he recovered from his surprise at such a proposition, Sewell adamantly shook his head.

"I don't want to go to Cleveland," he said.

"Why not?" asked Heinemann.

"I'm not good enough for the big leagues. Why, I've never even seen a big-league game."

"Joe, you can play shortstop in the major leagues," said Dobbs.

Sewell was unconvinced. He wanted to stay in New Orleans.

"You think it over, Joe," said Dobbs. "Then come back out to the park and play this afternoon. We'll have a ticket for you on the railroad just in case."

Sewell returned to his room in a state of shock. Unsure of what to do, he sought the advice of catcher Hank DeBerry, his roommate. DeBerry had played for the Indians in 1916 and 1917, and he knew what big-league ball was like.

"You're good enough to play up there, Joe," DeBerry assured him.

Finally, DeBerry and some of the other New Orleans ballplayers were able to persuade Sewell to accept the promotion. That evening, filled with apprehension, he reluctantly boarded a train and headed north. He never had been to a major-league city before, never even been out of the South, and suddenly he was about to be thrust into the midst of a heated pennant race. Even more staggering to the twenty-one-year-old ballplayer, he had become the heir to Ray Chapman's legacy. Sewell was overwhelmed by the enormity of his task.

*　　　*　　　*

In the face of public opinion following Chapman's death, Heinemann had been unable to reject Dunn's request for Sewell. Had the Pelicans owner refused to sell the player, he would have been subjected to a flood of negative publicity. Plus, he would have damaged his working relationship with Dunn, which had proven to be highly profitable for him.

Heinemann's reluctance to part with his shortstop stemmed from the needs of his own ballclub. New Orleans also was locked in a pennant race and was close on the heels of Little Rock. Also, several other big-league clubs had expressed an interest in Sewell. One club reportedly was willing to pay one hundred thousand dollars for the shortstop.

Heinemann at least was able to force the Indians to pay a steep price. They handed over six thousand dollars in cash and agreed to forfeit the rights to all options on New Orleans players in exchange for Sewell.

When the deal was done, Heinemann, who had worked closely with Cleveland ever since receiving financial assistance from Somers more than five years earlier, told the newspapermen he was only doing what he could to assist an old and trusted ally.

"We do not put dollars and cents above our friendliness for the Cleveland club, which has helped us many a time when we were sorely in need of help."

71

Sewell was an unlikely looking ballplayer. At five foot six and 155 pounds, he appeared better suited to follow his father into the medical profession. As recently as the spring of 1920, that was the path the younger Sewell had laid out for himself.

Joseph Wheeler Sewell was born October 9, 1898, in the small community of Titus, Alabama, where his father, Dr. Wesley Sewell, served as a country doctor for forty years. There were three other boys and two girls in the family, and all of them would receive college educations. As a youngster, Joe tagged along while his father made his rounds in the area, calling on his patients in a horse and buggy.

In 1916, Joe went to the University of Alabama in nearby Tuscaloosa to study medicine. When he arrived on campus, freshmen were called "rats" and were required to give their names when called upon by upperclassmen. Sewell had a standard reply he recited.

"Joe Sewell, sir, from Titus, Alabama. The latest census of Titus gives the place seventy-six people, sixty-two of whom are Sewells."

Sewell was elected president of the student body as a senior and was a member of several honorary and social societies. But his most notable achievements came on the athletic fields. Despite his lack of size, he was one of the top halfbacks in the South as well as a star on the baseball team.

In baseball, Sewell was Alabama's second baseman, and his best friend, Riggs "War Horse" Stephenson, was the shortstop. Joe's younger brother, Luke, was the catcher. The three of them attracted attention from the pro scouts while playing in some of the fast semipro leagues in the summers, but none was considering a baseball career. Joe and Luke were determined to become doctors, and Stephenson wanted to become a lawyer.

In the summer of 1919, the three were playing in the Tennessee Coal and Iron League when Ira Thomas, a scout for the Athletics, offered them a tryout in Philadelphia. They said they weren't interested. A few days later, Ward McDowell, the manager of their semipro team, took the three youngsters aside.

"You three kids are great natural ballplayers," he said. "Joe, you're not good material for a doctor. You haven't the personality. The same goes for you, Luke. And as for you, Riggs, if you'll make a lawyer, I'll make a balloon jumper.

"Now, you listen to me. There's a fortune awaiting you in baseball. Take my advice. Change your minds about your careers and let me see what I can do for you."

After talking it over, they agreed to give pro baseball a shot. McDowell then contacted Xen Scott, a Cleveland sports writer and scout who first had seen Joe at an Alabama football game. Acting on the tip from Scott, the Indians signed the three Alabama youngsters, selling Joe's contract to New Orleans on option and sending the other two to the Delta League.

Sewell joined the Pelicans in Nashville, Tennessee, late in May. In an effort to shake up his slumping team, Dobbs put him in the lineup at shortstop, and from that point on Sewell never missed a game for the Pelicans.

He was an immediate star, both at the plate and in the field. In one of his first series with New Orleans, he reached base twelve of thirteen times at bat. Most of all, he gained a reputation for almost never striking out, a talent he attributed to hitting rocks and bottle tops with a broomstick handle when he was a kid and to his superb eye.

"I have always made it a practice to follow the ball with the utmost care," he told his teammates. "I can even see the ball when it leaves the bat, although it is going like a flash. It never gets away from me. I follow the ball, particularly when it's breaking in a curve. I can see it, and when I swing I aim to hit it at that precise second."

By midsummer, reports on Sewell's progress began showing up in the Cleveland newspapers. The Indians planned to add both him and his pal Stephenson to their roster the following spring. When Chapman was killed and Lunte was felled by an injury, that timetable was accelerated for Sewell. Less than four months after leaving the Alabama campus, the young shortstop was headed to the big leagues.

72

The first leg of Sewell's journey north took him to Cincinnati. He arrived around nine o'clock on the night of September 7 only to discover he had missed his connecting train to Cleveland. Tired, lonely, and scared, he walked across the street to a hotel. It was a chilly night, and he was wearing only a seersucker suit and a straw hat.

"You know what, I'm going to Cleveland," Sewell said to the desk clerk. "Reckon I can get me a suit of clothes tonight?"

The clerk eyed him curiously for a few moments before answering.

"I know this boy around here who has a haberdashery. He might be able to get you a suit tonight."

Within an hour, the clothier arrived and Sewell was fitted with a new suit. He also bought a felt hat and high-button shoes, and pulled the money out of his pocket to pay for the purchase. Sewell thanked the two men for their kindness, then retired to his room.

He didn't sleep a wink that night. He could only lie there in the dark and wonder what it would be like playing big-league ball. The thought of trying to replace Chapman, one of the greatest stars in the game, frightened him. He didn't see how he could possibly measure up. Then he suddenly hit upon a solution to his dilemma. Instead of trying to replace Chapman, perhaps he could let the former shortstop guide him through the difficult days ahead. In the darkness of that hotel room, Sewell determined that he no longer was playing for himself. When he put on the Cleveland uniform, he would become the reincarnation of Ray Chapman. He would draw his strength from the dead ballplayer.

The next morning, Sewell caught a train to Cleveland, arriving at his destination at two o'clock in the afternoon. There was no one to greet him, and he had no idea where he was supposed to go. Not knowing what else to do, he flagged down a taxicab.

"Where's a good hotel around here?" Sewell asked the driver.

"What kind of hotel you want?"

"Do you know what hotel the ballplayers stay in?"

"Yeah, the Hollenden."

"Well," said Sewell, "let's go to the Hollenden."

At the hotel, he went to the front desk and asked for a room.

"I understand the ballplayers stay here. My name is Joe Sewell, and I'm a ballplayer."

Standing nearby was a husky, forty-year-old man with a prominent nose and ears, slicked-back hair, and round glasses. Overhearing the conversation, he walked over and extended his hand to Sewell. As nervous as he was, Sewell was put at ease by the air of friendliness about the man.

"So, you're Joe Sewell? We've been waiting for you."

It was Ed Bang, a jovial man who, in addition to his duties as sports editor of the *Cleveland Press,* went out of his way to become a friend and confidant of the Cleveland ballplayers. He had been staking out the hotel waiting for the new shortstop to arrive. With him were several other scribes looking for an interview.

Before Sewell knew what had happened, the writers began peppering him with questions. To the young ballplayer, still in awe of his surroundings, they seemed to descend on him like "a bunch of flies."

A few minutes later, Bang took Sewell under his supervision. He escorted him to League Park, introduced him to the office staff, and showed him the playing field. There was no game that day, so neither Dunn nor Speaker was at the park. Although Bang tried hard to make him comfortable in his new surroundings, Sewell's nervousness was evident. That evening, the ballplayer returned to the hotel, alone, with instructions to report to the ballpark the next morning, Thursday, September 9. He would get his first taste of big-league baseball at that time, when the Indians opened a three-game series. By chance, their opponents would be the New York Yankees.

73

The Yankees' arrival in Cleveland was preceded by an ugly rumor. The ballclub had stopped in Pittsburgh on Wednesday for an exhibition game with the Pirates. That afternoon, a story spread that several New York players, including Ruth, had been killed in an automobile accident. The report first surfaced in telegrams sent by unknown persons in Pittsburgh, Cincinnati, Cleveland, and Chicago to several Wall Street offices. Second baseman Pratt and outfielders Meusel and Lewis were the players besides Ruth who were supposed to have been badly injured or killed.

The initial reports came across private wires, then were transmitted over news tickers. It took several telegrams and phone calls to determine the stories were false, probably spread by gamblers trying to affect the odds of the upcoming New York–Cleveland series.

The Yankees had enough problems as it was. Not only did the stop in Pittsburgh deprive them of a much-needed day of rest before the series in Cleveland, they suffered two costly injuries in the meaningless game. Ruel split a finger and Bodie sprained an ankle.

Already, manager Huggins was without Mays. Now, he would be forced to use Truck Hannah behind the plate and juggle his outfield by shifting Ruth to center to replace Bodie and placing Meusel in Ruth's regular spot in right.

It was a dangerous time to do such shuffling. As the Yankees began their Western trip, the three contenders were running almost neck and neck in the standings. Cleveland led the league with a record of 81–49, and New York was just one-half game behind at 83–52. Third-place Chicago was only one game back with an 82–52 record.

Adding to the tension was the uncertain reception that awaited the Yankees in Cleveland, where feelings had been running high since Chapman's death. Mays might not be present, but no one knew just how the team would be received.

*   *   *

Sewell spent his first big-league game sitting at the end of the dugout by himself, trying to fade into the scenery. What he saw on the field confirmed all of the doubts he had about being able to measure up on this level of competition.

Sewell had showed up at the ballpark early that day, had been issued a uniform and introduced to his new teammates. He fielded some grounders, took a few swings in batting practice, and then was sent to the dugout by Speaker. "Don't worry about playing," Speaker told him. "You'll just be watching today."

A crowd of fourteen thousand turned out for the game, and Sewell was struck by the fans' sportsmanship. They cheered the Yankees when they arrived on the field, dispelling any fears of a demonstration against the visitors. The spectators even applauded politely when Pratt singled in the Yankees' first run and again when Meusel hit a sacrifice fly to score another.

The game itself seemed to be played out in front of Sewell at a dizzying speed by superhuman players capable of remarkable exploits, each one more amazing than the last. Ruth, waving his forty-two-ounce bat as if it were a toothpick, drove the ball over the right-field fence onto a porch across the street for his forty-seventh home run of the season. The ball sounded like a pistol shot as it left the bat. Later, Ward hit a shot to deep right field, where Elmer Smith raced back, leaped high against the wall, and somehow made a spectacular backhanded grab.

The Cleveland batters were even more impressive, pounding out fourteen hits against three New York pitchers to give Coveleskie a 10–4 victory. Four of the hits belonged to Johnston, who blasted two triples and two singles, then capped his day with a daring steal of home.

After each one of these long hits or one-handed grabs or bold baserunning maneuvers, Sewell found himself sliding down lower and lower on the bench.

"I don't belong up here," he kept repeating to himself. "It's too fast for me."

A day later, he found out firsthand what big-league baseball was all about. In the second game of the series, New York built up a 6–0 lead on the strength of a two-run homer by Ruth and a costly throwing error by Evans, the outfielder who had been pressed into service at shortstop. Going into the bottom of the fifth, Shawkey, who already had beaten the Indians five times in six tries, was pitching a two-hitter and seemed to have matters well in hand.

When the first two Cleveland batters went out meekly, Speaker decided the time was right to break in his new shortstop. He told Sewell to get a bat and go up to hit. The fans gave Sewell a loud ovation, but they were startled to see how small he was. The best he could manage was a weak foul pop, which Ward pulled down by third base.

On his first chance in the field, Sewell scooped up a grounder and heaved the ball wildly past first base for an error.

Two innings later, he came to bat for the second time. The Indians had scored one run and Johnston was on second base with two outs. Sewell hit a weak grounder to Pipp at first base to end the threat.

It was hardly an auspicious debut. Sewell's line score read two at-bats, no hits, and one error. The Indians lost 6–1, trimming their lead over the White Sox to just three-tenths of a percentage point.

The Yankees trailed by just one-half game and eight-tenths of a percentage point.

The lone bright spot for the Clevelanders had come in the ninth inning, when Mails redeemed himself for his poor showing in Washington by retiring all three batters he faced. He capped his performance by fanning Ruth on three pitches, a feat that he took delight in describing to the writers afterward.

"First, I threw him a fast one. He missed it. Then I tossed him a curve. He took a toehold and swung, the apple taking a nice hop as it crossed the plate, and the count was two and nothing. Ruth looked me over, and then settled for his home-run wallop. I took a long windup and busted one right through the center of the pan. Babe missed it from here to Frederick & Nelson."

But Mails's pitching was small consolation. It could not mask the disappointment over the poor performance of the Indians' two shortstops. In his report on the game, Wilbur Wood of the *News* echoed the despair felt by the team's followers.

"After watching Sewell and Evans at short, we can only pray that Harry Lunte will recover rapidly from the charley horse he sprung in the morning game Labor Day. The whole infield appeared more or less shaken with Lunte out of it, as was only natural."

On Saturday, Evans was back at short and Sewell remained on the bench as the Yankees beat the Indians 6–2 in the final game of the series to throw the standings into a jumble. The won-lost percentages now were being computed to four figures, and because of the difference in the number of games played the first-place Indians found themselves trailing the second-place Yankees in the "games behind" category. As listed in the newspapers Sunday morning, the standings read:

Cleveland	82–51	.6165	1/2
New York	85–53	.6159	—
Chicago	84–53	.6131	1/2

It was one of the tightest pennant races on record. With just three weeks remaining in the season, every game and every play was taking on exaggerated importance. While the Yankees, with their heavy hitting, and the White Sox, with their balance and championship experience, both had their supporters, just about all of the experts agreed on one thing. The Indians' problems at shortstop had tipped the scales against Speaker's team.

74

Sewell was in front of his locker putting on his uniform Sunday afternoon when Speaker approached him.

"How do you feel today, Joe?"

"All right," came the answer.

Speaker nodded his head and placed his hand on Sewell's shoulder.

"That's good. You're playing shortstop today."

The manager let the news sink in before continuing.

"I want you to have a good cut at every pitch you think is good enough to hit. Never mind too much about grabbing everything in the field. I'll help you from the outfield as much as possible."

There was little time for Sewell to think about anything but getting ready for the game. Nearby, George Burns, a veteran outfielder who had been purchased by the Indians midway through the season, pulled out a black bat from his locker and handed it to Sewell.

"Here, take this. It's a good bat. Make sure you take care of it."

Sewell named the bat "Black Betsy." It would become his Sunday bat—his most prized one—and it would last him throughout his career.

Jack MacCallister, the coach, came around and showed Sewell the lineup card. Joe was batting in the seventh spot, just behind

Johnston and just ahead of O'Neill. Cleveland's other newcomer, Mails, was scheduled to pitch.

Although the opponent was last-place Philadelphia, the Athletics had Scott Perry, one of the toughest right-handers in the league, on the mound.

Sewell still was trying to calm the butterflies in his stomach when the first batter of the game, Jimmy Dykes, hit a towering pop-up to the left side of the infield. Sewell circled under it and pulled the ball down, prompting a loud ovation from the crowd. Just executing the simple play helped calm him somewhat.

In the second inning, Sewell took a throw from Wamby to force a runner at second, but his relay throw to first went wild for an error to let in a run, tying the score at 1–1.

Sewell still was shaken by the play when he came to bat with one out and no one on in the bottom of the inning. He had run the count out to three balls and one strike when Perry threw a nickel curve, or what now is known as a slider, on the outside corner of the plate. The left-hand-hitting Sewell reached out and slapped the ball on a line over the third baseman's head and down the left-field line. The crowd roared when the ball hit in fair territory and rolled into the corner of the outfield. Sewell hadn't waited to see where the ball would land. He was out of the batter's box in a flash, and as he raced around the bases, he felt as if only his toes were touching the ground. He made it all the way to third, where he pulled in standing up with a triple.

As he stood there on the bag, Sewell could see third-base coach Chet Thomas clapping his hands and shouting something at him while the bugs in the stands tossed their hats in the air with joy. Looking around, Joe thought to himself, "Shoot, this ain't so tough!"

Two batters later, Jamieson knocked a single to right field and Sewell ran home with the first run of his career. He no longer was nervous. For the first time, he felt like a big-league ballplayer.

In the fourth inning, Sewell used his speed to beat out a grounder to third for another hit. O'Neill followed with a smash that third baseman Joe Dugan was able to knock down in time to throw across to first for the out. On the play, Sewell never hesitated as he rounded second and dashed for third. The Athletics were caught offguard by the brazen maneuver, and the hurried return throw across the diamond was barely in time to nip Sewell at the bag. The fans gave him a standing ovation, anyway. They recognized the daring play as a favorite stunt of Chapman's.

The Indians went on to win the game 5–2 behind the seven-hit pitching of Mails, who gained his third victory without a loss. In addition to his two hits, Sewell had seven putouts and five assists in the field to overcome his one error. He also displayed a strong throwing arm, twice throwing out runners from deep in the hole between short and third. Every time he fielded a grounder, Gardner would encourage him by shouting over from third, "Take your time now! Steady up!" Wamby also talked to Sewell throughout the game, making sure he was positioned correctly.

In the clubhouse afterward, Sewell was sitting in front of his locker accepting the congratulations of the other players when O'Neill walked up to him and smiled. "Chappie's looking down on you, Joe," said the catcher. "He's proud of you."

75

Mays rejoined the Yankees in Detroit and found the morale of the ballclub no better than it had been at the beginning of the season. Despite the two victories in Cleveland, the Yankees still were as divided as ever, with the players bickering among themselves and with their manager. Ruth had recovered from the notorious "chigger bite" on his arm, but there was a lingering unhappiness among some of his teammates over his role in the movie escapade. Lewis and Ruel were injured, Meusel was sulking, and to top off matters there has been an ugly showdown between Huggins and reserve outfielder Sammy Vick. Ever since the Western trip had begun, Hug had been goading the outfielder about his timid play, and Vick finally retaliated by slugging the manager in full view of the other players. Vick feared his career was over, but the next day Huggins startled him by remarking, "I'm glad to see you have some spirit in you after all."

Against this setting, Mays took the mound in Detroit on Sunday, September 12, to see how he would be received on Ty Cobb's home turf. There were twenty-nine thousand fans on hand at Navin Field, many of them sitting in roped-off sections of the outfield. They stood and booed him with such viciousness that even the normally unflappable Mays was visibly shaken. It immediately became evident that the reception hampered the pitcher's effectiveness. The first batter, Ralph Young, hit a high fly that was carried by the wind into the fans of the roped-off section of right field for a ground-rule double. Bush bunted Young to third, and Cobb ripped a single to right to make it 1–0.

That brought up Bobby Veach, and he hit another high fly to right. Again, the wind carried the ball into the crowd for a double. The next batter, Harry Heilmann, changed things up by driving the ball into the center-field crowd for yet another two-base hit to score Cobb and Veach, making it 3–0.

When Chick Shorten singled in Heilmann for a four-run Detroit lead, Huggins had no choice but to pull his pitcher. Mays walked to the bench with the boos rising in volume amid a scattering of cheers. What few cheers there had been were completely drowned out by the time he reached the dugout.

Detroit writer H. G. Salsinger could not help but gloat as he described the scene for his readers: Mays "was too frightened to pitch. He did not get a thing on the ball and it was probably a great relief for him when he was asked to retire. Some day the truth of Mays' acts will become known and when that happens Mays will undoubtedly depart silently. He has done nothing to help elevate the game in any way."

The Yankees, however, had the last laugh on this day. They hit five ground-rule doubles of their own to go with homers by Pipp and

Lewis for a 13–6 victory. They still trailed the Indians by seven-hundredths of a percentage point but they maintained their half-game edge in the games-behind column. The third-place White Sox fell 1½ games back after a 5–0 loss in Washington.

As for Mays, he was hardly as shaken as Salsinger and his other critics might have led themselves to believe. He secluded himself in his room after the game and thought over the events of the day. "What's the meaning of this?" he asked himself. "Are you losing your nerve?" Buoyed by his private pep talk, he sought out Huggins that evening and asked for another shot at the Tigers the next day. The manager agreed to give it to him.

On Monday, there were only ten thousand fans at the ballpark, but they immediately began to hoot and jeer when Mays took the mound. Their taunts became louder when he surrendered a first-inning run to the Tigers. Mays ignored them and kept on toiling, growing more effective the longer he worked. By the time he came to bat in the third inning, the mood of the crowd was beginning to change. He was given a generous ovation as he stepped to the plate.

The Yankees trailed 2–1 after five innings, but in the sixth Ruth hit a two-run homer—his forty-ninth of the season—to give New York a one-run lead. When Babe trotted back to the dugout after circling the bases, parents lifted their small children onto the field to shake the hand of the giant slugger.

By now, Mays had regained his rhythm. He blanked Detroit over the final five innings, and in the eighth he singled in the final run of a 4–2 victory. He walked off the field that afternoon feeling vindicated.

The other two contenders also won on Monday—the Indians beating the Athletics 3–2 and the White Sox downing the Nationals 15–6—so the standings remained unchanged. But on Tuesday, New York finally gained the upper hand in the race by defeating Detroit 13–3 while Cleveland lost to Philadelphia 8–0 and Chicago fell to Washington 7–0. The Yankees led the Indians by 1½ games and the White Sox by 2½.

76

The next day, Bagby pitched a three-hitter as Cleveland concluded the series against the Mackmen with a 14–0 victory while the Yankees and White Sox were idle. No one knew it yet, but it was to be the start of one of the great stretch runs in baseball history. At the time, all anyone could talk about was the hot hitting of Sewell. He had raked the Philadelphia pitchers for seven hits in sixteen at-bats over the past four games, and he was gaining confidence with each passing day.

On Thursday, the Great Mails pitched a four-hitter to beat Washington 1–0, with Sewell scoring the game's only run despite being victimized by one of the oldest tricks in the book. He was on first with a single when O'Neill hit a drive into right field. As Sewell raced toward third, coach Chet Thomas waved his arms for him to go home, but third baseman Frank Ellerbe pretended to be reaching for the throw. Sewell fell for the ruse and slid into the bag as the crowd groaned. Luckily, he scored anyway when Lefty Zachery threw a wild pitch to the next batter. The victory moved the Indians back into first, three percentage points ahead of the New Yorkers, who had lost 6–3 in Chicago.

Having regained the lead, the Clevelanders began picking up steam. They beat the Griffmen 9–3 on Friday as Sewell had two hits, one of them coming on a feet-first slide into first base. He also robbed Ellerbe of a hit by going deep behind second base to grab a hard grounder and flip the ball to Wamby to start a double play. "Once more, doff the chapeau to Joey Sewell, rookie extraordinary," praised Cleveland sports writer Ross Tenney. Even Mails got into the act, although he wasn't pitching that day. Speaker hurt himself sliding into home with Cleveland's first run in the second inning, and every one of the Indians came rushing out of the dugout to check on their leader. After a few moments, Speaker stood up, dusted himself off, and prepared to get back into action. The exuberant Mails was so happy to see his manager was all right, he slapped Speaker on the back and shouted encouragement to him. Back in the dugout, Mails walked around with a big smile on his face proclaiming, "I'd break my arm if necessary, pitching to win for Speaker." In Chicago, the Yankees lost again, 6–4, to fall a full game back of the Tribe and just a half-game ahead of the third-place White Sox.

Now, the victories started to roll in for the Indians. On Saturday, they beat Washington 7–5 while the White Sox were completing a three-game sweep of the New Yorkers with a 15–9 decision. The Red Sox arrived in town on Sunday, and the Clevelanders beat them 2–0. Back in New York, the movie, which had been renamed *Heading Home,* starring Ruth, opened on the big screen in Madison Square Garden, but in St. Louis the real-life Ruth couldn't prevent the Yankees from falling three games back with a 6–1 loss to the Browns. The White Sox stayed just 1½ games back with a win over the Mackmen, and it appeared to be shaping up as a two-team race. Even Joe Vila was ready to write off New York's chances, claiming that "only those blind to reason can see hope for the Yankees."

Strangely, Vila chose to lay the blame for the New Yorkers' demise on Mays, who had won six of his past seven decisions.

"There's another point worth remembering—the poor work of Mays during the first two months of the campaign," Vila reminded his readers in *The Sporting News.* "If Mays had shown his skill from the start the Yankees by this time would have been breezing along with a strangle hold on the leadership."

The day Vila filed his story, Mays, who would finish the season with a 26–11 record, beat the Browns 4–3 to end the Yankees' four-game losing streak. All the victory did was keep New York from losing any more ground, as Cleveland beat Boston 8–3 behind Mails's pitching and Chicago kept pace with a 13–6 victory over

Philadelphia. It was the Indians' sixth consecutive victory and their sixteenth in twenty September games.

On Tuesday, September 21, with just two weeks remaining in the season, the Cleveland winning streak reached seven with a 12–1 rout of the Red Sox. After a day off, the Indians prepared to meet the second-place White Sox, who had won six in a row, in a three-game showdown at League Park. After more than five months of battling for the championship, the Indians now had a chance to deliver a deathblow to their nearest rivals.

77

On the eve of the series, baseball was rocked by a statement released by Ban Johnson. For the moment, all thought of the pennant race was pushed into the background.

"I have evidence," stated the AL president, "and much of it is now before the Grand Jury, that certain notorious gamblers are threatening to expose the 1919 World Series as a fixed event unless the Chicago White Sox players drop out of the current race intentionally to let the Indians win. These gamblers have made heavy bets on the Cleveland team."

Johnson's startling revelation was the latest in a series of charges that had tainted baseball in recent days. There had been rumors of a fix during the previous Series, but most of the talk had been dismissed as sour grapes by those who had refused to believe the Red Legs were capable of knocking off the American League champions.

The scandal began to unfold the first week of September with reports that telegrams had been sent to William L. Veeck, Sr., the president of the Chicago Cubs, alerting him that hundreds of thousands of dollars had been poured into betting centers by gamblers wanting to wager on a Phillies' victory over the Cubs in their August 31 game. The news rekindled the suspicions over the 1919 World Series, and on September 7, Illinois State's Attorney General Maclay Hoyne bowed to public pressure by summoning a grand jury to investigate the charges.

Among the first to testify had been Comiskey, the pompous owner of the White Sox. He admitted hearing rumors of foul play in the Series, then charged that Johnson had refused to cooperate in investigating the matter. The league president lashed back at his rival with charges that Comiskey's players still were controlled by gamblers.

"I am determined that baseball shall be divorced from gambling," added Johnson, who had arrived in Chicago for the hearings.

An enraged Comiskey hotly retorted, "It was a terrible thing to report the blackmail of my players by gamblers just before they went into a series against Cleveland, a club in which Mr. Johnson has financial interests!"

In Cleveland, White Sox manager Kid Gleason found himself surrounded by reporters when he left his hotel room to head to the ballpark.

"I have nothing to say in the matter from any phase whatsoever except that we are trying our best to win the pennant, all reports to the contrary notwithstanding!" he said gruffly. "I know nothing of the reports that my players were involved in a gambling plot to throw away any World Series."

Speaker also feigned surprise at the charges.

"Such reports are entirely new to me, and I don't take any stock in them," he said. "In this series here, two great ball teams are fighting as hard as they know how, with the honor of getting into the World's Series as their stake.

"But the thing to do is to root out the baseball gambling that is responsible for all these stories. Suppress this evil and you'll kill off the thing that is now besmirching our great national game. That's the way to clean up all this mess of scandal."

*　　　*　　　*

The White Sox showed no signs of backing down in the face of either the gamblers' threats or the grand jury's investigation. They won the opener of the series 10–3 behind the pitching of Dickie Kerr to move within a half-game of the Indians.

With first place at stake, Mails was given the starting assignment for Cleveland in the second game. Warming up before the start of play, the brash southpaw turned to umpire Billy Evans and boasted, "I'm going to shut these bums out."

Evans laughed.

"Have you ever heard of Shoeless Joe Jackson, Buck Weaver, and Eddie Collins?" he asked.

"Sure," came the reply, "but have they ever heard of The Great Mails?"

Mails then set out to back up his words, keeping the White Sox scoreless through the first four innings. He opened the fifth by striking out Swede Risberg. But all of a sudden, Mails inexplicably lost his control. He walked Ray Schalk on four pitches. Then he threw four more balls to put opposing pitcher Red Faber aboard. When Mails's first two pitches to Amos Strunk also were wide of the plate, Speaker rushed in from center field to confer with his pitcher.

The crowd shouted at Speaker to leave Mails in the game, and after a lengthy deliberation the manager gave in to their wishes. When he returned to center field, Speaker nervously chewed on some grass while watching Mails throw two more balls to complete the walk to Strunk, loading the bases. Speaker started to call for a new pitcher, then chose to hold off before making the switch.

On the mound, Mails decided to abandon his sidearm pitches and go back to his overhand delivery. When he did, his control returned just as mysteriously as it had left. He blew three straight pitches past the hard-hitting Weaver for a strikeout. That brought up Collins, who fouled off four fastballs, then missed the next pitch by a foot for strike three. The side was retired without a run, and the crowd roared out its appreciation of Mails's feat.

That was the end of the White Sox for the day. Mails did not allow another baserunner the rest of the game. Meanwhile, Sewell rapped out three hits and stole a base to provide the offensive spark in a 2–0 victory by the Indians.

Although the White Sox won the next game 5–1 behind

Jackson's three hits, including a tremendous home run over the right-field fence, they left town still in second place, a half-game behind the Indians. In New York, not even Ruth's fiftieth and fifty-first home runs could keep the Yankees from losing two of three to the Griffmen to fall closer to elimination from the race.

*   *   *

With a week to go, the Indians traveled to St. Louis on Sunday and beat the Browns 7–5 behind seven strong innings of relief by George Uhle. A crowd of thirty thousand turned out to see the Clevelanders, and they spilled over onto the edges of the playing field, where they were held back by mounted policemen. At one point in the game, a drive by O'Neill struck one of the horses, resulting in a ground-rule double. The Indians wasted no time in jumping on the Browns, with Sewell's bases-loaded single in the top of the first driving in two runs to cap a three-run outburst. Speaker, who had been struggling at the plate recently, went out his first three times up to run his string to zero for eighteen before hitting a ninth-inning single. In Chicago, the White Sox kept the pressure on by besting the Tigers 8–1.

The next day, Speaker broke out of his slump with a pair of hits and Mails won his sixth straight by beating St. Louis 8–4. The White Sox kept pace with a 2–0 victory over the Tigers, but thanks to a quirk in the schedule they now faced the unpleasant prospect of four consecutive days off at this crucial time.

The Indians continued their relentless push on Tuesday, September 28, when Bagby beat the Browns 9–5 for his thirtieth victory of the season. That boosted Cleveland's lead to a full game over the idle White Sox and 3½ games over the Yankees, who now could do no better than tie the Indians for the pennant.

But there was little celebrating in Cleveland, or anywhere else in baseball. That same day, the grand jury in Chicago returned indictments against seven members of the White Sox plus one former player. The seven were pitchers Eddie Cicotte and Lefty Williams, outfielders Jackson and Happy Felsch, third baseman Weaver, shortstop Swede Risberg, and utility infielder Fred Mc-

Mullin. Also included in the group was Chick Gandil, the rugged first baseman who had retired from baseball after his role in the White Sox's loss in the World Series.

The lid was off the affair now. Cicotte, the star knuckleball pitcher, admitted: "[I] gave Cincinnati batters good balls to hit. I put them right over the plate. . . . I deliberately threw late to second on several plays."

Jackson said he "helped throw games by muffing hard chances in the outfield or by throwing slowly to the infield."

Comiskey had no choice but to immediately suspend the seven players still on his club. Gleason would have to throw together a patchwork lineup for the White Sox's final two games of the season.

Everyone had known it was coming, but the confessions of the crooked Chicago players were greeted with incredulity. No one had wanted to believe just how complete the sellout had been.

"It was like hearing that my church had sold out," said Ruth, speaking for players and fans everywhere.

*   *   *

For the Indians, one of the injustices of the scandal was that by the time the White Sox were gutted by the suspensions it really did not matter what Chicago did on the field. The Clevelanders were winning the championship on their own, leaving no opening for the White Sox. They completed their four-game sweep of the Browns with a 10–2 victory on Wednesday and headed to Detroit for the final four games of the season with twenty victories in their past twenty-six games. With Sewell in the lineup, Cleveland's won-lost record was an amazing 14–3.

The first game in Detroit was rained out on Thursday. Meanwhile, in Chicago, Gleason worked out with the patchwork lineup he had put together in the wake of the suspensions. He still had Schalk at catcher, Ted Jourdan at first base, and Collins at second base. To complete the infield, outfielder Shano Collins was moved to third and a seldom-used reserve named Harvey McClellan was stationed at shortstop. Veterans Nemo Liebold and Amos Strunk were joined in the outfield by Eddie Murphy. The pitching staff consisted of Kerr,

Red Faber, Tex Wilkinson, and Shovel Hodge. The makeshift squad departed that evening for St. Louis, where the White Sox would make their last stand.

78

Speaker could sense his players' uneasiness as they began play in a doubleheader against the Tigers on Friday, October 1. It was a cold, windswept day, and the Indians had a chance to clinch the pennant and earn a spot in the World Series opposite National League champion Brooklyn if they could win both games while the White Sox lost to the Browns.

For a while, it appeared that might happen. After seven innings, Cleveland held a 4–0 lead and Mails was blowing down the Tigers. But in the eighth, the Clevelanders suddenly fell apart. With one out, Howard Ehmke and Ralph Young hit singles for Detroit. The normally sure-handed Gardner booted Bush's grounder for an error, loading the bases. Cobb followed with a double to left, cutting the lead to 4–2. When Jamieson muffed Veach's liner to left, Bush scored to make it a one-run game and Cobb moved up to third. Heilmann then lined a single over second to tie the score.

That was all for Mails, who was replaced by Uhle. He promptly walked Ira Flagstead, forcing Speaker to call on Bagby to get out of the jam. In a rare relief appearance, the Sarge retired the next two batters to finally end the inning.

The game remained tied going into the bottom of the tenth when Flagstead opened with an easy roller to short. It should have been a routine play, but Sewell, who had been bothered by the cold weather, threw the ball into the Cleveland dugout for a two-base error. Babe Pinelli hit the next pitch into left field to score the runner and give Detroit a 5–4 victory.

Between games, the Indians were huddled dejectedly in their dugout shivering from the cold when Speaker called them together for a pep talk.

"We all blew up in that first game," he said. "Forget it now. It's over. We don't know what Chicago is doing, but it would be just luck for them to win. We've got to get this game if we want to see Brooklyn."

The second game started off poorly. Cleveland trailed 2–1 after two innings when word arrived from St. Louis that the White Sox were leading the Browns 3–0. The crowd, which had been rooting for the visiting Clevelanders all afternoon, cried out its disappointment as the score from St. Louis was announced.

Then things began to turn around for the Indians. They tied the game in the next inning and continued their assault by scoring in each of the next five innings. In all, they pounded out fifteen hits and had built up a 10–3 lead when umpire Brick Owens called the game after the eighth inning because of darkness.

The Indians rushed to the clubhouse, both to warm up and to celebrate. Word had just arrived from St. Louis that the normally reliable Faber had been unable to hold the White Sox lead and the Browns had rallied for an 8–6 victory. There were two games remaining in the season, and Cleveland held a two-game lead.

The task of pitching the clincher on Sunday went to Bagby, the thirty-game winner. He was not at his sharpest, giving up eleven hits, but he managed to keep the Tigers from scoring until the bottom of the ninth. By that time, the Indians had a comfortable lead.

The score was 10–1 and there were two outs when Clyde Manion lofted an easy fly ball to center field. As soon as the ball settled into Speaker's glove, the ten thousand Detroit fans were on their feet applauding the Indians' triumph. With the cheers ringing in his ears, Speaker jubilantly raced off the field clutching the ball and, with it, Cleveland's first pennant.

Back in Cleveland, the news of the Indians' victory was received with restrained enthusiasm. In the next day's edition of the *Plain Dealer,* Henry Edwards explained the calm reaction by the Cleveland fans: "It was simply a case of inability to believe the truth. They were just dazed. They will awake today."

The White Sox went down fighting, beating the Browns 10–7, but that was of little concern to the Cleveland players. They were able to celebrate their triumph that night, and they remained in a giddy mood as they arrived at the ballpark Monday for the formality of closing out the regular season.

"I slept a real sleep last night for the first time in many a night," Joe Wood told reporters. "When I wasn't lying awake thinking and planning and fighting over the next day's ball game in that furious pennant drive, I was dreaming restless dreams about it."

It was another frigid day, but the relaxed Indians played a peppery game, losing to the Tigers 6–5 in just one hour, twenty-eight minutes. That gave them plenty of time to catch a late afternoon train to Cleveland, and they arrived home shortly after midnight on October 4. Despite the late hour, there was an eager crowd on hand to welcome them.

Speaker, happy but weary, was called upon to make a statement.

"Of course, I'm glad that it's over and that we've won the league flag," he said simply. "There is nothing to say regarding our plans for the big series. I don't know who we will start."

With no further fanfare, the manager departed for the Hollenden, where he was greeted affectionately by a smiling Dunn.

"How do you feel, Tris?" asked the owner in his booming voice.

"Tired," was all Speaker could say.

The following day, the front page of the *Plain Dealer* featured a three-column by eight-inch drawing of a Cleveland ballplayer holding his cap to his side while leaning on a bat. The player was looking toward a giant pennant waving on the horizon. Looking down from the clouds was Ray Chapman. The inscription above him read, "Carry On." Beneath the illustration was the caption, "It pays to play clean."

79

For a thirty-two-year-old who had been cast aside by three different big-league ballclubs, Doc Johnston had done pretty well for himself. Inheriting the first-base job left vacant by Joe Harris's refusal to sign seven months earlier, he had overcome early-season injuries to finish with a .292 batting average and seventy-one runs batted in. Now, he had extra cause to celebrate. He was headed to the World Series and a reunion with his kid brother, Jimmy, the third baseman for the Robins. It would be the first time two brothers faced each other in World Series play.

On the train ride east, Johnston was in the midst of a raucous group of players and writers swapping stories, talking baseball, or engaging in spirited games of pinochle, checkers, or poker. Normally one of the most talkative players on the team, Doc was content to sit back and soak up the atmosphere for a while. Then he got to his feet, moved to the center of the crowd, and abruptly broke out singing. Several of the other players quickly joined in. The song Johnston had chosen was "Dear Old Girl," which had been one of Chapman's favorites.

At the back of the car, MacCallister leaned over to say something to Ross Tenney, one of the Cleveland writers assigned to cover the Series.

"You know, this is the first time the boys have done any singing since Chappie died."

It suddenly struck Tenney just how different the mood on the ballclub had been since Chapman's death. The Indians had been grim and businesslike in the final weeks of the season. What jokes had been told were whispered behind closed doors. There was no revelry on the bench or in the clubhouse. "A laugh was the exception," Tenney wrote.

Now, it was as if a huge weight had been lifted from the players' shoulders. They had fulfilled their mission. They had brought Cleveland the pennant Chapman had so desperately wanted.

80

It was a windy, chilly day in Brooklyn despite the bright sunlight that bathed Ebbets Field for the opener of the World Series on October 5. Hundreds of fans gathered outside the park early in the morning to claim the unreserved seats that went on sale at ten o'clock, but others were driven off by the gray sky and the sight of the huge American flag in center field being whipped about by the stiff wind.

Surrounded by tall apartment houses, rundown buildings, and a huge armory, the ballpark was situated in such a way that it "sucks in all the chilly drafts of Flatbush," according to Damon Runyan.

Long lines of fans trailed away from the park for blocks before making a dash for the bleachers when the gates were opened. Once inside, the people turned up the collars on their overcoats and eagerly awaited the showdown.

The Brooklyners were confident of victory. Under the leadership of Wilbert "Uncle Robbie" Robinson, the Dodgers had swept to victory in the National League, finishing seven games ahead of John Mc-Graw's Giants and 10½ up on the defending champion Red Legs.

The Dodgers were commonly known as the Robins in honor of Robinson, a short, fat man whose weight and comical behavior overshadowed his baseball knowledge and his considerable skills as a manager. Uncle Robbie, who had played with McGraw on the old

Baltimore Orioles and later served as McGraw's right-hand man with the Giants before a falling out between the two men, had taken over the Brooklyn ballclub in 1914. The Dodgers had been a perennial second-division finisher, but Robinson led them to the National League championship in 1916, only his third year on the job.

After three mediocre seasons, Brooklyn had returned to the top in 1920. But Robinson was known more for the things he said and did than for what his ballclubs accomplished. He was such a lax disciplinarian, his players often read newspapers on the bench. And when he instituted the "Bonehead Club" to eliminate mistakes on the team, he became the charter member by posting the wrong lineup card.

There were several holdovers from that 1916 club, most notably hard-hitting outfielders Zack Wheat and Hi Myers and pitchers Rube Marquard, Jeff Pfeffer, and Sherry Smith. The Robins also had one of the game's best spitball pitchers, Burleigh Grimes, who had won twenty-three games that season.

For the second year in a row, the Series would be played under a nine-game format. The first three games would be in Brooklyn, then the teams would travel to Cleveland for up to four games. If the issue still was not settled, games eight and nine would be held in Brooklyn. The Robins had gained the advantage of opening at home thanks to a delay in completing the renovations at League Park. Not only was the Series originally scheduled to open in Cleveland, the first game was to mark the renaming of the ballpark. Dunn had vowed to change the name to Dunn Field when the team won its first pennant, and now he was ready to go forward with the switch. Unfortunately, the new bleachers in center and right fields could not be completed in time, so the rechristening would have to wait.

There had been one other important matter decided before the Series opened. Under the rules of the National Commission, any player who joined the team after September 1 was ineligible for the World Series. Since Sewell had not been signed until September 6, his name was not on the list of eligible players the Indians submitted to the commission. The team had no recourse other than to petition for an exception to the rule because of the circumstances of Chapman's death. The commissioners refused to act on the request, instead turning it over to Brooklyn president Charles Ebbets for consideration. Whether because of public pressure or a strong sense of sportsmanship, the Brooklyn owner approved Sewell's addition to the Cleveland roster.

Or perhaps Ebbets did so because of the well-placed confidence he had in his club. In addition to their strong pitching, the Robins entered the World Series well rested, having wrapped up the National League flag more than a week earlier. The Indians, on the other hand, had battled right down to the wire before earning their spot in the World Series. In order to give his team a day of rest at home, Speaker had chosen to break precedent by not arriving at the playing site until the morning of the game. The Clevelanders did not step off the train until eight o'clock that morning.

Once at the ballpark, the Indians took their batting and fielding practice in their old and worn uniforms with the brown pinstripes, then retired to the clubhouse. At 12:45, they reappeared on the field wearing new gray uniforms that featured black mourning bands on the left sleeves in memory of Chapman. The surprise tactic had just the effect Speaker hoped it would. As one observer noted: "Their metamorphosis was as unexpected as it was startling, and their appearance brought a roar of approval from the stands."

The game itself reinforced Speaker's belief that his front-line pitchers were the equal of their Brooklyn counterparts. Both Coveleskie and Marquard threw five-hitters, but the Cleveland spitballer was aided by two spectacular fielding plays by Speaker as the Indians won 3–1. The Cleveland center fielder robbed Zack Wheat of an apparent double in the second inning, and he made a game-saving grab of Ernest Krueger's deep drive in the eighth inning.

Sewell also played a key role in the victory with a single and two outstanding fielding plays. Recalling the Dodgers' willingness to waive the rule that would have prevented the shortstop from playing in the Series, columnist Westbrook Pegler noted: "The way Sewell returned the favor to Ebbets' club indicates they don't know how to spell gratitude where Sewell went to school."

The next day, the Brooklyn pitching began to exert itself. Grimes tossed a seven-hitter to beat the Indians 3–0 to even the Series, and Sherry Smith followed with a three-hitter for a 2–1 victory in game three. Sewell's error in the first inning paved the way for the Dodgers to score both their runs.

As they prepared to depart for Cleveland that evening, the Dodgers were a confident ballclub. Their biggest concern appeared to be the loss of their mascot and batboy, a hunchback orphan named Eddie Bennett. Myers, the Brooklyn center fielder, had befriended the boy in April, taking him to the ballpark with him one day. The Dodgers won the game, and Myers brought the orphan back with him the next day. When the ballclub kept winning, the players elected to keep the boy around as their good-luck charm. The kindhearted Myers even went so far as to take Bennett home and pay for his room and board.

But Ebbets refused to allow the boy to accompany the team to Cleveland, leading to a tearful scene as Myers prepared to leave home for the train station. As the *New York Sun* reported it, the young orphan was sobbing as he told the pitcher: "Go to Cleveland and win, Hi. I'll stay here and pull for you. But, gee, how I wish I could go."

Had he known what awaited his team in Cleveland, Ebbets might have reconsidered his decision. His ballclub was going to need all the good-luck charms it could round up.

81

The first tipoff that the string had run out on the Dodgers came several hours before game four on October 9. Before the team left its downtown hotel for League Park, Marquard, a Cleveland native, wandered through the crowded lobby trying to unload his set of box-seat tickets. Spotting a promising-looking prospect, the lanky pitcher walked up to the man and offered to sell him the tickets for $350. It was Marquard's biggest blunder of the Series. His mark turned out to be an undercover policeman, who promptly arrested the pitcher on charges of ticket scalping.

Seven other men were arrested on similar charges, but Rube easily was the most prominent of the scalpers who were booked at the police station that morning. The pitcher appealed to Police Chief Smith to be released until after the game, and the chief good-naturedly granted the request.

"Under the circumstances, we could not delay Marquard from reporting at the ballpark," said Chief Smith. "That would hardly have been sportsmanlike."

Marquard arrived at the ballpark just in time to see the Indians even the Series with a 5–1 victory behind the five-hit pitching of Coveleskie.

The next day, a Sunday, the pitcher was arraigned in municipal court before Judge William B. Beebe on a charge of "violation of the exhibition ordinance." Marquard entered a plea of not guilty and left the courtroom surrounded by reporters. Although he hadn't pitched since the opener, Rube had become the most publicized player in the Series.

82

Across town, Bill Wambsganss sat in a hotel room and poured out his frustrations to his friend F. C. Lane, the editor of *Baseball Magazine*. The Cleveland second baseman was a deeply disappointed ballplayer. His hitting in the World Series had been weak and his fielding had not been as sharp as that of his Brooklyn counterpart, Pete Kilduff.

Already, Wamby had suffered through a subpar batting year. At a time when most players had seen their offensive statistics boosted through the use of the livelier ball and stricter pitching rules, his batting average had dropped from .278 in 1919 to a paltry .244. Visiting with him before game five of the Series, Lane could not recall ever seeing the ballplayer so despondent.

Wambsganss was quiet and reserved away from the ballpark, but on the field he was a vocal ballplayer always yelling encouragement to the pitcher. His father was a Lutheran clergyman in Indiana, and Bill had been expected to follow in his footsteps. Although he stuttered slightly and was terrified of speaking in public, he made it through two years of the St. Louis Theological Seminary.

Then, through a stroke of luck, one of his classmates who had played pro ball received a letter from the manager of the Cedar Rapids, Iowa, team saying he needed a shortstop. The classmate was Al Ward, third baseman and manager of the seminary team. He recommended Wambsganss, and in 1913 Bill got his start in organized ball with Cedar Rapids of the Central Association.

Pro baseball was quite an adjustment for the young seminary student. When he arrived at the hotel in Cedar Rapids, the other players pulled up in a horse-drawn van in front of the hotel. Wambsganss made his debut the next day in a Fourth of July doubleheader.

He returned to the seminary in the offseason and spent the winter in North Dakota doing field work as a schoolteacher. He rejoined Cedar Rapids in the spring of 1914 and quickly established himself as one of the smoothest fielders in the league. One day, he was discovered by a Cleveland scout who saw him handle fifteen chances without an error in a doubleheader.

When the scout reported his find, he was asked by the Cleveland owners, "What's he got?"

"Well, he has the funniest darn name I ever heard."

When it was reported on July 15, 1914, that the Naps had purchased Wambsganss for twelve hundred dollars, one scribe greeted the news with the notation: "Holy mackerel, what a moniker!" For the sake of brevity, the writers immediately shortened the name to "Wamby" to fit in the box scores.

Even Wambsganss marveled at his strange name. He claimed that when he was in school, a German professor once tried to analyze the name and finally determined it came from German words that when taken together give something of the meaning of the English term "overcoat."

"I don't know whether it fits me or not, but I have worn it all my life and will probably carry it with me to the end," Wambsganss said. "Anyway, it's a name that people don't confuse like Miller or Jones, even though there seems to be 96 different ways of pronouncing it.

"The umpires open their mouths, clear their throats, close both eyes and let out a bellow that sounds like Wamby-ganz. Probably that's the best they can do, but it was a real relief to me when people commenced to call me Wamby.

"That's a rather queer name itself, but at least they could pronounce it without choking and getting black in the face."

After that first season in Cleveland, Wamby went to his father and explained he no longer felt up to the task of being a minister and now wanted to pursue a career as a baseball player. The elder Wambsganss, a Cleveland baseball fan whose favorite player was Nap Lajoie, was thrilled by his son's decision.

By 1917, Wambsganss's slick fielding had earned him a starting position at second base. For three years, his spot on the team had been unchallenged, but his season-long batting slump in 1920 had made him the focus of criticism among the Cleveland fans. Some of his more vocal detractors even had called for him to be benched. His showing early in the World Series had done little to improve his status.

Listening to the dejected ballplayer talk on the morning of October 10, Lane could only offer encouragement.

"Stay with it, Bill," he said. "This could be your day."

Just talking to the writer had made Wamby feel better. He thanked Lane for his support, then got up to head to the ballpark.

In just a few hours, the man with the awkward name would earn himself a permanent spot in the baseball history books.

*   *   *

There were 26,784 fans on hand at League Park that Sunday afternoon, although later thousands more than that would claim to have been there. Bagby was scheduled to pitch for the Indians, and he was sitting in the dugout just before game time when Speaker walked over to see how he was feeling.

"Everything all right?" asked Speaker.

"Sure is," Bagby replied in his Southern drawl.

The manager then began to talk about how to pitch to the various Brooklyn hitters to prevent them from hitting the ball out to the temporary bleachers that had shortened the distance to the fence in right and center fields. After listening silently for a few minutes, the Sarge finally spoke up.

"I think I'll bust one out to those wooden seats. They seem just about right for me to hit."

Bagby got through the first inning, allowing only a harmless single, then retired to the bench to see how his teammates fared against Grimes. The spitballer had shut out the Indians in game two, but this time they jumped on him immediately. Jamieson and Wamby lined out singles, and Speaker crossed up the Dodgers by bunting for a base hit to load the bases. Smith, who had gone hitless against Grimes in Brooklyn, followed by hitting a 1–2 pitch high over the screen in right field for a grand slam—the first in World Series history.

That set the tone for one of the most amazing baseball games ever played. In the fourth inning, Bagby made good on his vow by hitting a drive that fell just over the shortened fence in right-center field for a three-run homer. It was the first roundtripper hit by a pitcher in Series competition. It also finished off Grimes, who was replaced by left-hander Clarence Mitchell.

The crowd still had not settled down from the excitement of the two blasts when the Robins came to bat in the fifth inning, trailing 7–0. Kilduff led off with a single and Otto Miller followed with another base hit to put runners on first and second with no outs. That brought up Mitchell, a good-hitting pitcher who was allowed to bat for himself.

Wamby stationed himself deep on the grass against Mitchell, a left-handed hitter who normally pulled the ball to right field. With the Indians leading by seven runs, Wamby wasn't concerned about the double play. He just wanted to prevent a base hit and keep the Robins from having a big inning.

The count was 1–1 when Mitchell lined the ball up the middle. Everyone in the ballpark thought the ball was a hit as it shot past second base and toward center field. Kilduff and Miller, believing the drive was out of any fielder's reach, took off running full speed. At the same time, Wamby took three steps to his right and threw his body toward center field, with his glove hand extended. Somehow, he pulled down the ball, cupping it in his mitt with his bare hand. That was one out.

As he landed on his feet, his momentum carried him toward second base. Kilduff was almost all the way to third by now, and all Wamby had to do was step on the bag for the second out. Turning to his left, he saw Miller standing just a few feet away. Startled, the runner had pulled up short of second and remained stationary, his mouth hanging open.

"Tag him! Tag him!" shouted Sewell.

Wamby needed no such prodding. Calmly, he walked over and gently touched the ball to Miller for the third out, completing the unassisted triple play, the rarest achievement in baseball.

As umpire Hank O'Day made the final out call, Wamby began running off the field. The fans were so stunned by what they had seen, they remained silent for a moment. Then, as Wamby neared the dugout, they began shouting louder and louder, and tossing their straw hats into the air.

Ring Lardner succinctly recorded the event with the notation: "It was the first time in world serious history that a man named Wambsganss had ever made a triple play assisted by consonants only."

The Indians won by a final score of 8–1, putting them ahead three games to two. It had been a remarkable day for the Clevelanders, and it would have a bizarre ending to it. That evening, reserve catcher Leslie Nunamaker went to bed and discovered a roll of bills under his pillow. Keenly aware of what had happened to the White Sox players involved in the 1919 World Series fix, Nunamaker rushed from his room to report the matter to Ban Johnson. The league president seized the bills for evidence. Later, when he inspected the money, he discovered the roll contained only sixteen Confederate dollar bills.

The way events had turned around so dramatically in the Series, Johnson thought that was about how much he would give for Brooklyn's chances at this point.

83

Mails, who had pitched in relief in game three, got his long-awaited start against Brooklyn in game six. After taking his pregame warm-up pitches, he strutted into the Cleveland dugout.

"Well, you boys get me one run today and we'll win. Brooklyn will be lucky to get a foul off me today."

The Great Mails proceeded to back up his bold prediction with a three-hit shutout for a 1–0 victory. The only run of the game scored in the sixth when Speaker hit a two-out single to left and scored on a double by George Burns. Mails, the former Brooklyn castoff, now had allowed only six hits and no runs in 15⅔ innings against his old teammates in the Series.

"I would pitch my arm off for Tris Speaker if need be," he boasted, "but I didn't need to strain myself in this game as I kept going along easy."

The Dodgers' humiliation continued on Tuesday morning, October 12. With the seventh and possibly final game of the World

Series just hours away, Marquard was found guilty in Police Court on a charge of ticket scalping. He was fined one dollar and costs by Judge Silbert.

"I am satisfied that Marquard violated the law and the spirit of the law," said the judge, "but I believe that he has been punished enough by being written up more than any presidential candidate and feel that this has been a lesson to him."

Referring to Detective Soukup's testimony that he told Marquard he was indeed the biggest rube in the hotel because of his attempt to sell the tickets, Silbert added: "I agree with Soukup's statements and feel that Rube has indeed been a rube, but think that hereafter he will stick to the game and try to keep it clean."

The costs amounted to $3.80. Marquard paid the money owed minutes after the trial ended and headed to the ballpark. That would not be the end of the Rube's troubles. He was the logical choice to pitch the seventh game in an attempt to prevent the Indians from clinching the championship, but Robinson was so mad at him he kept the big left-hander on the bench. Already, the decision had been made to unload Marquard, who would be traded to Cincinnati before the next season. But the worst blow was yet to come. Within a week of the final game of the World Series, Marquard's wife, who was better known as "Blossom Seeley" of the vaudeville stage, would divorce him.

Sensing a chance to finish off the demoralized Dodgers in the final game on the Indians' home grounds, Speaker was taking no chances of letting the Series return to Brooklyn. He named Coveleskie, who already had beaten the Dodgers twice, as his starting pitcher and informed him, "Stan, if you don't win today, you're pitching tomorrow."

Covey had no intention of letting that happen. He went out and blanked Brooklyn on five hits for a 3–0 victory. At 3:57 in the afternoon, the crowd of 27,525 watched as the Robins' Ed Konetchy hit a grounder to Sewell, who had the honor of flipping the ball to Wamby to force Myers at second for the final out of the season.

As soon as Wamby stepped on second base, Speaker raced from center field toward Dunn's box, where Mrs. Speaker, who once opposed her son's desire to become a professional ballplayer because he would be "sold into slavery," was waiting for him. Spoke dodged through the crowd on the field, went through an open gate to an adjoining box, and leaned across the railing to hug his mother.

Fred Charles of the *Plain Dealer* described the scene: "The embrace and the kiss awed the crowd into a moment of silence, and then a cheer went up. All over the stands women were standing on tip-toe or leaning across the railings, many of them with glistening eyes."

A crowd of fifteen thousand fans had gathered at the private box of the owner, and they were cheering themselves hoarse. Speaker turned and started back across the diamond to the clubhouse, again making his way through the throngs of people. Along the way, enthusiastic fans shook the manager's hand, slapped him on the back, and cheered him. The crowd parted to make a path for him, then clamored about him in his wake.

Once Speaker disappeared down the clubhouse steps, the fans turned their attention back to Dunn. They began chanting: "What's the matter with Dunn?! He's all right!" and "What's the matter with Speaker?! He's all right!"

Then came the cries of "Speech! Speech!"

Dunn responded by removing his hat and waving.

"I am the happiest man in the whole world today! I know you are happy, too! After all, it is your team! It is Cleveland's team more than it is mine! I thank you for your enthusiasm and for your loyalty!"

A small boy elbowed his way into the box and handed Dunn a scorecard and a pencil for an autograph. Dunn, his hands shaking from the excitement, wrote his name across the top of the card. For the next ten minutes, the team owner stood and signed more autographs.

As he did, Robins owner Charles Ebbets came to the box to shake his hand. Ebbets, too, was called upon to make a speech and, with his hat in his hand, he said: "I congratulate Mr. Dunn and the Cleveland boys. The best team won."

Throughout all this, Mrs. Speaker was alternately sitting and standing, with tears in her eyes and her hand at her throat. When she was called upon for a speech, the fans had to strain to hear her words.

"I am the happiest woman in the world. I am happy as only a mother can be happy—happy because of my son."

Then she sat down and cried.

Dunn brushed aside the last of the autograph seekers and, accompanied by a policeman, pushed his way through the crowd toward the clubhouse. Along the way, the excited fans pounded him on the back and attempted to hug him. Only when Dunn descended the steps did the crowd begin to head for the exits.

In the dressing room, Speaker drained two fountain pens while autographing scorecards and baseballs.

Half an hour later, almost four thousand fans still were standing in East Sixty-sixth Street, waiting for one more opportunity to cheer the players as they emerged from the locker room one by one and left the grounds.

84

One week after the World Series ended, the city of Cleveland held a public celebration at Wade Park to honor its championship ballclub. A stage was erected in a hollow of the park, which made a natural amphitheater, and long before sundown, hundreds of fans began assembling on the hillsides. By the time Mayor W. S. FitzGerald and Dunn arrived at seven o'clock in the evening, the embankments were packed. Estimates of the crowd size ranged from twenty-five thousand to fifty thousand.

The mayor and other city officials occupied the stage with Dunn and the players, while the players' relatives and friends sat in a semicircle in chairs in front of the stand. The crowd was kept back at a distance of fifty feet by a rope that stretched from the park lagoon to nearby Doan Brook.

Mayor FitzGerald began the proceedings by congratulating Dunn and the ballplayers. He then turned his attention to Ray Chapman.

"It was his manly spirit which dominated the game," the mayor said somberly. There was a moment of silence, after which the crowd could restrain itself no longer. The people began cheering and setting off firecrackers, and FitzGerald introduced the ballplayers, whose names were shouted through a megaphone by Harper Garcia Smyth.

In the excitement, the restraining rope was either broken or taken down, prompting the crowd to surge forward toward the stage, sweeping those who were seated from their chairs and causing a panic. In an effort to calm the people, Speaker, Wood, and Johnston stood to sing "Watching the World Go By."

It appeared that order had been restored, but when Johnston, Coveleskie, and Dunn leaned over the railing to shake hands, a new rush began. Fearing the situation might get out of hand, the players and others on the platform began to plead with the spectators to go home.

It was no use. Amid the screaming and shouting, the mob relentlessly pushed forward. In defense, several men near the stand formed flying wedges and charged through the crowd toward Euclid Avenue in an effort to turn the throng in the other direction. Still, the mayhem continued.

Hundreds of people were crushed against the platform, and chairs were trampled to splinters. The players grabbed their loved ones and fled for safety, while the mayor and other officials shouted for the crowd to disperse. As the people in the rear continued to push forward, those trapped in the middle of the mob lifted their babies above their heads and passed them forward to the stand in an effort to get them out of danger. On the edge of the crowd, several people were knocked into the adjoining lagoon and brook.

After escaping to higher ground, the Cleveland ballplayers turned and looked back at the scene in the park below them. To many of them, it seemed an appropriate ending for a bittersweet season, one they would remember more for its tragedy than for its triumph.

*   *   *

That night, the Cleveland ballplayers said their good-byes to one another and went their separate ways for the winter.

Several of them would remain in the city, among them O'Neill, Graney, Johnston, and Caldwell. Johnston would operate the billiard room he bought on Superior Avenue. O'Neill, who once had planned to go to work for Chapman at the Pioneer Alloys Company, instead would join Caldwell in entering the automobile business.

Speaker and Nunamaker would leave soon for a fishing trip in Canada before returning to Speaker's home in Texas for more hunting and fishing. Thomas wanted to head to Los Angeles, where he hoped to hook up with a movie company. Gardner would return to Vermont where he was co-owner of an auto repair and sales agency. Jamieson was going back to Paterson, New Jersey, where he would use his World Series bonus to buy a home to live in while he worked selling groceries. Wood also was headed for New Jersey, where he would work felling trees. Coveleskie would return to his home in Pennsylvania, then hook up with Wood for a hunting trip. "Doc" Evans would do his residence work in a St. Louis hospital. Bagby would work as a car salesman in Augusta, Georgia, while Guy Morton wanted only to hunt and fish near his home in Vernon, Alabama. The Great Mails was scheduled to marry Miss Grace Rippe of Seattle.

Sewell, the newest member of the club, planned to return to Alabama, anxious to get home in time to continue his studies at the University of Alabama and watch the Tide football team, which he had been a member of the previous fall.

Even if he never had played another game of major-league ball, Sewell's spot in Cleveland baseball history was assured. In the most difficult circumstances imaginable for an untested twenty-one-year-old rookie, he had far exceeded what Speaker or anyone else connected with the team had dared hoped for. In the regular season,

Sewell had a .329 batting average, .414 slugging percentage, and fourteen runs scored in twenty-two games. By comparison, Chapman's statistics for the season had been a .303 batting average, a .423 slugging percentage, and ninety-seven runs scored in 111 games.

Even Sewell's poor performance in the World Series, when he had batted just .174 and committed six errors in seven games, could not tarnish his contribution to the Indians' championship effort.

James Isaminger paid tribute to the young shortstop in the October 14, 1920, issue of *The Sporting News*: "Sewell must get full credit for breaking into the fast set in a pennant fight and then jumping into a World's Series. I don't believe there was ever an infielder who started a big-league career under the same circumstances. Only a rookie with lots of nerve could ever make good before howling World's Series mobs."

On his way to Cleveland more than a month earlier, Sewell had steadied his nerves by vowing to become the virtual reincarnation of Ray Chapman on the ballfield. He had kept his promise.

VII

The Aftermath

I intend to keep on and work as well as I can to provide a home and comfortable future for my family. This is what I shall try to do, for that is my lookout. What people may wish to think about me or say about me is their lookout.

Carl Mays

85

On August 17, 1921—the first anniversary of Chapman's death—the six thousand paying customers who arrived at the ballpark in Cleveland were greeted by young ladies from the local YWCA. The women, who were wearing shoulder sashes with the inscription "In Memoriam of Ray Chapman," handed out rosebuds to each fan passing through the gates.

The Indians were playing the Philadelphia Athletics in a doubleheader on an overcast and dreary afternoon, and no announcement had been made of the special ceremony that would be held to honor the deceased ballplayer. It was to be a quiet and simple tribute. That was the way Jim Dunn wanted it.

The Indians owner had invited Chapman's widow to attend the game as his guest, but she had declined. Kathleen had not seen a game since her husband's death, nor would she ever return to the ballpark. The task of representing the family had been left to her father, who sat with Dunn in the owner's private box.

The ballclub was much the same as it had been at the end of the previous season, excluding a notable change in cosmetics. In his boastfulness, Dunn had outfitted the players in garish new uniforms with the words "World's Champions" emblazoned across the fronts of the shirts.

On this day, Cleveland was in second place in the standings, trailing first-place New York by the scantest of margins—just a hundredth of a percentage point. Coveleskie, one of the heroes of the previous World Series, was on the mound to face Philadelphia's Lefty Moore. The Athletics quickly jumped on Coveleskie, scoring four runs on four hits and two costly errors in the top of the first inning.

The fans still were grumbling about the Indians' poor play when Jamieson, leading off the bottom of the first, took a hard cut at one of Moore's pitches and sent a vicious shot toward right field. Johnny Walker, Philadelphia's twenty-four-year-old baseman, lunged to his left in an effort to stop the drive. When he did, the ball struck the hard-baked ground near the bag and took a wicked bounce. Walker had no chance to protect himself as the ball shot up and struck him on the right side of his head just above his ear. There was a sickening crack as the force of the blow lifted him off his feet and spun him around. He already was unconscious as he fell headfirst to the ground.

Players from both teams rushed to Walker's aid, fearing the worst. Leaning over the stricken ballplayer, the Indians could not help but feel as if they were reliving that horrible moment from a year earlier when it was Chapman who lay injured in the dirt. For a full ten minutes, the two trainers and Cleveland outfielder Joe Evans, who had completed his medical studies at the University of Mississippi during the winter and now was a doctor in his residency, administered first aid to Walker.

Finally, the Philadelphia first baseman regained consciousness and was able to sit up. The relieved fans, who already were in a somber mood because of the tribute to Chapman, applauded with relief. Walker was in great pain, but with the aid of two of his teammates, he slowly made his way to the dressing room. A few moments later, the injured player, accompanied by Evans, was rushed to Lakeside Hospital to be treated by Dr. M. H. Castle, the Indians' physician. Before leaving, Evans confided to several players that he feared Walker's skull had been fractured and that his life was in danger.

After this grim beginning, the game proceeded. Jamieson's hit touched off a five-run rally by the Indians, chasing Moore from the mound. Slim Byron Harris, who earlier in the season had won eight consecutive games for the last-place Athletics, came in and got the final out of the inning.

Philadelphia briefly tied the score in the top of the second, but Cleveland scored four runs in the bottom of the inning to take a 9–5 lead. By the time the Indians came to bat in the bottom of the fifth, the score was 10–7 and Rollie Naylor was pitching for the Athletics.

No one in the ballpark needed reminding that it was while leading off the fifth inning against the Yankees one year earlier that Chapman had been fatally beaned. To the Indians, it seemed to be fate, not coincidence, that the first batter up now was Wamby, who had moved up to assume Chapman's number-two spot in the batting order.

Naylor delivered one pitch, which Wamby made no effort to hit. Behind the plate, umpire Billy Evans, also a friend of Chapman's, signaled ball one and then called for a timeout.

Silently, the Cleveland ballplayers stepped from their dugout, removed their caps, and stood with heads lowered. There had been no announcement that such a ceremony would be held, but the fans needed no urging to rise to their feet and bow their heads in silence. A stillness settled over the grounds, and the American flag fluttered weakly at half-mast just beyond the outfield fence. Sixty seconds passed before Evans raised his head and called out, "Play ball!"

Shortly after the tribute to Chapman, Doc Evans returned to the ballpark. He brought with him encouraging news: Although Walker had suffered a severe concussion, his skull had not been fractured as had been feared. His condition was listed as serious, but his life was not in danger.

The game itself was anticlimactic. Cleveland won 15–8. Wamby, batting in Chapman's spot, was two for four with two runs scored. Sewell, batting sixth, was one for five with one run scored.

The last out had just been recorded when a steady rain began falling, forcing the postponement of the second half of the double-header.

86

Rae Marie Chapman was born on February 27, 1921, a Sunday, at St. Ann's Maternity Hospital in Cleveland. The news of her birth commanded an eight-column, seventy-two-point headline across the top of the front page of the *Cleveland News.*

The newspaper called the seven-pound baby girl "a living monument to perpetuate the memory of Ray Chapman."

As a youngster, Rae Marie was described by her uncle, Dan Daly, as "an active child who was very musical. She liked to sing and dance. And she was quite clever in school."

Rae Marie was two years old when her mother remarried. Kathleen's second husband was one of her cousins—Joseph F. McMahon, a California oil man. The couple had one son and named him Joseph McMahon, Jr.

It had taken Kathleen a long time to recover from Ray's death, and her family hoped that her new marriage would help her regain the happiness she once had known. But on April 21, 1928, when she was thirty-four years old, Kathleen died suddenly in California.

The circumstances of her death were the subject of some controversy. The version repeated by the Daly family was that Mrs. Daly had gone to Los Angeles to accompany Kathleen on a trip to Hawaii. The trunks already were packed and ready to go when Kathleen, who had not been in good health, returned to the bedroom to take some medication. A few moments later, she suddenly called out, "Oh, Mother!" Mrs. Daly rushed in to discover Kathleen lying on the floor. According to Mrs. Daly, her daughter had gotten the bottles mixed up and accidentally poisoned herself.

"The medicine was in the cabinet, but she took a bottle of something else—cleaning fluid or something that looked the same," Dan Daly claimed years later. "In her weakened condition, it was just enough to kick her over the line."

However, the Cleveland newspapers attributed Kathleen's death to a "self-administered poisonous acid." The *Plain Dealer* added that she recently had returned from a hospital where "she had attempted to recover from a nervous breakdown."

A copy of the coroner's report attached to an insurance form sent to Chapman's mother also listed the cause of death as suicide.

Following Kathleen's death, young Rae Marie returned to Cleveland to live with her grandparents. That winter, there was an outbreak of measles in the city, so the Daly family sent the child to Florida to prevent her from catching the disease. Despite the precautions, Rae Marie contracted the measles shortly after her return to Cleveland in April. Complications set in, and Chapman's daughter, only eight years old, died on April 27, 1929—within six days of the first anniversary of her mother's death.

There was one other notation to the young girl's death. The nurse who cared for Rae Marie said that one day in Florida, the youngster told her, "I was talking to my mother last night."

"You mean Mrs. Daly?" asked the nurse.

"No, no. I mean my real mother."

Not knowing what to say, the nurse could only answer, "Oh."

"Oh, yes," said Rae Marie. "She talks to me once in a while. And she told me I'll be with her soon."

*   *   *

After returning from her son's funeral, Mrs. Chapman withdrew from contact with the outside world. She stopped going to church and abandoned all of her social activities. Only rarely did she leave the house.

"She gave up everything," recalled Margaret Chapman, who was fifteen years old at the time. "She just sat in the house. She never cried. She didn't cry, but she was very bitter. She was so introverted and bitter.

"It was seven years before she got over that. For seven years, she was in a deep depression. And it was hard on us. That's when I needed her the most. I was a young girl, getting ready to go to high school, and I needed her. I had a good friend whose mother was wonderful, and I used to think, 'Oh, I wish my mother was like that.' But she couldn't give it to me.

"Ray was her favorite. He always was her favorite. But that was okay. He was everyone's favorite."

87

With the memory of Chapman's beaning still fresh in their minds, the Indians experimented with a form of protective headgear during training camp in the spring of 1921. The head covering was made of leather and was similar to the football helmets then in vogue, but the players found it very unsatisfactory and soon abandoned its use.

It was not the first time such equipment had been tried by professional ballplayers. Perhaps the first actual headgear designed to protect the batter was patented January 24, 1905, by the A. J. Reach Company. The innovation was known as the "Reach Pneumatic Head Protector." Although it did not gain acceptance, a few players such as Roger Bresnahan, who was credited with popularizing the use of shin guards by catchers, did wear it on occasion.

Despite Chapman's death, it was not until 1941 that the Brooklyn Dodgers became the first team to be equipped with batting helmets. Larry MacPhail had his team outfitted with the helmets, made of a light plastic material, after Jake Mooty of the Cubs hit Pee Wee Reese in the head with a pitch. Reese had the honor of being the first batter to wear the headgear, in a spring-training game between the Dodgers and Indians on March 8 in Havana, Cuba.

Late in the 1952 season, Pittsburgh Pirates executive Branch Rickey issued plastic batting caps to his team. These caps, which fit lower over the temples and ears than the previous model and weighed six to seven ounces, had been tried earlier in the season by the Pirates' New Orleans farm team in the Southern Association. The helmets were made of fiberglass and polyester resin, and were produced by American Baseball Cap, Inc., of which Rickey also was president.

This earned Rickey the reputation as "the father of the batting helmet." At first, the Pirates were instructed to wear the helmets throughout the game, prompting the following observation from Pittsburgh catcher Joe Garagiola: "It was awful. You see, we wore them all the time, not just at bat. And in the bullpen, the kids would be bouncing marbles off our helmets all day long. The fans called us coalminers, and the things were really heavy to wear."

Before long, the Pirates switched to using the helmets only when batting.

Although several players vowed never to use them, batting helmets had arrived on the scene to stay. In 1956, the National League made their use mandatory. Before the 1958 season, the American League teams voted seven to one to follow suit. Boston general manager Joe Cronin cast the lone dissenting vote, believing the league was legislating against Red Sox star Ted Williams, who was adamant in his refusal to wear a helmet. Nevertheless, in March 1958, AL president Will Harridge notified his umpires that all players were required to wear the protective headgear.

88

Late one night after his team won the world championship in 1920, Indians owner Jim Dunn, fortified by liquor, walked out to the middle of his empty ballpark. He spread out his arms, threw back his head, and shouted out triumphantly, "I own the best damn baseball team in all the world!"

The Indians' glory would be short-lived. Dunn died in the spring of 1922, and his widow inherited control of the team. That marked the beginning of the ballclub's demise, and it would be 1948 before the Indians would win another league championship.

It did not take long for the breakup of the ballclub to begin.

Graney retired in 1922 and over the next few years he became a prosperous automobile dealer. He was wiped out by the stock market crash in 1929, and two years later turned to broadcasting the Indians' ballgames on the radio to earn money. He was the first ballplayer to move to the radio booth, where he served from 1931 to 1953. His popularity as an announcer was even greater than his popularity as an active player, although he rarely displayed the humor he had on the ballfield. When he retired in 1953, the Cleveland fans staged a special "night" to honor him.

Graney later moved to Missouri, where he died in 1978 at the age of ninety-one. In those final years, he enjoyed reminiscing about baseball, and he always said being a member of that 1920 championship team was his greatest achievement as a player. But to the day he died, he never forgave Mays for the fatal beaning of Chapman. In 1962, writer Regis McAuley asked Graney about the incident. The old ballplayer's words were as bitter as they had been more than forty years earlier: "People ask me today if I still feel that Mays threw at Chappie. My answer has always been the same—yes, definitely!"

O'Neill stayed with the Indians through the 1923 season, then went on to play for the Red Sox, Yankees, and Browns before retiring in 1928. He later spent fourteen years as a big-league manager with the Indians, Tigers, Red Sox, and Phillies, and he led Detroit to the world championship in 1945. O'Neill returned to Cleveland following his retirement in 1954 and died eight years later.

For Speaker, the 1920 championship was the pinnacle of his career, both as a player and as a manager. Over the next six seasons, he led the Indians to finishes of second twice, third, fourth, and sixth twice before a belated betting scandal forced him to resign his post as manager following the 1926 campaign. Former Detroit pitcher Dutch Leonard alleged that he had been involved in a scheme with Speaker, Wood, and Cobb to bet on the outcome of the final game of the 1919 season between the Tigers and Indians. The three men denied Leonard's charges, and Speaker pointed out in his defense that he had hit two triples in that game. The charges were dropped when Leonard failed to appear before commissioner Kenesaw Mountain Landis and repeat his allegations in front of the other three.

Having weathered the crisis, Speaker resumed his playing career with Washington in 1927 before joining his aging rival Cobb on the Philadelphia Athletics in 1928 for his final season. Speaker's twenty-two-year totals in the big leagues included a .344 batting average and 3,515 hits. Nine years after his retirement, he was among the second group of players elected to the Hall of Fame, where his plaque hails him as "the greatest center fielder of his day."

In 1945, while he was living in Cleveland, Speaker was setting out flowers for his wife one day when he fell from the porch roof of his home and fractured his skull. Although he would recover completely, at least one newspaperman felt compelled to remark on the similarity between Speaker's injury and the one suffered by Chapman twenty-five years earlier. Wrote Joe Williams: "Dark memories are stirred regarding the fate of Ray Chapman—the one great pal Speaker had in baseball. You can never tell what kind of a calling card the old G.R. (Grim Reaper) is going to use, can you?"

Even in retirement, Speaker remained an avid baseball fan. He and his wife, the former Mary Frances Cudahy, whom he had married in 1925, regularly attended the games in Cleveland and often traveled to the club's spring-training site. In 1958, Speaker celebrated his seventieth birthday at the Indians' training camp in Tucson. The following December, the couple went to his hometown of Hubbard, Texas, for a three-month vacation before again heading west for spring training. Speaker and a friend, Charles Vaughn of Hubbard, spent one day fishing on Lake Whitney, not far from the ballplayer's birthplace. They were about to return home at 5:30 in the afternoon when Speaker suddenly slumped forward in the boat. Vaughn and several other fishermen picked him up and carried him to the back of his car. When a doctor arrived a few minutes later, Speaker opened his eyes and whispered, "My name is Tris Speaker." Then he died, the victim of a heart attack.

89

After his spectacular debut with Cleveland in the fall of 1920, Joe Sewell returned to the University of Alabama to begin medical school. He also joined the Black Fryars, the university's drama group, and a few weeks after playing in the World Series he was playing a part in the group's road play.

The next spring, Joe's brother Luke and his best friend, Riggs Stephenson, joined him on the Indians, and each of the three youngsters went on to gain fame in his own right.

Stephenson played part-time for the Indians for five years before being traded to the Chicago Cubs. There, he batted over .300 for eight consecutive seasons. He retired following the 1934 season with a fourteen-year batting average of .336.

Luke Sewell, a catcher, played twenty seasons for four different teams in the big leagues, compiling a .259 average. In 1941, he became the manager of the St. Louis Browns, and three years later he led them to their first and only American League pennant.

A third brother, Tommy, briefly made it to the major leagues with the Cubs in 1927, batting one time.

But the most spectacular career belonged to Joe Sewell, who quickly proved that his performance in 1920 had not been a fluke. He batted .318 in 1921, and he remained the Indians' shortstop for ten seasons. His best year was 1923, when he batted .353 with 109 runs batted in. In 1931, he was traded to the Yankees, where he played three more years before retiring to become a coach for his new team.

Sewell's career was one of the most remarkable in baseball. Not only did he compile a lifetime batting average of .312, but he became known as the hardest man to strike out in the game's history. In fourteen seasons, he struck out only 114 times, or once every 62.8 times at bat. Once, he batted 437 consecutive times—from May 17 to September 29, 1929—without fanning, and in both the 1930 and 1932 seasons he struck out only three times.

Sewell also played in 1,103 consecutive games from September 13, 1922, through April 30, 1930—still the fifth-longest such streak in the major leagues. The flu and a 102-degree temperature finally forced him out of the lineup.

After leaving the Yankees, Sewell returned to Alabama. He stayed active in baseball by coaching the team at the University of Alabama and scouting for several major-league teams, among them the Indians.

In 1977, Sewell was voted into the National Baseball Hall of Fame. The young ballplayer who had gotten his start in the big leagues because of the game's greatest tragedy had earned himself a spot among the greats of baseball.

Even in his old age, Sewell remained an active and alert man. He already was seventy-eight years old when he was inducted into the Hall of Fame, yet for years afterward he continued to travel to Cooperstown, New York, for the annual ceremony. His wife of sixty-three years, Willie Veal Sewell, died in 1984, and Joe was left alone in his brick house just a few blocks from the University of Alabama campus. He had his two poodles—Rusty and Bo—to keep him company. He also had his baseball memories. More than fifty years after his retirement, he received a bundle of mail every day from fans wanting his autograph. He answered every request, but always there were piles of letters more than a foot high stacked on the counters in his kitchen. In his den were his trophies, pictures, and other baseball souvenirs. He still had his old pair of baseball shoes, as well as his bats.

"See that bat there," he would tell visitors, pointing to a

forty-ounce black bat enclosed in a glass case. "That was my Sunday bat—my best bat. I used that bat for fourteen years in the major leagues and never broke it."

It was Black Betsy, the bat George Burns had given Sewell before his first game with the Indians back in September 1920.

It was funny how things worked out, said Sewell. In some ways, he had enjoyed the type of career that had been predicted for Chapman. In other ways, he had outperformed his ill-fated predecessor.

"I never knew the man," said Sewell. "But Chapman must have been a great person. I never heard anybody criticize him."

Once, Sewell had told an interviewer he owed his success to Chapman. "As I look back, I know it was Chapman's death that made a star out of me," he had said in a 1933 interview. "If I had not pictured myself as his virtual reincarnation, I would have long since gone back to the minor leagues."

When asked about the quotation more than fifty years later, Sewell smiled and agreed that it was true. Often he had thought of himself as Chapman's reincarnation on the ballfield. And yet, he added, there had been more to it than that.

"I won't say that I was playing in Chapman's shadow because I was doing a job for myself. But there were a lot of people who were comparing me to Chapman, and Chapman to me. You know, who was the best and who could do the most things and stuff like that. We boys used to sit around the clubhouse, and they would talk about Chappie used to do this, Chappie used to do that, Chappie used to say this. He was well liked and he was a good ballplayer. His record holds that out.

"But I'm telling you what, the beautiful part about the whole thing was, when he got killed, I came right in there behind him, picked up the slack and just kept going. And when the smoke cleared away down at the end of the road, chances are I was a better ballplayer than Chappie was. The records, you know. Down the road, after several years, maybe I was a better ballplayer than Chappie. So you never know what's ahead of you until you try."

90

Chapman was buried in Cleveland's Lake View Cemetery, one of the city's most historic landmarks. Since its founding in 1869, it has been the final resting place for twenty-two of Cleveland's mayors and twenty of the thirty-two members of the city's Early Settlers Association Hall of Fame. Lake View also boasts the John D. Rockefeller memorial and the James A. Garfield Monument, a 180-foot-tall stone tower erected in memory of the nation's twentieth president.

Chapman's gravesite is not marked on any of the cemetery's brochures, and his tombstone says simply, "Raymond Johnson Chapman, 1891-1920." He rests there alone—four miles to the north of where his wife and daughter are buried in Calvary Cemetery.

Less than three miles west of Lake View Cemetery lies another famous Cleveland landmark—the remnants of League Park. The old ballpark, which reverted to its original name following Dunn's death, had been the exclusive domain of the Indians until 1932, when the city completed construction of a new Lakefront Municipal Stadium, which could hold three times as many fans. Although the ballclub divided its schedule between the two playing sites, the fate of League Park was sealed by the completion of the new facility. The wooden superstructure of the old ballpark was deteriorating rapidly and one year a windstorm blew down part of the outfield fence. In 1946, when Bill Veeck bought the Indians, the team moved into Municipal Stadium full-time.

The City of Cleveland bought League Park and demolished all but the Lexington Avenue wall and the two-story structure that housed the office buildings. The site fell into disrepair until 1979, when the Lexington Avenue neighborhood refurbished the park and declared it a Cleveland landmark. There now is a historical marker on the grounds explaining League Park's glorious history. Sadly, however, an important plaque from the old ballpark is missing. It was a bronze tablet, selected by Mayor FitzGerald's memorial committee from a group of nineteen designs and bought by the Cleveland baseball fans to be placed at the entrance to the park in 1921 in memory of Chapman.

Across the top of this tablet was the heading, "Chappie, The Idol of the Fans." Beneath these words was a picture of Chapman in uniform in the middle of a baseball diamond with a sprig of laurel on top. There was a glove thrown on the field at shortstop to mark the position he played. Two bats were crossed below home plate. At the bottom of the tablet was an inscription that could serve as the ballplayer's epitaph:

Raymond Johnson Chapman

This tablet erected by lovers of
Clean sport as an affectionate
Tribute to his inspiring enthusiasm,
Cheerfulness and unfailing
Loyalty to his club.

"He lives in the hearts of all those who knew him."

91

There was a special air of excitement surrounding the 1921 World Series. For the first time in history, the two New York teams were pitted against each other in the fall showdown for baseball supremacy. The Giants had won their seventh National

League championship in twenty years under the guidance of the legendary John McGraw. The Yankees, led by the slugging Ruth, finally had claimed their first American League pennant after a tight battle with the Indians. The World Series would be a confrontation between baseball's old guard and its team of the future.

Mays, who had won twenty-seven games that season, pitched a five-hit shutout for a 3–0 victory in the opener. His teammate, Waite Hoyt, followed with another 3–0 shutout the next day, and the Yankees had a 2–0 lead in the best-of-nine Series. The Giants rallied for a 13–5 decision in game three to cut the Yankees' advantage in half.

That was the situation when Mays faced the Giants' Shufflin' Phil Douglas in game four. In its own curious way, this game was to haunt Mays almost as much as the one fourteen months earlier when he had fatally beaned Chapman.

Through the first seven innings, Mays allowed only two harmless singles as the Yankees took a 1–0 lead on the strength of a run-scoring triple by Wally Schang. The American Leaguers appeared on their way to another victory when disaster suddenly struck in the eighth inning. The first batter up for the Giants was Emil "Irish" Meusel, a hard-hitting outfielder who had been acquired from the Phillies midway through the season. Miller Huggins signaled his pitcher to throw a fastball. Mays ignored the instructions, choosing instead to serve up a slow-breaking curve. Meusel lined the ball off the wall for a triple. In the Yankees' dugout, Huggins was furious.

Johnny Rawlings followed with a single to right to score Meusel and tie the game. The next batter, Frank Snyder, attempted a sacrifice bunt. Mays came off the mound to field the ball, but he fell down before he could make a play. Now, there were runners on first and second and still there were no outs. Douglas followed with another bunt to the mound. This time, Mays gloved the ball and threw to first for the out as the runners advanced. George J. Burns, no relation to Cleveland's George Burns, drove them both home with a double to left. Mays retired the next two batters, but in a matter of moments the Giants had taken a 3–1 lead.

The Giants added another run in the ninth when George "Highpockets" Kelly doubled and scored on a single by Meusel. The Yankees got one run back in the bottom of the inning on a home run by Ruth, but the Giants held on for a 4–2 victory. Although Mays had pitched well, allowing only nine hits and no walks, the game had turned around on Meusel's triple off the breaking pitch. Afterward, Mays explained that he had disregarded Huggins's instructions on the pitch because he had retired Meusel with a slow curve earlier in the game.

Among those who had reported on the game that day was Fred Lieb of the *New York Telegram*. Although only thirty-three years old, Lieb already was well established as one of the top baseball writers in the country. He had been covering the big leagues since 1911, first for the old *New York Press,* then for the *Morning Sun,* and now for the *New York Telegram*. He had a reputation as a straightforward, no-nonsense man, and his colleagues recently had elected him president of the Baseball Writers' Association. Because of his stature in the profession, Lieb's observations of what was about to unfold carry special significance.

In filing his story, Lieb attached little importance to Mays's sudden collapse in the game. That evening, he was back at the press headquarters in the Commodore Hotel when he was approached by George Perry, who was helping him with the accommodations for the writers in town to cover the Series. Perry was accompanied by a prominent Broadway actor who had an unusual story he wanted Lieb to hear.

According to the actor, Mays had been offered a large sum of cash if he could manage to discreetly lose any close game in which he was involved during the Series. At an appropriate time, the money would be handed over to Mrs. Mays while the game was in progress. She then would signal her husband from the stands that such a transaction had taken place. On this afternoon, claimed the actor, Mrs. Mays, who was sitting in the grandstand, had flashed the sign by wiping her face with a white handkerchief as the eighth inning was about to begin. A few moments later, Mays surrendered the succession of four hits and, as it turned out, lost the ballgame.

Lieb was skeptical of the tale. It had been only one year earlier that the exposure of the Black Sox scandal had resulted in the expulsion of the eight players involved in the 1919 World Series fix. And in the past twelve months, Judge Landis, the newly appointed commissioner of baseball, had suspended five other players involved in gambling. Considering the present mood in the sport, Lieb found it difficult to believe that Mays would become involved in such duplicity.

Still, the writer felt obligated to report the charges to the commissioner and the Yankees' owners. Although it was late, Lieb and Perry took the actor to see Colonel Huston at the Hotel Martinique. A member of the Yankees staff let the three men into the Colonel's suite, where they found Huston and his friend, Frazee, asleep on their beds. Both Huston and Frazee were fully clothed, and the room was littered with empty whisky bottles. Lieb finally was able to awaken the Colonel and introduce the actor.

"I'll let this man tell you his story," said Lieb.

Huston listened quietly as the actor repeated his allegations. When the man finished his story, the Colonel looked over at Lieb.

"This doesn't look too good for our club. Have you brought it to Judge Landis's attention?"

"No," answered Lieb. "I wanted to tell you first. But Judge Landis's quarters at the Commodore are our next stop."

Huston joined the group, which proceeded back to the Commodore. By now, it was well past midnight. The four men marched up to the commissioner's room and pounded on the door to his suite. After a few minutes, Landis, dressed in a flannel nightgown, opened the door and peered out.

"What in hell do you fellows want at this hour of the night?"

Lieb was the first to speak up.

"Judge, here's a man who thinks the game yesterday wasn't entirely on the up-and-up. He thinks Mays let up in the last two innings."

Suddenly, Landis was fully awake. He invited the men inside, then took the actor into one of the bedrooms and grilled him for almost half an hour. When they came back out, Landis was visibly concerned.

"I am making a full investigation of this man's story," he said. "I have already called up the detective agency that my office employs from time to time, and they will keep their eyes on Mays for the remainder of the Series."

Turning to Lieb, the commissioner added, "Freddy, don't you use this in your paper until there are further developments."

Lieb never wrote the story for his newspaper. Nor did he ask Landis what he thought after Mays lost the seventh game 2–1 when the Giants scored the tie-breaking run on a two-out double in the seventh inning. Instead, Lieb waited until the end of the Series, which the Giants won in eight games, before asking the commissioner about the progress of the investigation. Landis's only response was that the detective assigned to follow Mays had been unable to find any evidence to corroborate the actor's story. Lieb dismissed the tale as another of the many rumors that floated around baseball.

That is where the story would have died had it not been for a chance encounter between Lieb and Huston seven years later. It was in the offseason, and Lieb and his wife had accompanied National League secretary Harvey Traband and his wife to Dover Hall, a hunting lodge near Brunswick, Georgia. The lodge was shared by several baseball club owners, and Lieb and Traband ran across Huston, Dodgers manager and president Wilbert Robinson, Cincinnati baseball writer Frank Grayson, and their wives. One evening, the group gathered in the living room in front of a log fire and began swapping stories. It was during Prohibition, but there was plenty of rum and Coca-Cola to go around. By late in the evening, Huston, loosened up by several drinks, felt compelled to confide in Lieb.

"Freddy," he said, "I am going to tell you the damnedest story a baseball owner has ever told a reporter."

Robinson, who had also been drinking heavily, quickly snapped to attention.

"No, no, Colonel!" he said. "Don't tell him!"

Huston continued to repeat his remark, and every time he did Robinson pleaded with him not to say anything more.

By now, the party-goers had begun falling asleep one by one. Eventually, even Robinson dozed off. When he did, only Lieb, Huston, and Grayson still were awake. Grayson, who had overheard the conversation, tried to keep his eyes open, but soon he, too, gave out, leaving Lieb and Huston to talk in private.

"Now that we're alone," said Lieb, "what is this story you're holding back on me?"

"I wanted to tell you that some of our pitchers threw World Series games on us in both 1921 and 1922," answered the Colonel.

"You mean that Mays matter of the 1921 World Series?"

"Yes, but there were others—other times, other pitchers."

Huston was too tired to elaborate. Exhausted, he got up and made his way to bed. Again, Lieb failed to follow up on the story. The next morning, he departed before he had occasion to see the Colonel.

When he arrived back in New York, Lieb dug out his old scorebooks from the 1921 Series. In studying them, it occurred to him that virtually the only damage done to Mays by the Giants had been in those two late innings, including the one in which the actor had alleged foul play. Mays's total pitching line for his three games in the Series was: 26 innings pitched, 20 hits, 6 runs, 5 earned runs, no walks, 1 victory, 2 losses. His feat of not allowing a base on balls in 26 innings is a Series record that still stands. However, in the two suspicious innings, the Giants scored 4 runs on 7 hits. In the other 24 innings, they managed only 2 runs on 13 hits.

The next time he was able to speak to Huston alone, Lieb pressed the owner for more information on Mays and the 1921 Series. The Colonel refused to elaborate, stating only that he stood by what he had said that evening at the hunting lodge.

There was one final footnote to the incident. It happened during a conversation with Miller Huggins shortly before the Yankee manager's death in 1929. Lieb and a few other writers were talking to Huggins about the financial problems of some of the game's retired stars. It was a subject dear to the heart of Huggins, who prided himself on his loyalty to his players.

"Any ballplayers that played for me on either the Cardinals or Yankees could come to me if he were in need, and I would give him a helping hand," stated the former manager.

Huggins paused for a moment before adding: "I made only two exceptions—Carl Mays and Joe Bush."

The old man was not in good health, but as he spoke he rose from his chair to emphasize his point.

"If they were in the gutter, I'd kick them!" Huggins said bitterly, punctuating his words by swinging his leg back and forth as if he were kicking someone.

The sudden outburst shocked Lieb. "How can such a kindly gentleman carry such a deep hatred?" he wondered.

92

If Mays was aware of the suspicions the Yankees' owners had about his actions in the 1921 World Series, he showed no sign of it the following spring. Although he already was under contract for ten thousand dollars, he refused to report to training camp until he received more money. Mays got his new contract, but in the process he further alienated the team's management.

It did not help that he rewarded his bosses with a subpar performance. He had a losing record of 13–14 and his earned run average soared to 3.60—more than one-half run per game more than he had allowed the previous year and the worst of his career.

Early in the season, Mays even found himself in the peculiar position of being the target of another pitcher's bean balls. It happened against his long-time detractors, the Browns, who would battle the Yankees all the way to the wire in the pennant race that year. St. Louis pitcher Urban Shocker knocked down Mays on three straight pitches. After the third one, Mays charged the mound and challenged Shocker to a fight. The two men were separated before any blows were exchanged, and Mays went back to the plate. He walked on the next pitch. Shocker then hit the next batter, Whitey Witt, touching off a twenty-minute brawl between the two teams.

With Mays suffering through an offseason, the hard-throwing "Bullet" Joe Bush stepped to the front as the Yankees' top pitcher. Bush was the latest acquisition from Boston, and he turned in a won-lost record of 26–7 in his first season with New York.

Behind the pitching of Bush, the Yankees edged the Browns for the championship by one game. That set up a rematch with the Giants in the World Series. This time, the Giants won four games to none with one tie under a best-of-seven format.

Mays made only one appearance in the postseason competition, losing 4–3 and again giving up all of his runs in one inning. Bush lost both of his games, and his performance led to his fallout with Huggins. In the first and last games of the Series, Bush held leads entering the eighth inning. Both times, he surrendered three runs to lose close decisions. In the final game, the Yankees were on top 3–2 in the eighth when the Giants put runners on second and third with two outs. Huggins ordered Bush, a right-hander, to walk left-hand-hitting Ross Youngs in order to pitch to the right-handed Highpockets Kelly. When Bush got the sign for the intentional pass, he turned toward the dugout and yelled at Huggins in a voice loud enough to be heard all the way to the press area, "What for, you stupid [expletive]?" Bush issued the free pass as ordered, then threw one down the middle to Kelly, who banged out the game-winning hit. The next batter also singled in a run, and the Giants wrapped up the championship with a 5–3 victory.

That November, the Yankees put Mays on waivers, which meant that any team in the majors could put a claim on him. Their intent was to see if the other fifteen big-league teams would pass on him, enabling them to ship Mays to the minor-league team in St. Paul, Minnesota. Only one team claimed Mays. Although that blocked the move, it indicated a curious lack of interest for a pitcher who had won sixty-six games in the past three seasons.

Baseball writer Frank G. Menke believed he knew why the Yankees wanted to get rid of the pitcher—and why almost no other team wanted him.

"His fits of temper, his outbursts of rage, his petty fault finding, made life a rather miserable proposition for Miller Huggins. The conduct of Mays came about as close to cracking the morale of the team as any human agency could."

The bottom line, surmised Menke, was: "Mays is . . . one of the most fervently hated men in diamond annals. It wouldn't require the use of many fingers to count up his total of baseball friends."

*   *   *

In 1923, Huggins made no attempt to hide his dislike of Mays. Hug used the submarine pitcher sparingly, and he seemed to take special pleasure in humiliating him.

Mays pitched so infrequently, he began taking his complaints to the writers.

"What's wrong with me?" he would ask them. "Why won't Huggins pitch me?"

After an extended period of inactivity, Mays finally got a starting assignment in Cleveland on July 17. It would be one of the low points of his major-league career.

The Indians jumped all over Mays, who was left on the mound to take his lumps despite giving up twenty hits and four walks in addition to hitting a batter. The final score was 13–0, and Mays was forced to endure the entire ordeal.

When it was all over and the writers asked Huggins why he refused to change pitchers, the manager answered sarcastically, "He told me he needed lots of work, so I gave it to him."

In the locker room, shortstop Everett Scott attempted to console Mays.

"Carl, I just want to tell you that in all my years in baseball, I've never seen anything so rotten as this. But don't worry. The worm will turn. It always does."

"What's the use?" said Mays. "A worm is the same on all sides—especially that worm."

Another time, Mays was talking to the Boston writers before a game with the Red Sox. Burt Whitman of the *Boston Herald* asked why Mays was being used so sparingly. Spotting Huggins, Mays said he would let the manager provide an explanation.

"Hey, Hug!" Mays called out in front of the writers. "Why won't you let me pitch?"

Huggins looked over at the pitcher and feigned surprise.

"Why, Carl, are you still with the club?" Then he turned and walked away.

Mays pitched only 81⅓ innings that year. His won-lost record was a respectable 5–2, but his ERA had soared to 6.20. In the offseason, Mays again was placed on waivers. No other American League club claimed him, allowing the Yankees to ship him to Cincinnati in the National League for the paltry sum of seventy-five hundred dollars.

When Mays reported to Cincinnati to discuss his contract for the 1924 season, Reds president Garry Herrmann greeted him warmly. After a few minutes of idle conversation, the two men got down to business. Herrmann opened the negotiations by pulling out a piece of paper and handing it across the desk to the pitcher. It was a letter from Huggins. Mays was stunned by what he read: "Dear Garry: Just a note to tell you that in selling Mays to you I may be selling the best pitcher I've got. But I don't want him pitching for me and I don't want him pitching against me. He is a very hard man to handle and I suggest that you begin by cutting his salary in half."

Mays ended up signing for a cut in pay, but before leaving the room he made a pledge to his new boss.

"If you give me thirty starts, I'll win twenty games."

Mays made good on his vow, winning twenty games while losing only nine, earning him a five-hundred-dollar bonus from the grateful Herrmann. Two years later, he won nineteen games to keep the Reds in the pennant race before he was knocked out of action by a shin injury. Without him, Cincinnati faded in the final two weeks of the season to finish second. That was Mays's last hurrah in the big leagues. Plagued by injuries, he hung on for three more years, winning a total of only fourteen games. He went 7–2 with four saves and a 4.32 ERA for the Giants in 1929 and then called it quits.

Toward the end, he offered perhaps the best summation of his brilliant yet stormy career. While reminiscing with F. C. Lane of *Baseball Magazine,* the subject turned to a rival pitcher Mays respected. In discussing this pitcher's success, Mays said admiringly: "This fellow has no friends and doesn't want any friends. That's why he's a great pitcher."

As he listened, Lane realized that Mays was describing himself.

93

Following his departure from big-league baseball, Mays returned to Oregon to live. For the next few years, his life would be marked by a series of tragedies. First, he lost his savings of $175,000 in the stock-market crash, forcing him to go back to work for two more seasons pitching in the minor leagues. Next came the death of his mother. Then came the worst blow. In 1934, his wife, Freddie, only thirty-six years old, died unexpectedly following complications from an eye infection. Mays was left alone to raise his two children, Betty, twelve, and Bill, seven.

As he had throughout his career, Mays fought back from adversity. Shortly after his wife's death, he was remarried to Esther Ugsted, a former schoolteacher who had moved in to take care of his house and children. Mays ran a fishing resort, and he scouted for several major-league clubs. Ironically, one of them was Cleveland. For fifteen years, he also conducted a baseball camp. Among his pupils was shortstop Johnny Pesky, who went on to star for the Boston Red Sox from 1942 to 1954.

Always, Mays took special pleasure in working with younger

players. "I try to teach them everything," he once said, "but the big thing I do is teach them safety in baseball."

As time passed, Mays's greatest desire was to be chosen to the Baseball Hall of Fame. It was an honor he believed he deserved, and his statistics seemed to back him up. Mays had a fifteen-year won-lost record of 208–126 for a winning percentage of .623. His earned run average was 2.92.

Yet, year after year, Mays watched as some of his contemporaries with lesser credentials were inducted into the baseball shrine while he continually was overlooked. Among those voted in were two of his teammates on the old Yankees staff—Waite Hoyt and Herb Pennock. Although both men won more games, neither had a winning percentage above .600 or an ERA below 3.50.

"I think I belong," Mays continued to insist. "I know I earned it. Just look at my record. But just because I killed a man in an accident, they keep passing me up."

Lieb, a long-time member of the Hall of Fame's Veterans Committee, denied such charges. To the contrary, said the news-paperman, the suspicions surrounding the 1921 World Series were what kept Mays out. Lieb had first made the allegations public in 1949 in his book *The Story of the World Series.* Mays never bothered to contact him to dispute the story. In a later book, *Baseball As I Have Known It,* Lieb wrote: "Carl Mays's name has frequently come before the committee, but no one has ever brought up the Chapman tragedy as a reason why Carl should not be in the Cooperstown shrine. Rather, the question mark has often been his performance in the Series of 1921."

*   *   *

In his old age, Mays became increasingly resentful about his plight. In 1963, when he was seventy-one years old, he collaborated with Bob Burnes on an article for *The Sporting News.* Mays began by stating, "Nobody ever remembers anything about me except one thing—that a pitch I threw caused a man to die."

It had been more than forty years since that awful day in the Polo Grounds, yet Mays still was haunted by the stigma of the beaning.

"It was an accident, nothing else," he said. "But what happened to me in August of 1920 is the only thing anybody remembers."

Burnes noted that as Mays spoke "his words welled up in bitterness."

Eight years later, in 1971, Rube Marquard, who had won 201 games with a winning percentage of .532 and an ERA of 3.08 in an eighteen-year career, was voted into the Hall of Fame. A writer contacted Mays for his reaction.

"Rube Marquard was a great pitcher and I'm glad he made it," said Mays. "But my record is so far superior to his that it makes me wonder. I guess the answer is they just don't like me."

By now, Mays was seventy-nine years old and he had to walk with a cane because of arthritis. He also was hard of hearing, which led him to shout when he talked.

"If I don't talk loud I can't hear myself."

Otherwise, he had made few concessions to his age. He continued to hunt and fish near his home in Dayville, Oregon. In the winters, he traveled south to San Diego, where he would help one of his former students, Jerry Bartow, coach the Hoover High School baseball team. Mays would talk to the players about the old days and the greats he had played with and against—Ruth, Cobb, Speaker. He even told them about Chapman and that fatal pitch.

"I don't mind discussing it," Mays told Jack Murphy of the *San Diego Union*. "It's not on my conscience. It wasn't my fault."

On March 19, 1971, Mays got to see one of the Hoover pitchers throw a no-hit ballgame. Because he had been battling a virus all week, Mays watched the game from his pickup, which he had parked near the bullpen area. Afterward, he drove to a spot near third base, where he called out to the young pitcher.

"Rick, you pitched real well today. You kept your curveball down and your fastball tight. Now you can see all the hard work you've done has paid off. You'll be a good pitcher if you can remember to keep ahead of the hitters and throw your curve."

One week later, Mays wrote his biographer, Bob McGarigle, "I haven't been well the past week, been in bed with severe chest pains, and I want to go home."

He never made it. On April 3, Mays was admitted to El Cajon Valley Hospital in San Diego. He died the next day. In reporting his death, the Associated Press began its story: "Carl Mays, the New York Yankees pitcher who threw the fastball that hit and killed Cleveland batter Ray Chapman in 1920, died yesterday."

To the end, he never was able to escape that pitch.

Bibliography

Books

Alexander, Charles. *Ty Cobb* (New York, 1984).

Asinof, Elliott. *Eight Men Out: The Black Sox and the 1919 World Series* (New York, 1963).

Barrow, Ed. *My 50 Years in Baseball* (New York, 1951).

Blackwood, William. *Sketch Book of the Cleveland Indians* (Cleveland, 1918).

Brown, Warren. *The Chicago White Sox* (New York, 1952).

Cobb, Ty, with Al Stump. *My Life in Baseball: The True Record* (Garden City, N.Y., 1961).

Coberly, Rich. *The No-Hit Hall of Fame* (Newport Beach, Calif., 1985).

Coffin, Tristam. *The Old Ball Game* (New York, 1972).

Cohen, Richard M., David S. Neft, and Jordan A. Deutsch. *The World Series* (New York, 1979).

Creamer, Robert. *Babe: The Legend Comes to Life* (New York, 1974).

———. *Stengel: His Life and Times* (New York, 1984).

Crepeau, Richard C. *Baseball: America's Diamond Mind, 1919–1941* (Orlando, Fla., 1981).

Durso, Joseph. *Baseball and the American Dream* (St. Louis, 1986).

Eckhouse, Morris. *Day by Day in Cleveland Indians History* (New York, 1983).

Einstein, Charles, ed. *The Baseball Reader* (New York, 1980).

Farrell, James T. *My Baseball Diary* (New York, 1957).

Fitzgerald, Ed, ed. *The American League* (New York, 1952).

Green, Paul. *Forgotten Fields* (Waupaca, Wis., 1984).

Gropman, Donald. *Say It Ain't So Joe: The Story of Shoeless Joe Jackson* (Boston, 1979).

Heilbroner, Louis, ed. *The Baseball Blue Book 1920* (Fort Wayne, Ind., 1920).

Honig, Donald. *The Boston Red Sox: An Illustrated Tribute* (New York, 1984).

Honig, Donald, and Lawrence Ritter. *Baseball: When the Grass Was Real* (New York, 1975).

James, Bill. *The Bill James Historical Baseball Abstract* (New York, 1986).

Jedick, Peter. *Cleveland: Where the East Coast Meets the Midwest* (Rocky River, Ohio, 1980).

Johnson, Harold (Speed). *Who's Who in Major League Baseball* (Chicago, 1933).

Lewis, Franklin. *The Cleveland Indians* (New York, 1949).

Lieb, Fred. *Baseball As I Have Known It* (New York, 1977).

————. *The Boston Red Sox* (New York, 1947).

————. *The Detroit Tigers* (New York, 1946).

————. *The Story of the World Series* (New York, 1949).

Lowenfish, Lee, and Tony Lupien. *The Imperfect Diamond* (New York, 1980).

MacFarlane, Paul, ed. *Daguerreotypes of Great Baseball Stars* (St. Louis, 1981).

Mack, Connie. *My 66 Years in the Big Leagues* (New York, 1950).

Mathewson, Christy. *Pitching in a Pinch* (reprint, New York, 1977).

McGarigle, Bob. *Baseball's Great Tragedy: The Story of Carl Mays* (New York, 1972).

Meany, Tom. *Babe Ruth: The Real Story of the King of Swat* (New York, 1948).

Menke, Frank G. *Sports Tales and Antecdotes* (New York, 1953).

Murdock, Eugene. *Ban Johnson: Czar of Baseball* (Westport, Conn., 1982).

Okrent, Daniel, and Harris Lewine. *The Ultimate Baseball Book* (Boston, 1984).

Porter, David, ed. *Biographical Dictionary of American Sports: Baseball* (New York, 1987).

Powers, Jimmy. *Baseball Personalities* (New York, 1949).

Reach Official American League Base Ball Guide, 1920–1921 editions (Philadelphia).

Reichler, Joseph L., ed. *The Baseball Encyclopedia* (sixth edition, revised, New York, 1985).

Reidenbaugh, Lowell. *Baseball's 50 Greatest Games* (St. Louis, 1987).

———. *Take Me Out to the Ball Park* (St. Louis, 1983).

Rice, Damon. *Seasons Past* (New York, 1976).

Rice, Grantland. *The Tumult and the Shouting: My Life in Sport* (New York, 1954).

Ritter, Lawrence. *The Glory of Their Times* (New York, 1966).

Ritter, Lawrence, and Donald Honig. *The Image of Their Greatness* (New York, 1979).

Rose, William Ganson. *Cleveland: The Making of a City* (Cleveland, 1950).

Rubin, Bob. *Ty Cobb, The Greatest* (New York, 1977).

Ruth, George Herman (Babe), and Bob Considine. *The Babe Ruth Story* (New York, 1948).

Salant, Nathan. *Superstars, Stars, and Just Plain Heroes* (Briarcliff Manor, N.Y., 1982).

Seymour, Harold. *Baseball* (two volumes, New York, 1960).

Smelser, Marshall. *The Life That Ruth Built: A Biography* (New York, 1975).

Smith, Robert. *Babe Ruth's America* (New York, 1974).

———. *Baseball's Hall of Fame* (revised, New York, 1973).

———. *Heroes of Baseball* (Cleveland, 1952).

———. *Pioneers of Baseball* (Boston, 1978).

Sobol, Ken. *Babe Ruth and the American Dream* (New York, 1974).

Spink, J. G. *Judge Landis and 25 Years of Baseball* (Binghamton, N.Y., 1947).

Sullivan, George. *The Picture History of the Boston Red Sox* (New York and Indianapolis, 1979).

Van Tassel, David D., senior editor, and John J. Grabowski, managing editor. *The Encyclopedia of Cleveland History* (Bloomington and Indianapolis, 1987).

Voigt, David Quentin. *American Baseball* (two volumes, Norman, Okla., 1969).

Zoss, Joel, and John S. Bowman. *The American League* (London, 1986).

Articles

Burkholder, Ed. "McGinnity Was a Man of Iron" (*Sport,* April 1954).

Burnes, Robert L. "50 Golden Years of Sports" (*Rawlings Magazine,* March 1949).

Cashman, Joe. "Bill Carrigan: My Days With the Red Sox" (a ten-part series, *Boston Daily Record,* January 1943).

Cerrone, Rick. "Stan Coveleskie: The First Great Indians Pitcher" (*Baseball Quarterly,* Fall 1977).

Chapman, Kathleen Daly. "Memorial of Ray Chapman" (from "In Memory of Ray Chapman" memorial publication, Cleveland, 1920).

Crosby, S. "Charles Jamieson of the World's Champions" (*Baseball Magazine,* June 1921).

"Dead or Alive: The Evolution of the Baseball" (*Rawlings Roundup,* 1959).

"The Death of Chapman, Killed by a Pitched Ball" (*Literary Digest,* September 1920).

Eller, Hod. "Why the New Pitching Rules Are Unjust" (*Baseball Magazine,* August 1920).

Foster, John B. "Evolution of the Baseball" (*Baseball Magazine,* March 1936).

Foster, Mark S. "Foul Ball: The Cleveland Spiders' Farcical Final Season of 1899" (*Baseball History,* Summer 1986).

"A Good Word for the Spit Ball" (an interview with Stanley Coveleskie, *Baseball Magazine,* February 1920).

Groh, Henry Knight. "Who's Who on the Diamond" (*Baseball Magazine,* June 1918).

Joyce, W. L. "Never a Wild Pitch" (*Yankee,* October 1973).

Kofoed, J. C. "The Unluckiest Pitcher in the American League" (*Baseball Magazine,* August 1915).

Lane, F. C. "Baseball's Most Sensational Shortstop" (*Baseball Magazine,* June 1918).

———. "Carl Mays' Cynical Definition of Pitching Efficiency" (*Baseball Magazine,* August 1928).

———. "A Catching Hercules (Hank Severeid)" (*Baseball Magazine,* October 1924).

———. "Graney, a Player Who Bats With His Brains" (*Baseball Magazine,* July 1920).

———. "The Man Who Made That Wonderful Triple Play" (*Baseball Magazine,* December 1920).

———. "The Man Who Never Strikes Out!" (*Baseball Magazine,* February 1927).

———. "My Attitude Toward the Unfortunate Chapman Affair" (*Baseball Magazine,* November 1920).

———. "A Startling Baseball Tragedy" (*Baseball Magazine*, October 1920).

———. "Tris Speaker Traded" (*Baseball Magazine*, June 1916).

Mays, Carl. "A Good Ending" (*Baseball Magazine*, November 1918).

———. "What I Have Learned from Four World's Series" (*Baseball Magazine*, November 1922).

Murphy, Jack. "Carl Mays Recalls That Tragic Pitch" (*Baseball Digest*, May 1971).

Patterson, Ted. "Jack Graney, the First Player-Broadcaster" (*Baseball Historical Review*, 1981).

Pfeffer, Jeff. "How a Single Pitched Ball May Upset a Pennant Race" (*Baseball Magazine*, June 1920).

Phelon, W. A. "How the World's Championship Was Won" (*Baseball Magazine*, December 1920).

———. "Who Will Win the Big League Pennants?" (*Baseball Magazine*, May 1920).

"The Pitcher Who Cinched Cleveland's First Pennant" (an interview with Duster Mails, *Baseball Magazine*, December 1920).

"Ray Chapman's Story . . . And His Roots" (from *Once There Was a Dam*, author and date unknown).

Sanborn, Irving E. "Consider the Pitchers" (*Baseball Magazine*, September 1920).

Speaker, Tris. "How I Spend My Annual Vacation" (*Baseball Magazine*, March 1923).

Thomas, James S. "Where Ball Players Graduate from College to the Majors" (*Baseball Magazine*, 1921).

Trachtenberg, Leo. "The Travails of Miller Huggins" (*Baseball History*, Summer 1987).

"Tris Speaker Explains" (an interview with Tris Speaker, *Baseball Magazine*, September 1916).

"Tris Speaker, the Star of the 1920 Baseball Season" (an interview with Tris Speaker, *Baseball Magazine*, December 1920).

Ward, John J. "Carl Mays" (*Baseball Magazine*, June 1955).

———. "Important Changes in the Baseball Rules," in two parts (*Baseball Magazine*, May–June 1920).

———. "Joe Sewell—Steady and Dependable" (*Baseball Magazine*, November 1932).

———. "The Man Who Made Record Homers" (*Baseball Magazine*, December 1920).

————. "The 'Pinch Pitcher' of the World's Champions" (*Baseball Magazine,* December 1916).

————. "Who's Who on the Diamond" (*Baseball Magazine,* August 1917).

Williams, Joe. "Speaker Describes Chapman's Death by a Bean Ball" (*New York World-Telegraph,* September 24, 1941).

Miscellaneous

Jamieson, Charlie. Text of interview, unpublished (National Baseball Hall of Fame Library files).

Wambsganss, Bill. Text of interview, unpublished (National Baseball Hall of Fame Library files).

Newspapers

Boston Globe, 1919–1920.

Cleveland News, 1912–1928.

Cleveland Plain Dealer, 1912–1928, 1958.

Cleveland Press, 1912–1928.

Detroit Free Press, 1920.

Hartford (Kentucky) *Republican,* 1920.

Illinois State Journal-Register (Springfield, Ill.), 1910.

New Orleans Times-Picayune, 1920.

New York Herald, 1920.

New York Sun, 1920.

New York Times, 1919–1921.

New York Tribune, 1920.

New York World-Telegraph, 1920.

Owensboro (Kentucky) *Messenger-Inquirer,* 1891–1892, 1920.

Philadelphia Inquirer, 1919–1921.

St. Louis Globe-Democrat, 1920.

St. Louis Post-Dispatch, 1920.

Southern Illinoisan (Carbondale, Ill.), 1920.

The Sporting News, 1905–1977.

Toledo (Ohio) *Blade,* 1911–1912.

Personal Interviews

Daly, Dan. Carmel, Calif., September 13, 1985.

Joy (née Chapman), Margaret. Huntington, W. Va., August 8, 1985, November 15, 1985.

Sewell, Joe. Tuscaloosa, Ala., October 17, 1985.

Wambsganss, Bill. Cleveland, Ohio, August 3–4, 1985.

Index

319